The publisher gratefully acknowledges the generous support of the Lisa See Endowment Fund in Southern California History and Culture of the University of California Press Foundation.

Holy Hip Hop in the City of Angels

Holy Hip Hop in the City of Angels

Christina Zanfagna

UNIVERSITY OF CALIFORNIA PRESS

University of California Press, one of the most distinguished university presses in the United States, enriches lives around the world by advancing scholarship in the humanities, social sciences, and natural sciences. Its activities are supported by the UC Press Foundation and by philanthropic contributions from individuals and institutions. For more information, visit www.ucpress.edu.

University of California Press
Oakland, California

Suggested citation: Zanfagna, Christina. *Holy Hip Hop in the City of Angels*. Oakland: University of California Press, 2017. doi: https://doi.org/10.1525/luminos.35

Library of Congress Cataloging-in-Publication Data

Names: Zanfagna, Christina, 1980- author.
Title: Holy hip hop in the City of Angels / Christina Zanfagna.
Other titles: Music of the African diaspora; 19.
Description: Oakland, California : University of California Press, [2017] |
    Series: Music of the african diaspora; 19 | Includes bibliographical
    references and index. |
Identifiers: LCCN 2017026657| ISBN 9780520296206 (pbk.) | ISBN
9780520968790   (e-edition)
Subjects: LCSH: Rap (Music)--Religious aspects--Christianity. | Rap
    (Music)—California—Los Angeles—History and criticism.
Classification: LCC ML3921.8.R36 Z36 2017 | DDC 306.4/
842490979494—dc23
LC record available at https://lccn.loc.gov/2017026657

See, they call Los Angeles the City of Angels; but I didn't find it to be that, exactly.

—THE BIG LEBOWSKI

This is a multi-layered city . . .
Layers of history reach deep,
Run red, scarring the soul of the city . . .
How I love it, how I hate it . . .

—LOUIS RODRIGUEZ, "LOVE POEM TO LOS ANGELES"

To live and die in L.A., it's the place to be
You've got to be there to know it

—TUPAC, "TO LIVE AND DIE IN L.A."

CONTENTS

Introduction

Earthquake Music and the Politics of Conversion

*For it is not light that we need, but fire; it is not the gentle shower, but thunder.
We need the storm, the whirlwind, and the earthquake.*
—FREDERICK DOUGLASS

Pastor Graham waited for me at a table in the International Food Court in downtown Los Angeles. A week earlier, in the spring of 2007, I met the former gang-banger-turned-preacher at a Hip Hop Church L.A. Friday night service in Inglewood, where he delivered a powerful sermon on the nature and importance of compassion. His hair tightly braided in cornrows and his skin heavily inked with tattoos, Pastor Graham—at thirty years old—was one of a growing cadre of young black hip hop pastors and gospel rappers in Los Angeles. When he was not delivering the Word, he was rapping with members of Hood Ministries—a collective of gospel MCs and street disciples whose sound more closely resembled gangsta rap than gospel music. Over a slice of pizza, I asked him, "What do you call your music?" He contemplated while finishing his mouthful, then answered, "I don't like to call it Christian rap or gospel rap or even holy hip hop 'cause that sometimes scares people off." A few bites later, he proudly declared, "I call it *earthquake music,* because this music shakes our souls and moves the ground we walk on." *Earthquake music.*

Our conversation grew more intensely personal. I learned about his turbulent upbringing during the 1980s and '90s at the height of L.A.'s gang wars and police raids: how an older gang member introduced him to using a gun on the streets of Compton, California, when he was just nine years old and how he ended up in jail at age seventeen. His hustling lifestyle brought him fast money, cars, and women, but he lost it all as quickly as he made it. After staring down the barrel of his own gun, a trigger pull from ending his life, he awoke to a new spiritual path. "To find a way through these streets, I had to look to the sky, but also dig deep," he uttered as he recalled this seismic shift in his life. His gaze dropped to the ground. "God kept me moving out here, but my heart is scarred from everything I've been through—all the tragedy around me. That's why we gotta make this *earthquake music.*"

SOUTHLAND ERUPTIONS

Hip hop, since its fabled birth in another devastated city—the Bronx, New York—has been both a disruptive and transformative force. In the 1970s, amidst postindustrial neglect, white flight, extreme poverty, street gang wars, and the looting and arson associated with ongoing New York City blackouts, black and brown youth turned violent and competitive energies into artistic expression. DJs created funky beats out of preexisting technologies and old records while MCs developed raw, rhythmic rhymes that voiced their daily lives and future aspirations. East Coast politicians and media sources typically "wrote off" or demonized this burgeoning youth arts culture, criminalizing its graffiti as public defacement and its music as disorderly "black noise."[1] In spite of, or perhaps because of, its unruly reputation, hip hop has spread to become a lingua franca for youth around the world, spawning numerous subgenres and variants. Among these is Christian rap or holy hip hop—an inevitable development especially given the historic centrality of both Jesus and avowedly religious music in black communities.

Emerging in the mid-1980s, holy hip hop (also known under the monikers gospel rap, Christian rap, Christ hop, worsh-hop, and hip *hope*) refers to a musical genre and cultural movement that integrates Christianity and hip hop.[2] As a musical practice used to articulate both a spiritual and social conception of self, gospel rap features biblically informed and Christ-centered lyrics over hard-hitting hip hop beats. The first holy hip hoppers came of age during the geopolitical and economic shifts of the post–civil rights years and comprise what many refer to as the "Hip-Hop Generation."[3] As this diverse subculture of predominantly black youth explored and converted to Christianity, they in turn brought hip hop worldviews and aesthetics to their worship practices. While Islam—and in particular, the Five Percent Nation—has historically been the most prominent religious ingredient in hip hop's diverse religious stock, explicit references to Christianity found a home in the steadily growing culture of holy hip hop, especially in Southern and West Coast hip hop scenes.[4]

But the story of holy hip hop in the City of Angels is unique. Since taking shape in the Inland Empire in 1986, it has developed alongside and in reaction to L.A. gang culture and the hypercommercialized West Coast gangsta rap that both critiqued and glorified the violence, drugs, death, and misogyny associated with it. The year following holy hip hop's initial Southland sounding, the 1987 antigang task force, Operation HAMMER, subjected black and brown youth to increasingly harsh state laws. The Los Angeles Police Department (LAPD) initiated an assault upon ten square miles of South Los Angeles between Exposition Park and North

Long Beach. In a single weekend in 1988, a thousand police officers arrested 1,453 people. Referring to it as "Vietnam in the streets," historian Mike Davis remarked, "As a result of the war on drugs every non-Anglo teenager in Southern California is now a prisoner of gang paranoia and associated demonology."[5] By 1990, over fifty thousand people had been arrested in raids, resulting in the most arrests of black youth since the 1965 Watts Rebellion.[6] Meanwhile, members of the black clergy and black middle and upper classes wielded God's Hammer—the Bible—to make their own accusations about the moral depravity of inner-city youth in relation to God's law.

More upheavals of nature and culture followed. Four major earthquakes rattled Southern California: the Joshua Tree earthquake (M6.1), Landers earthquake (M7.3), and Big Bear (M6.5) earthquake, which all struck in 1992, and the Northridge earthquake of 1994 (M6.7).[7] Mass flooding and fires ensued, causing severe damage throughout greater Los Angeles. The year 1992 also witnessed the rioting, looting, and arson that exploded in the wake of the Rodney King beating by five LAPD officers and their subsequent acquittal by a mainly white jury.[8] In just three years, the Land of Sunshine endured some of the most costly and calamitous national disasters since the Civil War.[9] Aside from $500 million of flood damage, the 1992 riots cost the city $1 billion, while the 1992 firestorms totaled $1 billion and the 1994 earthquake caused a staggering $42 billion of damage. In the face of repeated environmental eruptions, increasing poverty and unemployment, gang violence, police brutality, mass incarceration, intergenerational social alienation, and neoliberal efforts to make the state less responsive to people's needs, certain black Angelenos turned to holy hip hop for spiritual salvation, artistic expression, financial opportunity, and local community. In fact, many of the veteran L.A.-based gospel rappers converted to Christianity in the years surrounding the four major earthquakes. Religious conversion became a way to make sense of and move through these disastrous circumstances and shattered grounds. Hip hop, again, became a way to transform violence and chaos into art and healing. But this time it was *holy*. And Pastor Graham, with his *earthquake music,* was speaking to this renewal of spirit in calamitous times.

Holy hip hop groups that emerged during the 1990s in L.A. took such names as Sons of Disaster, Sons of the Cataclysm, and Apokilipz, while the Compton-based group Gospel Gangstaz named their reunion album *The Flood.* Even Tupac foreshadowed this "end of times" with his 1991 album *2pacalypse,* in which the MC returns to destroy the earth with a final party for all those in the Thug Life. Los Angeles in the 1990s also witnessed the emergence of the production team, Earthquake Brothers, who produced many of the beats for Freestyle Fellowship's 1993 album, *Innercity Griots*—a classic of L.A.'s burgeoning underground hip hop scene. The press release for *Holy Hip Hop,* a 2006 documentary hosted by Christopher "Play" Martin (formerly of the rap duo Kid 'n Play), ended with the line: "With unimagined earthquakes and other fatalistic aspects permeating our very existence, holy hip hop, Christian hip hop, spiritual spitting, whatever you want to label it, will remain, just for the certain fact that it can uplift a downtrodden people."

To further develop Pastor Graham's metaphor of musical disruption, *earthquake music* signifies multiple and intersecting processes throughout the Southland: the "underground" explosion of holy hip hop in Los Angeles; the holy hip hop artists who live in predominantly black communities that sit astride the lethal Newport-Inglewood fault; the harsh apocalyptic beats that permeate gospel rap tracks; and the hip hop ministries that continue to shake up and polarize traditional church congregations and communities. The confluence of these developments in relation to the increase in conversions to Christianity by young hip hop "heads" in Los Angeles during the early 1990s reveals an assemblage of practices, spaces, and traversals that only holy hip hop can *sound out.*[10]

To talk about holy hip hop as *earthquake music* is to explore how landscapes of urban peril and instability produce sound worlds that integrate styles such as gangsta rap, urban gospel, neo-soul, Jamaican dancehall, local street vernaculars, black preaching, and sampled soul, funk, and R&B tracks. To talk about holy hip hop as *earthquake music* is to explore the ways that natural disaster, migration, racial segregation, civil unrest, and continued urbanization in Los Angeles formed a unique terrain for the emergence of devoutly religious subjects in the later part of the twentieth century. It is to talk about how American cities are giving rise not necessarily to secularization but to new forms of pop music worship both in the pulpit and on the streets. It is to talk about how this holy hip hop emerges not only in areas of unpredictable seismic activity, but is also a sonic and spatial practice that embraces a social imaginary of both turmoil and transformation. That's why Pastor Graham has to make this *earthquake music.*

CONVERSION, EARTHQUAKE MUSIC, AND SEISMIC SOUNDINGS

Religious *conversion* was a seismic event in the lives of gospel rappers—an event that sometimes struck suddenly like an earthquake or built up over time as repeated rumblings and aftershocks. Once converted, L.A. gospel rappers performed *earthquake music*—a sacred form of hip hop born from the grounds of a city shattered by social and environmental ruptures that in turn both moved and mended those very grounds. Holy hip hoppers navigated the "hip" and the "holy" in lyrical street-corner battles, during church services, and on hip hop dance floors, unsettling the boundaries between the church and the streets, missionizing and marketing, pop music and worship, performance and praise, entertainment and evangelism. These boundaries were not only performed and repositioned through a variety of tactics, but they were also lived, suffered, and resisted.

FIGURE 1. Pastor Graham at his clothing store, Ms. Anne's Sons, in Inglewood, c. 2016. Photo courtesy of Tiana Adams.

I offer *seismic soundings* as a term that links music, geography, and conversion. This idea is predicated on the understanding that music provides frameworks and tactics for navigating uneven and shifting grounds wrought with racial and religious fissures. L.A. gospel rappers made music that pulsed through and reshaped specific urban spaces in relation and reaction to episodes of environmental and social upheavals. They enacted a kind of musical tectonics. Just as seismic waves trigger earthquakes through the sudden movement of underground rock along a fault, gospel rap performances released transformative and ecstatic energies through the friction of hip hop and Christianity at the fault lines of so-called "sacred" and "secular" spaces.

The metaphor of *earthquake music* underscores a set of terminologies and concepts that both earthquakes and music have in common. Sound waves, like seismic waves, are measured by their amplitude and volume. Earthquakes, like music, have *pulse* effects and *resonance* effects. I pull out these connections in an effort to underscore both the sounded nature of L.A.'s shape-shifting, power-laden geography and the dynamic groundswelling force of holy hip hop. When certain cultural energies and musical practices coincide, *shifts* are produced that can be destructive. But within this destruction lies the possibility for transformation as well as the repositioning of social and physical borders. *Earthquake music* captures this power, thereby creating new centers and also new forms of marginality.[11] In this way, holy hip hoppers also sound out underground or unseen geographies of black Los Angeles.

By integrating the fields of ethnomusicology, critical human geography, African American studies, urban studies, and anthropology, this book explores how ethnomusicological studies can expand discussions of the cultural politics of religiosity, race, and place, further probing how *sound* provides unique perspectives on contemporary urban religious phenomena. Drawing on over two years of continuous ethnographic research in L.A. from 2006–8 (and ongoing conversations over the past ten years) with gospel rappers, Christian DJs, pastors and clergy members, street evangelists, local activists, and fans, *Holy Hip Hop in the City of Angels* illustrates how conversion—as a religious, musical, and spatial practice—enables pathways and possibilities for black Angelenos amidst the radical postindustrial transformations, environmental cataclysms, and culture wars of Los Angeles in the late twentieth and early twenty-first centuries. The struggle of holy hip hoppers is not a politics of protest, but rather a *politics of conversion.* These street evangelists convert existing scriptures into hip hop rhymes, urban spaces into "airborne churches," and commercialized gangsta rap beats into anthems of praise. Here, conversion becomes both a religious transformation of healing and a daily practice of possibility within a multitude of constraints. While most academic studies of conversion focus on the human agent in relation to a religious change, I also attend to the conversion of nonhuman entities, material objects, sonic resources, and urban spaces. In this way, I conceive of conversion as both an analytic and an idiom of transformation.

For gospel rap artists, hip hop is not only a modality for expressing sudden or ongoing and messy religious conversions, but also one of the essential threads that links holy hip hoppers' pasts to their present. Hip hop in L.A. has become an idiom of widespread religious conversion, and *earthquake music* is how holy hip hoppers navigate and sound out invisible fault lines in the City of Angels. Just as the Northridge earthquake occurred along a fault that no one knew existed, invisible ruptures—social, musical, and physical—crisscross the shifting grounds of Los Angeles. Conversions, like earthquakes, can arrive as divine shakings along active faults. After they strike, people and places undergo seismic shifts and collective upheavals—new identities and new structures often emerge, even as these identities and structures are necessarily grounded in the same broken earth from which they are pushed upward. In following holy hip hop back to one of its initial soundings in Fontana, California, in the 1980s, we realize how this "Junkyard of Dreams" on the edges of the City of Angels became the birthplace of both the Hell's Angels and the early self-titled "Thug Angels" of holy hip hop.[12]

The specters of black poverty, hypersegregation, and racial terror have always haunted visions of L.A. as a Promised Land of the American Dream. African Americans in L.A. make up almost half of the city's homeless population, and approximately one in four black Angelenos live below the poverty line.[13] And yet, L.A. has historically boasted one of the largest, long-standing, and politically powerful black populations in the nation, making up almost 10 percent of the region's overall population.[14] When El Pueblo de Nuestra Señora la Reina de Los Angeles Del Río de Porciúncula (The Town of Our Lady the Queen of the Angels on the River Porciúncula) was established in the late eighteenth century under the Spanish flag, the majority of the Spanish founders were of mixed and African descent.[15] By the time the United States seized control of California in 1846, the multicultural pueblo had become an expansive, ethnically diverse city with significant nonwhite geographies and an atypical and flexible racial order.[16] Throughout the twentieth century, a steady influx of immigrants from Central and South America, Asia, and elsewhere transformed the Los Angeles metropolitan area into an urban mosaic with people hailing from all over the world speaking well over two hundred languages. The black population of L.A. had always been diverse, but by the early 2000s, new black immigrants from the Caribbean, Africa, and the Americas rapidly moved into the region. Nigerians, Ethiopians, Ghanaians, Belizians, Jamaicans, Haitians, and Trinidadians all clustered in and around existing African American communities. This diversity disrupted common assumptions about what constituted black L.A.

Holy hip hop continues to challenge unitary notions of blackness in L.A., painting a picture of black religious diversity not bound by certain orthodoxies. As holy hip hoppers continue to seek Zion—a spiritual home for which there is no single route—their migrant journeys can be traced from Caribbean childhoods to Los Angeles upbringings to missionary trips in Africa, and through reggae dancehalls, hip hop clubs, Nation of Islam meetings, political marches, and black Lutheran churches. Los Angeles is also home to a unique "musical *mestizaje*," creating cross-cultural currents that are particular to this city.[17] For example, the gangsta rap that many gospel rappers previously performed is informed by the *cholo*-inspired attire, tattoo art, and lowrider culture of Southern California Chicanos, revealing how black and brown diasporas also find their overlap through holy hip hop.[18] I explore how the multiple diasporic routes that holy hip hop brings together speak to the persistent search for Zion through black religion and popular music. Given the dearth of scholarly works that link significations of Christianity, Islam, and Rastafarian culture in black popular expressions, *Holy Hip Hop in the City of Angels* offers a unique perspective on how these religions intertwine in people's everyday musical experiences.[19] Hence, I allow music's role in the mutual construction of both diasporic urban spaces and new religious subjectivities to resonate.

Holy hip hop subjectivities assemble a unique arrangement of spiritual, musical, and political sensibilities informed by positions of race, gender, and class.[20] While holy hip hop is not an overtly politicized movement, many of the gospel rap artists featured in this book grew up in hip hop culture, amidst the deeply wrought race politics of L.A. in the 1980s and '90s, and under parents who honored and explored both the militant Muslim teachings of Malcolm X and the Christian peace-seeking philosophies of Martin Luther King, Jr.—in addition to other spiritual traditions. Young black Angelenos used gospel rap to interface with diverse black religiosities and navigate the complicated social and spiritual realities that they confronted in their daily lives. As Pastor Graham said, finding God was what allowed him to "move through these streets" and gospel rap was what moved the ground he walked on. In the spirit of hip hop's unruliness and extending the legacy of Christian liberation politics, gospel rap provided new possibilities for engaging with multiple key black cultural entities—African American churches, gospel music markets, hip hop scenes, and political movements from Civil Rights to Black Power to Black Lives Matter.[21] Conversions, of all kinds, opened up these possibilities. But more than anything, gospel rap gave young hip hop heads seeking God a way to participate in the cultural movement and musical language they knew so well: hip hop.

WHAT IS HOLY HIP HOP?

Gospel rap, on the one hand, is an extension of black sacred musical styles, considered a subgenre within the ever-proliferating sound world of contemporary urban gospel.[22] It reaffirms music's historically central role in African American religious culture as a medium of worship and community building. On the other hand, gospel rap is an expression of hip hop aesthetics and practices associated with street life and, oftentimes, gang culture. Gospel rappers remain committed to "taking the gospel to the streets" as well as seeking relationships with "unchurched" and marginalized populations in ways that traditional churches and gospel music artists have failed to do. This is in part due to how hip hoppers have become *holy* hip hoppers: in most cases, their initial and primary commitment was to hip hop music and culture; then, they gave their lives to Christ. As L.A. holy hip hop artist Soup the Chemist once told me, "I'm not a Christian rapper. I'm a rapper who's a Christian. I was a rapper first and then I became born-again." While many of the gospel rappers I met attended church services occasionally as youth, most of them would say that they were first *baptized* in the streets of Los Angeles. This is why their holy hip hop sounds more like gangsta rap than gospel music.

Musically, gospel rap is squarely planted in the sound world of hip hop, embodying a diversity of regional hip hop styles and variations from Southern bounce to Los Angeles gangsta rap to New York street aesthetics. There is no singular "holy hip hop" sound. Nor are there specific sonic signifiers that distinguish holy hip hop from "secular" rap. Holy hip hop, like most hip hop music, is driven by the dynamic fusion of beats and rhymes. Gospel rap beats, whether created from samples, music software programs, and/or live instrumentals, provide the musical foundation over which gospel MCs spit (i.e., rap) their spiritually inspired lyrics. It is the lyrics—usually expressions of belief or personal testimony—that make holy hip hop *holy*. Despite the importance of lyrics in distinguishing holy hip hop as a sacred genre, I do not analyze the religious meanings expressed in gospel rap lyrics at great length. Most scholarly studies on hip hop focus on lyrical analysis—a tendency that has often produced limited interpretations and discussions about hip hop music and culture. To avoid this tendency, I focus on the musical and spiritual practices of holy hip hoppers. While I describe the sound of certain holy hip hop tracks and performances throughout the text, I encourage readers to explore the musical links listed in the back of the book in order to experience the music itself.

Stephen Wiley is recognized as the first artist to commercially record and distribute a gospel rap cassette with his 1985 release *Bible Break*—a fact acknowledged by California Christian rapper T-Bone in his song "Our History" on his own 2002 album entitled *GospelAlphaMegaFunkyBoogieDiscoMusic*. Hailing from Oklahoma, Wiley is often referred to as the "Godfather of Gospel Rap." While the title track of Wiley's album reached the #14 spot on Christian radio in 1986, many gospel rappers have called his style "soft" or "homogenous." New York's Michael Peace followed in 1987 with *Rock It Right* and Dallas's P.I.D. (Preachers in Disguise) in 1988 with their Run DMC–inspired street style and the addition of clergy collars. Two years later, multiracial Christian rap trio DC Talk released their self-titled debut album. The late Danny D-Boy Rodriguez emerged on the scene with *Plantin' a Seed*.[23] While mainstream media and press generally focus on these few artists as the forerunners of holy hip hop, the Los Angeles–based gospel rap group SFC (Soldiers For Christ) was also producing gospel rap as early as 1986. Early Christian rappers from the Southland, such as Gospel Gangstaz, L.A. Symphony, the Dynamic Twins, and I.D.O.L. King, have generally not been acknowledged among the likes of Wiley, Peace, DC Talk, and Rodriguez.

Although sufficiently below the radar of mainstream visibility and simultaneously marginalized by both religious music circuits and commercial hip hop scenes, the holy hip hop movement now boasts its own annual awards show, several national festivals and conferences, online music archives, a slew of hip hop preachers, independent record labels, numerous radio programs, and hip hop ministries and churches—a growing trend most recently celebrated by *USA Today*, *Vibe*, *Vanity Fair*, and numerous local newspapers. The increasing number of FM, internet, and satellite gospel radio stations throughout the 1990s and early 2000s has been critical to exposing gospel music audiences to holy hip hop. Categories for gospel music awards have been expanded to include Christian rap by the National Academy of the Recording Arts and Sciences (the Grammy Awards), the Stellar Awards, and the Gospel Music Awards.

Christian rapper Lecrae won the "Best Gospel" album for his 2012 release, *Gravity*, at the 2013 Grammy Awards, "Best Artist of the Year" at the 46th Gospel Music Association (GMA) Dove Awards, and "Best Gospel Artist" at the 2015 BET Awards. Lecrae's awards (all won in religious categories) reveal that while gospel rap sonically registers as hip hop, the audience it cultivates commercially is a holy one. Lecrae's recent success, along with his 2015 performance of "Welcome to America" on the *Tonight Show* with Jimmy Fallon and 2016 performance at the BET Hip Hop Awards, has brought unprecedented exposure to the subgenre in the years since I first began this research, and contributes to its slow but steady commercialization.

Despite these developments, Christian rap has generally not been well received by mainstream or commercial hip hop culture. "Secular" hip hop artists, fans, and industry professionals often view the infusion of a hip hop sensibility with Christian morals as gimmicky, soft, and musically subpar. In some ways, holy hip hop artists find themselves in a triple bind: considered musical mavericks in the church, corny Bible-thumpers in the streets, and criminal youth by law enforcement in the hyper-ghettos of L.A., they are constantly fighting against accusations that their ways of being and expressing are blasphemous and/or inauthentic. These competing critiques constitute their struggle to move freely across social, spatial, and sonic borders—a border crossing that has generally been the norm in black music.

Holy hip hop practitioners are part of a genealogy of African American artists who have blurred the lines between the "sacred" and the "secular" within churches, nightclubs, and the music industry at large. Holy hip hop, as it extends these practices of musical border-crossing, is really nothing new. Pop stars such as Ray Charles, Sam Cooke, Al Green, Aretha Franklin, Curtis Mayfield, Stevie Wonder, and Donny Hathaway, among others, merged gospel music sensibilities with R&B and soul.[24] While pop music has drawn inspiration from the church, black Christianity has long absorbed the sounds of popular music. Gospel icons such as Thomas Dorsey, Andrae Crouch, the Staple Singers, the Edwin Hawkins' Singers, and Kirk Franklin have all incorporated "secular" music forms into "sacred" worship, whereas Sister Rosetta Tharpe took church music to the nightclub. Styles such as the blues, jazz, R&B, soul, rock, funk, and even punk music have found their way into the church, but generally not without a thunderous backlash of skepticism that has often re-polarized religious discourses on the permissibility of sacred/profane border crossing.

One is immediately reminded of the shocked and horrified reactions of churchgoers when pianist Thomas Dorsey brought blues music into the church in the 1920s and '30s, boldly ushering in the sound that would become standard gospel music.[25] Similarly, some members of an older generation as well as more traditional adherents of black Christian worship have expressed an aesthetic aversion to the "noise" and iconography of hip hop, seeing it as an unorthodox presence in the church. For them, gospel rap literally brings the street sensibility of Bronx block parties and schoolyard battles associated with early hip hop into the sanctuary. Despite hip hop's impressive ingenuity, it has not broken free from some of its unlawful and immoral associations. In Los Angeles, gospel rap also carries the controversial stigma of West Coast gangsta rap and the sounds of black masculine rage and pleasure that accompanied it—sounds that were met with both forceful condemnation and unprecedented commercial success.

And so, perhaps, nothing quite as unabashedly commercial as hip hop has entered the pews, nothing that displays materialism and violence so dramatically or employs such forceful modalities (e.g., *scratched* vinyl, *break*dancing, *explicit* lyrics). And perhaps this is why G. Craige Lewis of EX Ministries, an African American preacher who has been deemed holy hip hop's number one "public enemy," preaches his anti–hip hop gospel to congregations of one to two thousand people every weekend. When Lewis finishes his sermons, he calls congregants who have purchased hip hop CDs to pile them on the altar, where they will be smashed to pieces, sometimes with sledgehammers. Those with tattoos—what Lewis calls "marks of Cain" and "emblems of the occult religion of hip hop"—are called to kneel before the altar so that Lewis can pray for God to save their souls before it's too late.[26] It is not surprising that some gospel hip hop artists choose not to perform in church.

The emergence and rise of holy hip hop coincides with both national and global revivals of fundamentalism, contemporary apocalyptic movements in the United States (especially Los Angeles) at the turn of the century, trends toward religious pluralism, and the new sense of radical individualism ushered in by 1980s consumerism. In this pluralizing environment, there is both a greater openness and increased vehemence towards new, unorthodox, and individualized expressions of religious belief. In addition, holy hip hop's minimal yet slowly increasing presence in the commercial marketplace has been made possible by the growth of Christian Lifestyle Branding,[27] Prosperity Theology, and the proliferation of "hip" religious commodities (e.g., "Jesus Is My Homeboy" and "Mary Is My Homegirl" T-shirts, diamond cross medallions, etc.).[28] Cornel West argues, "Never before has the Nation (or world) been so seduced by markets and so hungry for spirituality," which begs his haunting question: "Why is the United States the most market-driven *and* religious nation of modern times?"[29] Indeed, there are myriad instances of religion being expressed through popular culture, from sports events to movies, TV shows, and large-scale concerts and festivals. Scholars continue to identify the presence of religious and ritual behavior in contemporary musical youth subcultures and analyze how popular music is an arena through which religion is mediated.[30] Given this renewed presence of religion in the public sphere, both in the United States and globally as expressed through mass social movements and antigovernment protests, we must acknowledge the extent to which postwar modern individualism and continued urbanization in American cities are giving rise not to secularization, but to new modalities of worship both inside and outside the institutional context and creating expanded possibilities for the emergence of devoutly religious subjects.

That said, for the purposes of this book, I am less interested in situating holy hip hop within larger national trends in institutional religion and evangelical Christianity. While I draw occasionally from religious studies scholars who address hip hop culture,[31] I do not prioritize comparisons between holy hip hop and other genres of Contemporary Christian Music (CCM), such as Christian rock, Christian heavy metal (or "Heavenly Metal" as some have dubbed it), and Christian New Age.[32] In addition, the majority of the musicians I worked with were grassroots artists that often also maintained day jobs. As such, they were mediating a much different set of situated circumstances, localized constituencies, and shifting locations than commercially viable CCM artists in California and beyond. The economic, racial, and gendered differences and asymmetries of power between commercial CCM and grassroots gospel hip hop are significant, warranting more culturally and geographically specific readings.

LOCATIONS AND LOCOMOTIONS

Occasionally, I will draw links to holy hip hop in cities such as Atlanta, Harlem, Chicago, and Houston, but I will focus on how Los Angeles's specific arrangement of earthquakes and natural disasters, populations, policing practices, violent crime, factory closures, and gang culture makes holy hip hop in the City of Angels a distinct phenomenon on its own terms. The sprawling, fragmented quality of Los Angeles's geographic terrain—a decentralized, polynucleated, and automobile-oriented city—poses different spatial and organizational challenges for studying holy hip hop culture. What does it mean for holy hip hop to be emplaced on grounds that are so unstable and constantly moving?

To study cultural phenomena in Los Angeles, one must acknowledge a specific tension about the experience of place—that is, place as both physically situated and shape-shifting, both located and locomotive. To this end, I have found several different bodies of literature to be useful. While the frameworks of urbanization and "suburbanization" as proposed by Edward Soja, Allen Scott, and Mike Davis of the Los Angeles School of Urbanism have helped me situate holy hip hop within historical sedimentations, state policies, and patterns of African American migration specific to Southern California, I depart from their emphasis on political economy to also consider the cultural politics of place.[33] In trying to account for the way that power relations, social dynamics, and everyday practices produce our sense of space and place, I have looked to the field of critical human geography, and specifically the work of British and French geographers such as Henri Lefebvre, Michel De Certeau, Doreen Massey, Michael Keith, and Steve Pile.[34] Synthesizing the above work, I aim to hold the tension of physical locatedness *and* the unfixed, relational aspect of space.[35] To understand urban life is to deal with the empirical aspects of specific places, the abstract notions and stories that we attach to those places, and the social relations and activities that create and define them.

Given the challenge of holy hip hoppers to find spaces of acceptance and belonging—to find Zion—I became particularly interested in tracking when and where holy hip hop was performed. This prompted a deeper curiosity about the mediating effects of place on music and vice versa. There is a rich and expanding literature that connects notions of space and place to music.[36] While many of these studies have provided historical and ethnographic accounts of music's relationship to specific localities, few of them engage directly with scholars from critical human geography, and in this way, do not connect music to the social interactions and spatial practices that shape space.[37]

City space also shaped the social interactions and spatial practices of this musical ethnography. It shaped how holy hip hoppers and I both lived and conducted our respective work in the city, allowing for certain kinds of movement and prohibiting others. Spanning 4,060 square miles, Los Angeles County is the most widely dispersed metropolis in the country, while Los Angeles city proper covers 469 square miles. And yet, until the late 1970s, the majority of black Angelenos lived in a few densely populated neighborhoods in South Los Angeles—still commonly referred to as South Central despite undergoing an official name change in 2003. During the years I lived in Los Angeles, holy hip hop—while concentrated in a handful of neighborhoods—was spread across this vast metropolis. Inglewood became one of the main geographical foci of my research because it was home to the Hip Hop Church L.A., but no central hub existed. Holy hip hop's fragmented, translocal community contributed to its uniquely ruptured soundings and sensibilities, but also to its capacity to span multiples spaces.[38]

Throughout my research, I conducted interviews and attended holy hip hop events, concerts, and church services across greater Los Angeles—from Lancaster to Long Beach, Inglewood, Moreno Valley, Compton, Rancho Cucamonga, Fontana, Leimert Park, Watts, Santa Monica, downtown Los Angeles, Carson, Culver City, Bell Flower, Gardena, and Northridge. In the following chapters, I will illuminate how these disparate localities within Southern California are linked to one another through musical and spatial practices, constituting a kind of audibly rendered (sub)urban archipelago.[39] Los Angeles, long touted as a diffuse concrete sprawl epitomizing the ethics and aesthetics of "car culture" immortalized by the G-Funk–inspired gangsta rap of Dr. Dre and Snoop Dogg, is often overlooked as a place of sociality, spirituality, and artistic communion.[40] In Los Angeles, hip hop and automotive spaces are inextricably intertwined. The car became a critical locomotive and location during my research on holy hip hop—a process that was as much a pedestrian and vehicular voyage through L.A.'s archipelagic geography as it was a musical journey through sound.

I began to see my research as an effect of ethnographic *locomotion* as much as ethnographic *location*.[41] My research field was a mobile, heterogeneous terrain of encounter comprising many fields as opposed to a physically bounded space. My ethnographic experience was one of navigation—navigating diverse populations and urban spaces, but also the borders between sacred and profane musical practices and vernaculars. Travel *between* various research sites and fields throughout Los Angeles became as critical to my understanding of gospel rappers as spending time with them in fixed locations.

A significant amount of my field research and ethnographic work—conversations, observations, listening to music, processing information and experiences—was conducted from and inside automobiles. Over time, I began to treat *driving*, both alone and with holy hip hoppers, as an interdisciplinary methodology that privileges practice and traversal. Driving to particular events and interviews, I witnessed the physical Los Angeles that my informants did: the same streets, signs, buildings, churches, communities, and hip hop spaces that made up their current daily movements as well as their pre-gospel rap pasts. The specific routes I took to events in Inglewood, Watts, or Compton provided much different experiences of urban geography and also helped to defetishize space. The mental geography created by driving into Inglewood from the 405 Freeway along Manchester Boulevard is very different than the one created by driving south down Sepulveda Boulevard. Different routes to and from holy hip hop locations highlighted different spatial segregations, different densities of population, different ethnic and racial groupings, and different kinds of commerce. There are many L.A.'s—many versions of the city. Depending on whether or not I took streets or highways, chose to cut through certain neighborhoods or even drive down specific blocks, I witnessed the compression and exaggeration of social difference in distinct ways. By driving these various routes, I was able to get a better sense of how holy hip hoppers experienced negotiations of time, space, and bodies from the quasi-privacy of cars, and how our travel and movement across the city was raced and gendered in specific ways.

We listened to holy hip hop tracks on their car stereos. We talked about things we saw on the streets. Cars were where a lot of misrecognitions of gospel rappers took place as well. From the passenger side of their rides, holy hip hop music blasting out of the windows, I observed how black men playing hip hop music at loud volumes are often seen and heard as gangsters, gangsta rappers, or more generally, criminals. That is, driving around Los Angeles with gospel rappers was often where I witnessed firsthand how they were interpellated by both police and city residents. The hypervisibility of black bodies in commercial media has rendered invisible important truths about everyday racial subjugation.

Christian rapper Lecrae, on his 2006 track "Jesus Muzik," raps about the confused reactions he receives as he drives his pale yellow convertible down the street:

> Plus I'm bumpin dese Jesus beats whenever they seein me
> People lookin all confused, cuz every one of my tunes is screamin Jesus peeps

Then the hook, which features a "screw" technique of making the words super low in register and hyper-slow in delivery, drops in: "Ridin wit my top down listenin to this Jesus music." Fast driving cymbal hits gallop across a surging and synthesized melodic loop. Lecrae refers to the bewilderment that his music and his identity create for those witnessing him ride through the neighborhood "bumpin dese Jesus beats." The song's instrumentals, like most gospel hip hop, sound just like any other commercial hip hop track. Expecting to hear the profane language so common to gangsta rap and other forms of commercial hip hop, passersby often do a double take upon hearing the religious message booming from his car speakers.

More spiritual clues awaited inside the cars of gospel rappers. Gospel rap automobiles also doubled as mobile spiritual altars traversing the city, leaving the resonances of "Jesus beats" in their wake. Crosses dangled from their rearview mirrors. Small pictures of Jesus were affixed to their dashboards. Cars served as a portable "merch table" or literal marketplace of holy hip hop music sales. Gospel rappers sold their homemade CDs out of the storefront of their car trunks at flea markets, in church parking lots, or on street corners. It was also important to play holy hip hop music on car stereos as this was often the intended listening environment. While most L.A. residents do not necessarily own homes, many own cars and spend a significant amount of time in them.

The cars of holy hip hoppers became spaces of rumination, prayer, music making, consumption, marketing, and missionizing. They became a part of L.A.'s shifting landscapes as they were *converted* into roaming offices, record stores, or music studios. I would like to highlight the ways in which the "automobility" of this particular ethnography became both a literal and symbolic vehicle for grounded forms of listening, looking, mapping, relating, and witnessing—a vehicle for *driving as interdisciplinarity.* "Automobility" was how the archipelagic geography of Los Angeles was connected. *Earthquake music* was how gospel rappers navigated those moving grounds, even as they let Jesus "take the wheel."

Los Angeles's development coincided with the American automobile era.[42] Studies and writing abound on the pedestrian experience or the act of strolling through the city, whereas cars have been absent from the analysis of the urban.[43] And yet, cars and the modes of mobility they make possible reconfigure both urban and suburban life and enable certain kinds of "dwelling, traveling, and socializing" in the "automobilized time-space."[44] While scholars and Southland residents alike have often lamented the privatizing, segregating, and alienating effects of the car on city life—particularly in relation to the preservation of public spaces and associational life—the car has been hailed as an emancipatory object and transcendent space in African American cultures. This is especially true for Los Angeles–based gangsta rap. Paul Gilroy, critiquing what he calls "American automotive utopianism,"[45] argues that African Americans' experiences of "racial terror, brutal confinement, and coerced labour must have given them additional receptivity to the pleasures of auto-autonomy as a means of escape, transcendence, and, perhaps fleetingly, also of resistance."[46] But the search for such automotive pleasures has often resulted in ostentatious displays of conspicuous consumption.

Returning to the gospel rappers whose automotive altars bump "Jesus beats," how can we understand cars as the quintessence of consumer capitalism as well as important spaces of spiritual practice? Further, how does the automobility of holy hip hop culture in L.A. make possible certain movements across the city *and* demonstrate how specific music cultures and racial subjects are constrained by local geometries of space and power? What kinds of "black cultural traffics" are produced through the mobilities and immobilities of holy hip hop culture?[47]

WHAT IS THIS "BLACK" IN HOLY HIP HOP?

To say that a significant part of my research was conducted in cars is not to imply that holy hip hoppers exclusively "trafficked" in the local, or even the regional.[48] While most holy hip hoppers clearly defined themselves as Christian, their every-day lives and practices revealed the mixing of diverse transnational spiritualities and sound worlds: gangsta rap, urban gospel, Nation of Islam–inspired hip hop, Five Percent Nation lyrical tropes, Jamaican dancehall, African American preach-ing, street vernaculars, and sampled soul, funk, and jazz music. Throughout the book, I foreground these sonic and linguistic intersections of Islam, the Rastafarian movement, and Christianity in the lives of gospel rap practitioners—intersections that highlight sympathies and circulations among black religious forms as they challenge Christianity as a fixed category. Sometimes, holy hip hop expressions that are inflected with multiple religious sensibilities are done so in a self-conscious manner, such as a Barbadian-born Christian rapper's identification as "The Pastorfarian." Most often, such expressions are highly encoded and unintentional, illustrating be-low the radar cultural intimacies and borrowings.

Many scholars have argued the point of black American diversity and hetero-geneity as it is linked to the cultural repertoires of the African diaspora.[49] While this point may seem obvious, it deserves restating, as the tendency to equate race and nation in black American musical performance remains seductive from many different vantage points. Riffing on Stuart Hall's well-known essay, "What Is This 'Black' in Black Popular Culture?" I argue that this "black" that we hear echoing through holy hip hop is an expression not just of *multiple L.A.'s* but also of *multiple Americas* enmeshed in the soundscapes of the Caribbean and Africa.[50] Holy hip hoppers might not define themselves as part of a diaspora, but their discourses and practices transcend biologically driven and ahistorical renderings of race and nation.

The diasporic routes and resonances of gospel rap suggest how an ethnomusicology of contemporary black sacred music may expand the self-definition of academic fields such as American Studies and African American Studies. That is to say, while the African diaspora has often been theorized through black popular music, studies on black sacred, and specifically Christian, music also have a theoretical intervention to make vis-à-vis the black Atlantic. Los Angeles–based gospel rap, in somewhat paradoxical fashion, helps to unsettle the frame of black American particularism, especially in regard to notions of black Christian uniformity *and* U.S. hip hop superiority as it is circumscribed by national boundaries.[51] But this focus on the diasporic routes and resonances of holy hip hop does not mean that it loses its cultural identity as African American.[52] Many of the global connectivities sounded through holy hip hop take shape in what we consider highly localized spaces, such as Inglewood and Compton—spaces that are also iconically rendered as black American in the popular imagination.

Here, I must return to the premise of black American diversity and heterogeneity.[53] Holy hip hoppers have developed a position that certain kinds of black Christian orthodoxies and respectability politics have deemed incomprehensible. Their music poses a challenge to existing racial and moral hierarchies as it radically expands notions of black worship. While scholars have often described black popular culture as a diasporic and contradictory space, studies of black religion have generally been articulated through a nationalist frame that does not acknowledge the internal splintering within African American communities, nor the presence of certain global syncretisms and linkages.

In trying to challenge assumptions of African American homogeneity, there is always the danger of reifying the very categories and signifiers one attempts to unsettle. The reification of both "the black church" and the signifier "black" is something that troubles me in my own work and the work of others. The study of black religion has been, as Anthony Pinn states, "hopelessly biased towards Christian sensibilities and themes," leading to "the myopic depiction of black religion as synonymous with the Black Church tradition."[54] As the holy hip hop stories and soundings herein suggest, the church is a highly mobile, porous, and transnational configuration composed of many different individuals, communities, organizations, governing principles, agendas, sentiments, musical genres, and ministerial practices. Sometimes "the church" can even refer to a particular state of mind or religious awareness; other times it refers to a shared space of intimacy between a group of people and/or God. Rarely does it simply refer to the actual structure of a freestanding church building that houses a homogenous all-black congregation. I am interested in the religious sensibilities, experiences, and practices of holy hip hop as opposed to institutional structures of Christianity.

Meanwhile, the debates surrounding African American Christianity (i.e., resistance vs. accommodation, liberation vs. oppression, white vs. black) have also failed to yield more complicated and historically up-to-date understandings of the diverse experiences associated with being religious, musical, and African American in America.[55] Taking a complex, diasporic (and locomotive) framing of black Christianity seriously, we must then consider how holy hip hop is implicated in many global histories of racial and economic injustice as well as black freedom struggles that have engendered connections, conversions, and contradictions among people of African descent. In this way, gospel rap—like the spirituals and hip hop—is part of a far-reaching arc of black theological and liberation thinking from James Cone to Black Lives Matter.[56]

Another influential and deadly framing of black Americans has been the "culture of poverty"—a postwar phenomenon gaining traction in the 1970s that has been hegemonic in the social sciences and domestic politics as expressed through conservative policies on welfare.[57] The "culture of poverty" posited that poor people, especially people of color, exhibited monolithic and pathological beliefs and behaviors such as being unmotivated, violent, abusive of drugs and alcohol, and linguistically deficient, among others. Many scholars have critiqued the fatalistic myths and stereotypes articulated and reinforced under this model, providing real-world data that goes against the corrosive ideas associated with the "culture of poverty." Holy hip hoppers provide another real-world example that challenges and disrupts these long-standing theories about the cycle of poverty, the perpetuation of the underclasses, and more specifically the pathologies associated with gangbanging and gang cultures.[58] Conversion, as a constitutive component of *earthquake music*, is not just an important focus of this book, but is also a generative analytical tool for examining the transformative practices and effects of holy hip hop that seek to break free of such demonizing and incarcerating discourses.

THE POLITICS AND PRACTICES OF CONVERSION

During most of my interviews with gospel rap artists, talk of conversion took center stage. For L.A. gangsta rappers–turned–gospel rappers, holy hip hop nurtured a politics of conversion that attempted to move beyond the polarizing vocabularies of "secular" and "religious" in order to create passages across the fault lines of generation, genre, and geography amidst L.A.'s particular conditions and constraints. Instead of getting boxed into either hip hop or Christianity, they converted themselves, their music, and their surroundings into something wholly new. Practices of conversion, whether they involved a spiritual change, a change from one viewpoint to another, a physical transformation, a change in function, or even just a turn of phrase, made possible certain moments, sites, and experiences of transition, rebirth, and changeover.[59]

My interest in conversion emerges out of the centrality of these conversionary practices in the lives of holy hip hoppers—conversion as a religious transformation, a musical transposition from secular rap to gospel rap, and a spatial tactic of creatively repurposing the urban environment for spiritual aims. Gospel rappers also converted common hip hop aphorisms, slang terms, and lyrics into expressions evoking religious connotation. When they used the term MC—an abbreviation for "Master of Ceremonies" but in hip hop cultures thought to mean "Microphone Controller"—they understood this to signify "Minister of Christ." In a series of similar linguistic re-significations in holy hip hop, "player hater" became "prayer hater," the lyric "Baby Got Back" was changed to "Baby Got Book," and "BYOB" was an acronym for "Bring Your Own Bible" instead of "Bring Your Own Booze." These clever linguistic turns, what I refer to as *flippin' the script(ure),* were part of a larger set of multimodal and intersecting conversionary practices across varied temporal and spatial terrains in which gospel rappers harnessed conversion as a technology of transformation in order to precipitate acts of rebuilding, reinvention, and integration.[60] In addition to converting to Christianity, young black hip hop artists—some of L.A.'s most policed and yet simultaneously ignored citizens—enacted spiritual, spatial, and sonic transformations through their *seismic soundings.*

Conversion is a word at once practical and irrational, objective and subjective, worldly and otherworldly, shadowy and illuminating. It is the multi-resonant nature of conversion—its capacity to enunciate and join together bodies and beliefs, politics and the divine—that makes this word so ambiguous and powerful. The vocabularies and phrases signifying conversion are vast and equally vague, aggregating an active and ever-changing lexicon of conversion-related expressions. *I got saved. God got a hold of me. I've been delivered. Born again.*[61] *Born from above. Raised from the dead.* In this way, conversion is both an experiential idiom of religious transformation and a generative concept shaping everyday idioms and expressions. Interestingly, converts rarely use the term to refer to their exact moment of conversion; rather, conversion has become a way to understand this process after the fact, both instant and gradual, which gives insight into the importance of narrativizing, retelling, and interpreting conversion experiences.

Scholars have exposed and debated the challenges in using "conversion" as an analytical tool.[62] The Comaroffs argue that the term conversion "carries a common-sense European connotation" that oversimplifies a complex and partial process.[63] They question the extent to which "conversion" fully grasps "the highly variable, usually gradual, often implicit, and demonstrably 'syncretic' manner in which so-cial identities, cultural styles, and ritual practices" are transformed by evangelical encounters.[64] Acknowledging the potential of conversion to mask, simplify, and naturalize complex social processes, I have tried to avoid the teleological tendency of conversion, which often posits conversion as a final destination or quest for meaning in the face of modernization. I have also attempted to disentangle the word itself from holy hip hop practices of conversion in order to position conver-sion not as a definitive breach with an amoral and "unsaved" past, but rather as a set of ongoing transformative events, acts, and narratives—a series of rumblings expressed through *earthquake music* that "shakes our souls and moves the ground we walk on."

The etymological origins of the word contain many spatial resonances: to turn, return, turn around, reorient, and change directions. Conversion is a movement, "a form of passage," and a "turning from and to" that can open a path to a par-ticular future, to humanity, or to belonging.[65] As anthropologist Diane Austin-Broos argues, "Conversion is a type of passage that negotiates a place in the world. Conversion as passage is also quest, a quest to be at home in a world experienced as turbulent or constraining or, in some particular way, as wanting in value."[66] Conversion is not a quest for utopia, but rather a quest for "some place rather than no place."[67] It is the creation of new, provisional, and often mobile places of belonging outside of the church or the club that constitutes gospel rap's unique geographies of conversion—geographies of mobility not captured by city maps or visual renderings of black L.A. Conversion, like automobility, is also a way to link the archipelagic spaces of the Southland through passages and traversals. And like driving through the city, holy hip hop conversions involve the navigating of mul-tiple routes, mergings, blockages, and impasses.

In the following chapters, I explore articulations and manifestations of con-version in the lives of holy hip hoppers—*rites/rights of passage, geographies of conversion,* and *the evangelical hustle.* Each of these ideas builds on the concept and practice of conversion, exploring the intentional and unintentional conver-sions of peoples, places, objects, and sounds through *earthquake music.* Here, conversion illuminates how the cultural, political, and religious are interrelated in holy hip hop practices and how those practices emerge from structures of dis-crimination and stigmatization that are at once highly localized and *resoundingly* global.

FINDING ZION, SOUNDING PLACE

The term Zion has often been used by gospel rappers to denote a place of spiri-tual and musical belonging that was not necessarily afforded those who partici-pated in *both* hip hop and Christianity. Not a physical place, per se, Zion was an abstraction, a feeling, "a quest to be at home" amidst L.A.'s Babylons. Zion and Babylon are spatial imaginaries that have been significant in the formation of transatlantic solidarities as well as multiple searches for liberation and salvation that no doubt implicate imperialism, colonialism, and African dispersal. Holy hip hoppers sounded these global connections as they simultaneously localized these biblical terms to signify the harsh realities of the L.A.'s postindustrial landscapes, racial segregations, policing practices, and pop culture excesses.[68] For holy hip hoppers, the Zion they sought was not about the formation of statehood or even a return to some distant motherland; rather, it was about creating the conditions of possibility for certain kinds of black becoming. Holy hip hop's search for Zion involved a series of twists and turns instead of the notion of simple return to a distinct homeland. Conversion was about conceiving of more liberated Afro-futures as opposed to reclaiming roots.

Holy hip hop subjectivities were produced in and through a number of different locations—street corners, churches, parks, schoolyards, cultural centers, clubs, and theaters—but more importantly, gospel rap artists, in their quest for Zion, created alternative spaces that linked the seemingly disparate elements of Christianity and hip hop. These spaces assembled and blurred racial, spiritual, and musical geographies, producing heterogeneous social arrangements that were often highly mobile and fleeting. They were not permanent physical locations. In this way, I draw from Jacqueline Nassy Brown's assertion that place must be understood "first and foremost as an abstraction, not a set of physical properties just there for the eye to see."[69] Holy hip hop's geographies of conversion were constituted more through spiritual ideas and musical sounds than physical properties and visual forms. As such, they denaturalized the idea of *place as matter,* even as the very real material conditions of specific places were crucial in the formation of gospel rappers and their music—and even as the volatility of L.A.'s physical and social landscapes in the 1990s were wreaking havoc on the lives of its residents.

Holy hip hop's geographies of conversion often left no visual trace, sometimes fading out as quickly as they were sounded into existence. These sonic geographies spoke to the larger invisibility and impermanence of multiple black L.A.'s. Recall the painful transformation of Central Avenue from a dynamic epicenter of black music and interracial socialization to a desolate and abandoned thoroughfare. Once the heart of Los Angeles's African American community during the 1920s–50s, Central Avenue was home to a vibrant jazz and R&B scene that flourished until the LAPD carried out a series of systematic and racially motivated crackdowns on the nightclubs and bars, forcing many of them to shut down. Many histories of black Los Angeles, although now invisible to the eye, reside in genealogies of sound. Unearthing these histories involves acts of listening rather than seeing. Here, popular music practices are generative of critiquing academic tendencies that perpetuate the hegemony of vision.

As storms, earthquakes, and riots altered and destroyed the physical terrains of greater Los Angeles, holy hip hoppers began to sound out new geographies of possibility in their aftermath. Their expressions made audible certain histories, practices, places, and daily realities, giving prominence to the experience of *place as sounded*. Their expressions mapped the complex historical, spatial, and political relationships between the 1992 L.A. riots, Ice Cube's Nation of Islam–inspired song "We Had to Tear This Muthafucka Up," and the "House of Judah" church standing on the former site of a Western Surplus gun store. In particular, the entangled soundscapes that holy hip hop assembled, from gangsta rap to urban gospel to dancehall, epitomized the tension between the leakiness of these sound worlds and the acute spatial distinctions and segregations that constitute the physical and social geography of Los Angeles.[70] While the city is often *read* by urban planners, visual artists, and creative writers who offer optic experiences of urban life, I underscore its acoustic legibility. Call to mind the many misrecognitions of gospel rappers as "gangsters" in their cars in which the visual fails. The conceptual stakes of sound *matter*. The audible city has something unique to say.

CHAPTER BREAKDOWN

The musical stories relayed herein tell us what holy hip hoppers say and do in the name of the Jesus and in allegiance to hip hop music. The diversity of holy hip hop subjects, spaces, and sounds is only partially captured here, and yet black religious heterogeneity is one of the major ideas at stake in this book. When possible, I emphasize how black diasporic religious sensibilities circulate and infuse one another through hip hop performances in Los Angeles. Readers should not expect a linear history of holy hip hop or a full-fledged portrait of L.A.-based gospel rap. Instead, this is an ethnography of holy hip hoppers' transformative soundings and practices of conversion that produced specific musical, spatial, and spiritual possibilities and pathways through the City of Angels. Rather than arguing for the valorization of holy hip hop and gospel rappers, I am interested in how holy hip hop expressions sound out injustices and inequalities within black musical communities, segregations, and integrations across urban geography, and new social and spiritual imaginaries.

Chapter 1, "'Now I Bang for Christ': Rites/Rights of Passage," focuses on the making of holy hip hoppers through an amalgamation of stories about *saving* Los Angeles. I foreground the conversion narratives of holy hip hop artists as they intersect with certain discursive formations shaping and policing the geopolitical and social landscapes of the Southland in the 1980s and '90s. Discourses of urban reform and regeneration during these years were spiritually charged and linked to imaginations of disaster and apocalypse in the wake of major earthquakes and floods as well as the 1992 riots. The ideologies and mythologies at work in these tales of urban anxiety reveal the relationships between discourses regarding the "saving" of black youth from gang life, rescuing hip hop from its increasing profanity and commercialism, and rehabilitating and incarcerating criminals. For certain self-proclaimed gangbangers-turned-churchgoers, "bangin'" was a way to represent their faith through music and fervently enact their loyalty to Christ. Hence, the common gospel rap turn of phrase emerging from the turning point of conversion: "Now I Bang for Christ."

Chapter 2, "Hip Hop Church L.A.: Shifting Grounds in Inglewood," chronicles the trials and triumphs of the Hip Hop Church L.A. in Inglewood—a monthly Friday night hip hop ministry started in 2007 by local activist-pastor Carol Scott and hip hop star–turned-pastor Kurtis Blow. Housed within the Holy Trinity Evangelical Lutheran Church, the hip hop ministry became a deeply contested terrain for members of the clergy and congregation. Conflicts over who was allowed entry into the realms of power and authority within this predominantly black church were often forged through ideological struggles over what constituted appropriate music and language in the pulpit. I situate gospel rap performances, sermons, and social interactions within the hip hop ministry in relation to the changing demographics and politics of Inglewood as a "fallen" city of African American upward mobility.

Building upon theories from critical human geography, chapter 3, "Beyond Babylon: Geographies of Conversion," explores how holy hip hoppers made use of urban spaces in unconventional ways, creating lively and experimental zones of social and musical contact. These zones were characterized by a surprising heterogeneity and intersectionality where multiple religious sensibilities mingled, sometimes coexisting, sometimes colliding, sometimes converting both people and places. While the social and territorial instability of Los Angeles has historically been managed and manipulated by state bureaucracies to implement specific agendas of urban reform, this same instability provided the conditions of possibility for city dwellers to radically re-vision and remake the existing urban milieu. Whether converting a Skid Row street corner into an "airborne church" or transforming the burned-out carcass of a gun store into a holy hip hop club, gospel rap artists animated "off the map" levels of urban history and experience.

Chapter 4, "The Evangelical Hustle: Selling Music, Saving Souls," examines how gospel rappers enacted what I term the *evangelical hustle*—that is, the daily moves they made to manage money, morality, and musical creativity through the twin pursuits of missionizing and marketing as well as how they "got their hustle on" for Christ instead of cash. The everyday flows and monetary exchanges involved in gospel hip hop performances and street evangelism—from the allocation of "formal" church offerings, to informal "love offerings" given to artists, to gospel rappers' repeated denials of payment for their CDs and musical services, to spontaneous gestures of generosity and resource sharing—complicated purely

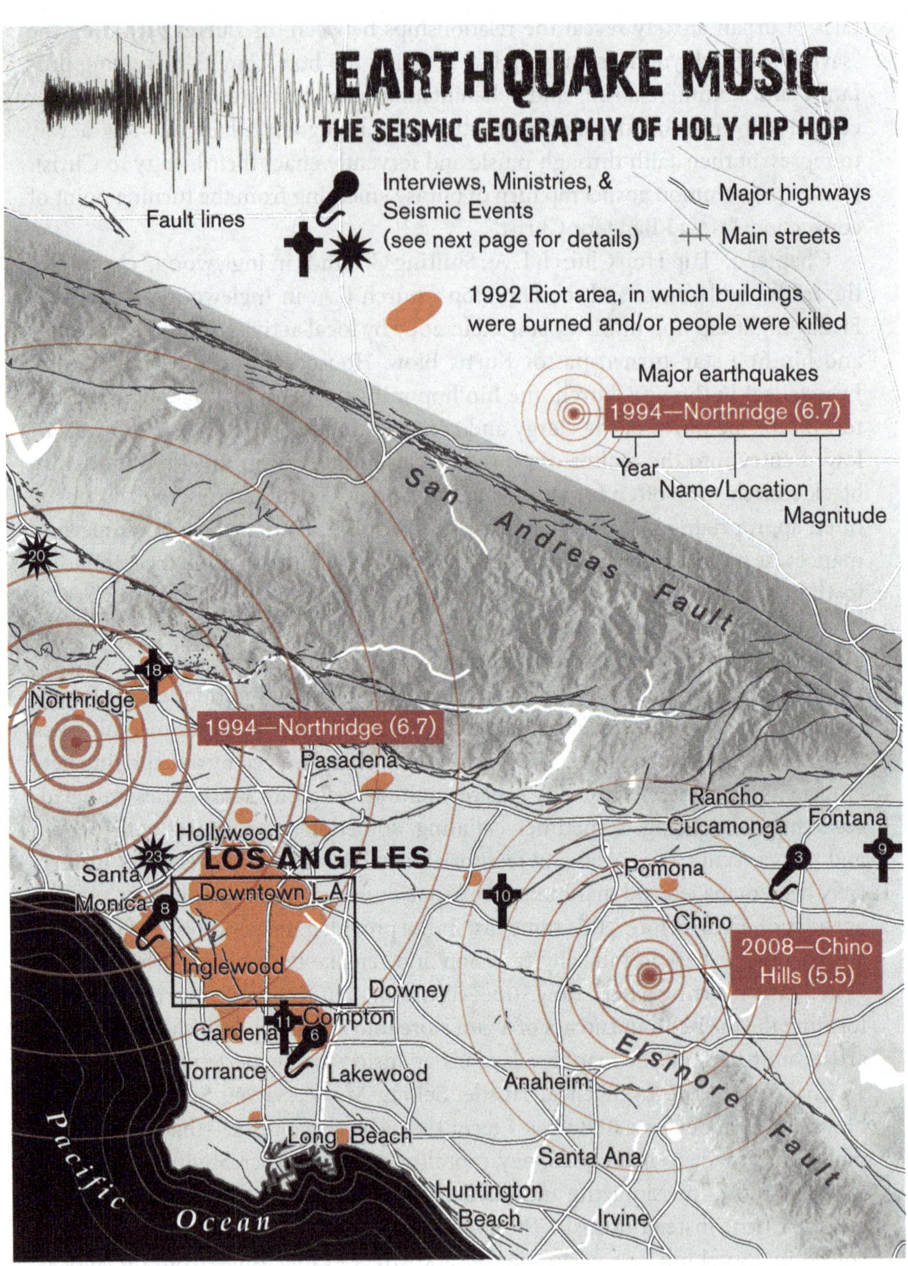

MAP 1. "Earthquake Music" map by M. Roy Cartography (refer to page 26 for map legend).

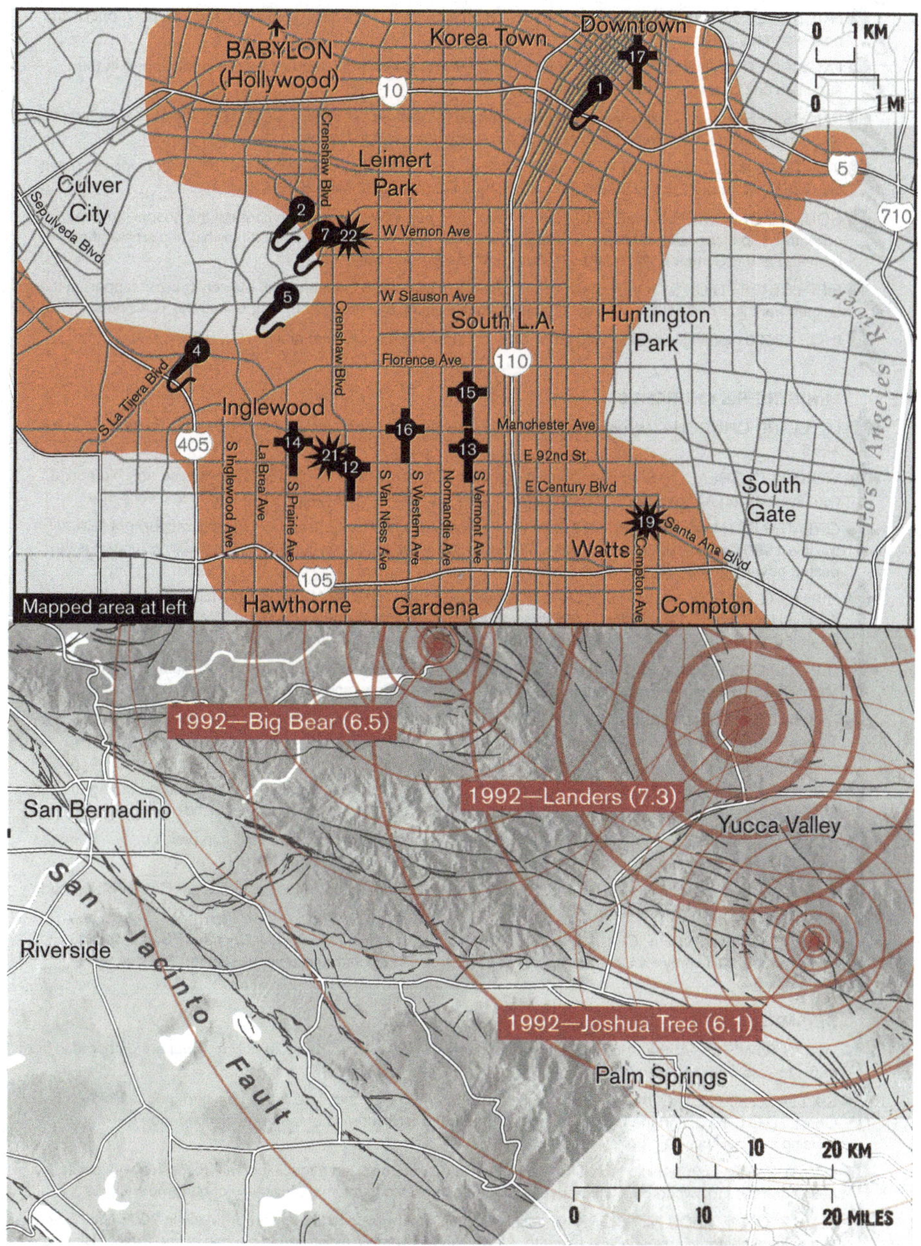

MAP 2. "Earthquake Music" map by M. Roy Cartography (refer to page 26 for map legend).

1 INTERNATIONAL FOOD COURT—2007 interview with Pastor Graham (hip hop pastor & gospel rapper) in downtown Los Angeles during which he called holy hip hop "earthquake music"

2 FATBURGER AT BALDWIN HILLS CRENSHAW PLAZA—2007 interview with Khanchuz (gospel rapper); first post-war retail complex in California

3 FATBURGER IN RANCHO CUCAMONGA—2007 meeting with Soup the Chemist (gospel rapper) in the suburban city located in San Bernardino County

4 PANN'S RESTAURANT—Interview with Cue Jn-Marie (gospel rapper, pastor & activist) at the 1950s coffee shop and diner; location of the famed Samuel L. Jackson scene from Pulp Fiction

5 WESTSIDE BIBLE CHURCH—First meeting and interview with Celah (gospel rapper from Hip Hopposite) and Slack (gospel rapper from IDOL King); now renamed Community of Faith Bible Church

6 SOUND DOCTRINE'S HOME STUDIO—Location of group interview with members of the gospel hip hop collective, Hip Hopposite: DJ Heat, Celah, B-Love, Sound Doctrine, and Crossfire; holy hip hop artists often gathered at the Compton home for bible study and to record tracks

7 FIFTH STREET DICK'S COFFEE AND JAZZ EMPORIUM—2008 interview with Majesty (gospel rapper) at the Leimert Park jazz hotspot founded by a former homeless man, Richard Fulton, right before the 1992 riots

8 IHOP—2008 meeting with Holy D (gospel rapper) at the well-known diner chain

MINISTRIES & CHURCHES

9 LOVELAND CHURCH—Gospel rapper Soup the Chemist first performed holy hip hop at this Fontana church in 1986

10 VICTORY OUTREACH—Soup the Chemist and his group Soldiers for Christ (SFC) performed holy hip hop at numerous Victory Outreach churches throughout San Bernardino County in the late 1980s and early 90s

11 GREATER BETHANY COMMUNITY CHURCH—Gardena church where B-Love (gospel rapper) got "saved" in the late 1990s and where Bishop Jones - brother to Jamaican singer, model, and actress, Grace Jones - is the pastor; now renamed City of Refuge Church

12 HIP HOP CHURCH L.A. @ HOLY TRINITY EVANGELICAL LUTHERAN CHURCH—Initial Inglewood home to the Hip Hop Church L.A.; started in 2006 by rap legend-turned-minister Kurtis "Blow" Walker, Pastor Carol Scott, Sharon Collins-Heads, and Mike Green; now housed at Inglewood's Faith Lutheran Church

13 HIP HOP CHURCH L.A. @ TOTAL RESTORATION MINISTRIES—Hip Hop Church L.A. mobile ministry event on March 7, 2008 at a storefront church where Pastor Graham rapped and delivered a sermon

14 FAITHFUL CENTRAL BIBLE CHURCH @ THE FORUM—Famous Inglewood indoor arena and home to "The Takeover" Youth Ministry, a hip hop-inspired service established in 2005 and formerly pastored by newjack gospel icon, Kirk Franklin

15 CRENSHAW CHRISTIAN CENTER—Home to Pastor Fred Price, Jr.'s "Hip Hop Sunday" service during the early 2000s; the first event drew nearly 10,000 to the megachurch structure known as the Faithdome

16 CLUB JUDAH @ LOVE & FAITH CHRISTIAN CENTER—Weekly Saturday night hip hop praise party that began in 2003; hosted in a church building that was formerly a Western Surplus gun store

17 THE ROW (THE "CHURCH WITHOUT WALLS")—An "airborne" church that pastor/rapper Cue Jn-Marie leads every Friday night on the corner of Wall Street and Winston Street on L.A.'s Skid Row

18 FREEDOM FELLOWSHIP CHURCH—"Youth and Young Adult Hip Hop & Rock Church" in San Fernando and home to Klub 20/Twenty - a Christian open-mic party where Khanchuz and other gospel rappers perform

SEISMIC EVENTS

19 WATTS TOWERS—At the height of gang-related violence in the late 1980s, 75 holy hip hoppers gathered in front of the towers with their bibles

20 SIX FLAGS MAGIC MOUNTAIN—During the 1995 Holy Hip Hop tour, L.A. gospel hip hop groups Soldiers For Christ, I.D.O.L. King, and the Gospel Gangstaz performed for hundreds of fans who climbed atop the stage, causing it to collapse

21 DARBY PARK—In 2004, Hip Hop Church L.A. pastor, Carol Scott, led a mock funeral procession with several hearses to the Inglewood park where people buried guns in a coffin to mourn victims of gang violence

22 KLUB ZYON @ KAOS NETWORK—A gospel hip hop open-mic founded by Cue Jn-Marie in 2006 and housed at a cultural center in Leimert Park; home to the well-known weekly underground hip hop event, Project Blowed

23 SCHOENBERG MUSIC BUILDING, UCLA CAMPUS—Gospel rappers B-Love and Khanchuz had performed for my "Cultural History of Rap" class at the UCLA Herb Albert School of Music when the 2008 Chino Hills earthquake struck (5.5M)

MAP 3. "Earthquake Music" map by M. Roy Cartography.

economic notions of success and visibility. In this unique spiritual economy, gospel rappers transposed words and actions from the realm of gangbanging to street evangelism.

In the final chapter, I return to the broader themes of conversion and black liberation through an exploration of the multiple "Roads to Zion" that crosscut gospel hip hop. I link polyvalent renderings of Zion in L.A.-based holy hip hop to the spiritual traversals and tracks of rap stars such as MC Hammer, Nas, Snoop Dogg, Lecrae, and Kendrick Lamar. These intersecting quests for Zion through Christian, Muslim, and Rastafarian spiritual and musical sensibilities are creating new mappings of black diasporic religiosity. They point to new questions in the study of American popular music and religion that go beyond the categories of oppression and resistance, the religious and the secular. Further, they unveil how conversion—as a transformative practice in the lives of hip hoppers of various religious affiliations—is but one way to *sound out* life's path through the terrors and triumphs in the City of Angels, in America, and beyond.

"Now I Bang for Christ"

Rites/Rights of Passage

How can I live hip hop and still be Christian?
—RALPH C. WATKINS (HIP HOP DJ AND MINISTER)

God give free will, I choose to walk in love
But don't think 'cause I'm a Christian I forgot how to thug
—KHANCHUZ (GOSPEL RAPPER)

On a sunny and smog-heavy afternoon at Fatburger, Khanchuz and I leaned over greasy cheeseburgers, French fries, and my audio recorder. With eyes closed, he prayed over the hum of traffic: "Father God, thank you for this food we are about to receive. Lord, let it be nourishing to our bodies and strengthening to our spirits, Father God. We invite you to be in our conversation today, Father God. In Jesus's name, we pray. Amen."[1] Khanchuz, a former gangbanger and now gospel rapper, offered this "fast food" blessing on the small, caged-in sidewalk patio of a burger chain nestled in the sprawling Crenshaw Plaza shopping complex. Despite our surroundings, in that moment, all felt sacred. While we had only met briefly a week before in July of 2007—where rap star–turned-preacher Kurtis "Blow" Walker was delivering a sermon at the Hip Hop Church L.A. in Inglewood—Khanchuz immediately launched into the intimate details of his life story between slow sips of Sprite. He paused occasionally to wipe back a tear as I struggled to pose careful questions in response to his twisting tale of conversion.

Over a decade earlier in the early 1990s, at the height of the Los Angeles gang wars and amidst recurring environmental disasters, Khanchuz was a gangsta rapper who went by the name "Sleep." He earned the title from repeatedly passing out in a drunken stupor with his friends. After Khanchuz "got saved," he contemplated changing his MC name to "Awake," but eventually settled on "Conscious" after searching an electronic thesaurus. As is typical in hip hop naming practice, he altered the conventional spelling to "Khanchuz"—something, he recalled, that he used to do with his "homies" when he was "bangin." Khanchuz's first God-inspired rap was delivered inside a jail cell in Colorado to the rhythm of his fellow inmate's plastic spoon tapping against the bars. "And now I bang for Christ," he told me zealously, which constituted performing his street-hard brand of gospel rap with his hip hop crew ADK (Any Demon Killa) in between part-time work as a youth counselor for a South L.A. group home and a drug test administrant in Long Beach. For Khanchuz and many other gospel rap practitioners, "bangin" was not about selling drugs, pimping women, and toting guns but rather about how he represented his religious beliefs and fervently enacted his loyalty to Christ.[2] His spiritual repurposing of the term "bangin" was a jab at many of the demonizing discourses associated with "culture of poverty" politics.

Khanchuz was used to fielding questions about his commitment to both hip hop and Christianity. Given his "hardcore" look—tattoos, shaved head, goatee, gold tooth, baggy hip hop attire, requisite black sunglasses, and imposing hyper-masculine stance—most people were surprised to discover that he was a righteous and committed Christian. Across the way from Fatburger, Khanchuz once applied for a job at Wal-Mart where his interviewer asked him if he was "ghetto." Just south of the Crenshaw Plaza outside his former apartment in Inglewood, prostitutes repeatedly asked him if he wanted to "take a ride" while local drug dealers offered him weed. He would tell them, "Dude, I'm so cool off that. You don't even know." And they didn't. These were the continual acts of questioning and misrecognition that Khanchuz negotiated in his everyday life—on the streets but also in the church as congregants, clergy, and pastors often assumed he was just another impious rapper. As I sat across from him, I couldn't help but feel that my interview questions were somehow linked to other forms and sites of questioning that he had been involved in with landlords, bosses, passersby, judges, reporters, ministers, police, pimps, and prostitutes.[3]

Another sip of soda prompted him to rap one of his lyrics: "Obey my thirst like Sprite and thirst for what's right. I lay hands like Tyson in a spiritual fight." As Khanchuz spoke of multiple conversions—the transposing of hip hop lexicons and street slang into religious settings, the transformation from performing gangsta rap to gospel rap, and the social and spatial changes that dramatically altered the historically segregated neighborhoods where gospel hip hop practitioners resided and worked—he mapped out a city at once profane and sacred, a city of catastrophe and renewal, a city of incarceration and possibility.

CATACLYSMIC CARTOGRAPHIES

This chapter focuses on the emergence of holy hip hop practitioners, recognizing that hip hop, as a genre and practice, "goes gospel" because people *convert* to Christianity. Rather than mere autobiography, holy hip hop conversion narratives articulated complex and cataclysmic entanglements of nature, technology, culture, and the divine.[4] Amidst narratives and discourses of urban peril and racial uplift, holy hip hop subjects and subjectivities emerged through an assemblage of agential forces and fields of power: the LAPD's policing practices throughout the 1980s and '90s as they represented an increasingly punitive criminal justice system, events and imaginaries linked to environmental disaster, forms of black Christianity, social programs of urban reform, the role of individual social actors, and the agency of religious beings.

In particular, the conversion narratives of gospel rappers such as Soup the Chemist, Khanchuz, B-Love, and Cue remapped and reinforced similar discourses of salvation regarding the *saving* of black youth from the perils of inner-city life, *rescuing* hip hop (especially gangsta rap) from its increasing profanity and commercialism, and *rehabilitating* parts of historically black L.A., especially Inglewood as a "fallen" city. These intersecting stories shared specific narrative parallels of fall and resurrection, disaster and rehabilitation, death and rebirth, mutually reinforcing each other and powerfully shaping how Angelenos defined and experienced L.A. as both utopia and dystopia, heaven and hell.[5] In particular, this city of sunshine and beaches was the breeding ground for a host of urban anxieties linked to gang violence, natural disaster, inner-city poverty, and rioting throughout the 1980s and '90s. Mike Davis, in *Ecologies of Fear: Los Angeles and the Imagination of Disaster* (1998), examined the barrage of earthquakes, floods, and fires that tormented Southern California during the early 1990s, remarking, "Cataclysm has become virtually routine."[6] Davis continued:

> This virtually biblical conjugation of disaster, which coincided with the worst regional recession in 50 years, is unique in American history, and it has purchased thousands of one-way tickets to Seattle, Portland, and Santa Fe. After a century of population influx, 529,000 residents, mostly middle-class, fled the Los Angeles metropolitan region in the years 1993 and 1994 alone. Partly as a result of this exodus, the median household income in Los Angeles County fell by an astonishing 20 percent (from $36,000 to $29,000) between 1989 and 1995. Middle-class apprehensions about the angry, abandoned underclasses are now only exceeded by anxieties about blind thrust faults and hundred-year floods.[7]

What were the *effects* and *affects* of this level of disaster and tragedy on people and places? What stories were told, championed, and circulated in the wake of loss, dislocation, and hostility? How were certain city inhabitants grouped, labeled, and treated in moments of instability? How did people make sense of this landscape of uncertainty through music and other forms of social life? How did individuals, communities, and institutions enact agendas of change and rehabilitation, and which people and places were deemed worthy of such efforts at transformation?

The anxious and fearful rhetorics and imaginaries surrounding these events were articulated and deployed through the often racially inflected lenses of religion, science, art, and the economic market. The practical and material responses to natural disasters and cultural uprisings—responses of rescue, rehabilitation, lockdown, and evangelism—were shaped by these powerful rhetorics. And yet, the imaginary of "paradise lost" pervaded the varied responses of religious leaders, scientists, musicians, and city officials, among others, as they struggled to "save" their own versions and visions of paradise. In the 1980s and '90s, the Los Angeles Police Department scapegoated black and brown youth for the ills of urban existence, scientists blamed urban developers for transgressing environmental common sense, and religious radicals pointed the finger at the moral depravity of the entertainment industry. A 1995 *Los Angeles Times* article speculated, "There's no question that [we are] caught in the middle of something strange . . . maybe God, as the biblical sorts preach, is mad at us for making all those dirty movies."[8] In turn, Hollywood has also played a prominent role in promoting and propagating the concept of apocalypse or "Last Days" through the genre of Los Angeles disaster fiction and film.

Along these lines, holy hip hoppers prefigured the City of Angels as modern-day Babylon in their everyday conversations and music. Many gospel rappers emerged in Los Angeles at this particular conjuncture, in the midst of environmental eruptions, social unrest, culture wars, and a web of discourses and debates around urban renewal and redemption unique to California's Southland. Their holy hip hop soundings were audibly entangled in these complex social assemblages and cartographies of catastrophe.[9]

FONTANA FOUNDATIONS

The story of holy hip hop in the City of Angels begins appropriately with an aural misrecognition and a case of mistaken identity. Soup the Chemist, one of the first African American hip hop MCs to "go gospel" in the 1980s, was in route to a youth church service in Fontana, his new religious hip hop track, "Listen Up," booming from his car speakers as he pulled into the church parking lot. The year was 1986 and Soup had just committed his life to Jesus.

Soup had been interested in God since boyhood; it was his uncle's death that first caused him to question the existence of Heaven. He studied many different religions throughout the Inland Empire as a youth, becoming a Jehovah's Witness, then a follower of the Nation of Islam, and eventually a student of metaphysics. Christianity was difficult for Soup to accept as he did not resonate with the picture of a white Jesus and felt that it was a white man's religion. He recalled, "I can remember feeling angry after watching *Roots*, and studying the history and philosophy of the Black Panther Party for Self-Defense."[10] But after suffering through and surviving a violent head injury, Soup felt that God had saved him.

In the early to mid-1980s, during this time of religious exploration, Soup was equally compelled by hip hop music and culture. Influenced by the early hip hop sounds of Grandmaster Flash, the Cold Crush Brothers, Double Trouble, Run DMC, and Rakim, Soup began training as a DJ at the Delmann Heights Community Center in San Bernardino. He had made his first mixtape in 1983 in remembrance of his musical mentor, DJ Tracy Houston, who was shot to death. In 1986, after a drug-addicted crew member stole all his DJ equipment, he began to question his life of partying and ceased making and listening to hip hop altogether. He sold all his vinyl records and became a member of Loveland church in Fontana. Soup recalled for me the time period following his conversion (also over a Fatburger, but this time fifty miles east of Crenshaw Plaza in Rancho Cucamonga): "For a whole year I did no music, no nothing, but I was going crazy. I hate choir music. It was killing me, so I started writing my own gospel raps. I started writing rhymes for me. I was studying a lot—just trying to understand what the heck I was doing."[11] He then lamented that nobody was making gospel rap in those days except for Stephen Wiley, whom he felt lacked a street sensibility so inherent to hip hop.[12] Two other God-inspired hip hop tracks emerged that same year—Doug E. Fresh and the Get Fresh Crew's "All the Way to Heaven" (1986) and MC Hammer's "Song of King" (1986)—but both releases were squarely planted in the commercial hip hop market. Soup remained apprehensive about integrating hip hop aesthetics with his newly devout lyrics.

Hip hop and Christianity finally merged musically for Soup on his gospel rap track "Listen Up," where he unveiled a moment in his conversion story on the last verse. Aside from tackling topics such as war, poverty, and terrorism, he rapped about his days as a party animal and how he "couldn't wait to hit all the clubs, flirt with the freaks and get a buzz." He pinpointed the moment of his conversion:

> Flopped on the couch and turned on the TV
> But there really wasn't nothing for me to see
> Till this guy on TBN started getting to me
> He said either you will go to heaven or hell
> And if you don't believe me, time will tell

He fell to his knees and began to pray in front of the Trinity Broadcasting Network—the world's largest religious network and America's most-watched faith channel.

Once parked outside the Fontana church, Soup sat in his car with the windows rolled down and listened to some gospel rap tracks he had mixed earlier that day. His slow "old school" rhyming couplets traversed a simple Casio keyboard bass line and sparse, hard-hitting hip hop snare and bass drum hits. A man parked next to him, overhearing the hip hop beat and muffled lyrics of "Listen Up," approached Soup's car to reprimand him for playing "that stuff out loud like that" near a house

FIGURE 2. Soup the Chemist above the Los Angeles skyline, c. 2013. Photo courtesy of Daley Hake.

of prayer. But as the man came closer and *listened up* to the exact words, he paused. "Man, are they talking about God in that?" he uttered in surprise. "That track is tight! Who is that?" Soup, still skeptical of how his gospel rap might be perceived by churchgoers, replied cautiously, "Oh, this dude I know. You really like it?" The man asked for a copy of the cassette, which eventually found its way into the hands of the youth pastor at the church.

A few days later, Soup received a call from his new fan, youth pastor Kevin Schubkegel: "Hey man, that guy who's rapping on the cassette, do you know him?" Soup finally came clean and admitted, "That's me, man." Pleased to have located the mystery MC behind this new brand of pious hip hop, Schubkegel immediately invited Soup to rap for the youth of Loveland, who, while somewhat shielded from the gang wars and aggressive policing practices that terrorized residents of South Los Angeles, were also experiencing the effects of racial segregation, deindustrialization, and joblessness.

In the 1940s, Fontana—a historically blue-collar and working-class city east of Los Angeles that Mike Davis refers to as "Junkyard of Dreams"—once offered African Americans the promise of new life in the Citrus Belt: upward mobility, agricultural abundance, and resplendent respite from the urban swarm of inner-city life. The *Eagle,* Los Angeles's progressive black paper, featured prominent ads for "sunny, fruitful lots in the Fontana area" during this time. Davis explains:

> For pent-up residents of the overcrowded Central Avenue ghetto, prevented by restrictive housing covenants ('L.A. Jim Crow') from moving into suburban areas like the San Fernando Valley, Fontana must have been alluring. Moreover, Kaiser's Richmond Shipyards were the biggest employer of Black labor on the coast, and there was widespread hope that his new steel plant would be an equally color-blind employer. The reality in Fontana was that Blacks were segregated in their own tracts—a kind of citrus ghetto—on the rocky floodplain about Baseline Avenue in vaguely delineated "north Fontana."[13]

It is fitting that holy hip hop in the City of Angels would emerge in Fontana—a city in the heart of the Inland Empire that "has been both junkyard and utopia for successive tropes of a changing California dream" and is still suffering from sedimentations of class inequality and racial segregation.[14] This time the dream was holy hip hop, which signaled a larger dream to reconcile Fontana's seemingly insurmountable juxtapositions. That gospel rap would share the same birthplace as the Hell's Angels (emerging just forty years earlier in 1946) is also fitting as they both epitomize the hard-edged, fraternal grace of outlaw culture. Even notorious gangster and bootlegger Al Capone once owned a home there. The house still stands, with a large "C" on the chimney. Soup also used to identify himself with a capital "C" when he was doing secular rap, going by the name Super C. Some say it stands for Super Christian, although Soup later explained that the "er C" stands for "everyday remembering Christ." To be sure, the emerging sounds of holy hip hop in Fontana sat somewhere between Capone and Christ, gangsterism and grace.

Soup too was caught in between his *street* aesthetic and his newfound loyalty to the *church.* "I'm not a Christian rapper," he reflected. "I'm a rapper who's a Christian. I was a rapper first and then I became born-again. I didn't want to be put in a box where every rap I write had to be about Jesus because that's not how I live. I wrote songs that dealt with all sorts of situations—money, all kinds of things."[15] The first few times Soup performed at youth services in Fontana, he and the congregation were both "tripping out." This was the first time anyone had heard gospel rap.

> Everybody was tripping out. You know, they had never heard Christian rap. It was 1986. So I was like, man, this is a trip. But I was scared to talk because I was still *street*. I wouldn't talk. And everybody kept saying, "Hey, give your testimony." I was like, "No no no." I said, "I go to church but I'm still trying to get myself, you know … I ain't on that level." "Just rap then," they said. It made such noise that they wanted me to do it at Sunday service too. I was like, "Aw, I ain't rapping in no Sunday service, man!" Dude was like, "Nah nah, I'm telling you. Everybody is raving about it. Just do that same song you did." So I did it again. The beat was real old school—drum machine.[16]

An experienced MC and hip hop artist, Soup was still learning how to express himself in the language and format of testimony, unsure whether he could articulate his story and himself in the parlance of the church without resorting to certain kinds of hip hop slang and terminology that might be deemed inappropriate in such a holy setting. For Soup, religious conversion took time and practice.

Eventually, Soup and his gospel hip hop crew—Soldiers For Christ (S.F.C.), which included DJ Dove and emcees Brother G and QP—started getting calls from churches throughout San Bernardino and Ontario. They performed at many different youth services for Victory Outreach churches throughout the area. At one such service, the three hundred young people in attendance rose to their feet, clapping their hands and shouting in praise. One teenage boy was inspired to start writing his own gospel rap lyrics. The next time Soup performed at a Victory Outreach service he pressed up one thousand cassettes of S.F.C.'s first, self-produced gospel rap album, *Fully Armed* (1987). Like "Listen Up," the album featured the "old school" hip hop drum machine and Casio sounds of the 1980s and contained a wide range of samples from the Philadelphia sound of Gamble & Huff to the theme song from *Happy Days*. A couple tracks featured Soup rhyming in a distinctive reggae-dancehall style and even shouting down "Babylon." The title track featured a drum machine, record scratching, and a simple four-beat rock guitar riff with Soup delivering faster, more complex rhymes in a more distinctive East Coast style of delivery reminiscent of KRS-One.

The next time S.F.C. performed at Victory Outreach, they sold every last album out of the trunk of Soup's car in the church parking lot. Soup's gospel rap was producing cataclysmic reactions throughout the Southland. In order to capture the burgeoning spirit of this new movement, he and DJ Dove coined the phrase holy hip hop. "We started it right there in West Covina. Victory Outreach presents Friday night Holy Hip Hop. They tried to put me in the box of 'Christian rap,' so we had to come up with our own saying."[17] He also changed his name to Soup the Chemist to invoke a new intention behind his music.

An interesting fact about me is that I love clam chowder. I would be on the school bus when I was a kid and while everybody had their potato chips or candy, I'd whip out my can of clam chowder. They called me Soup. That name stuck with me; I dropped the "o" and just kept "Sup." As for the Chemist part, in science, chemistry causes a reaction. I wanted to be a musical scientist or chemist so to speak. When my lyrics hit the ears, a reaction occurs.[18]

Later, he would reincorporate the "o." Soup's statement paralleled Pastor Graham's invocation of holy hip hop as *earthquake music*—"music that shakes our souls and moves the ground we walk on." Inspired by his new musical science and the social possibilities of merging hip hop and Christianity, Soup the Chemist began a California movement, Raising a Nation That Will Obey, among the newly emerging Los Angeles–based holy hip hop groups that followed in S.F.C.'s wake. In the late 1980s, the movement was seventy-five strong. Soup assembled all of them in front of the Watts Towers to take a photo for his new album cover. The towers, made of found rebar, steel rods, and glass from soda bottles, have held an important place in the imagination of black art and politics. In the 1960s, "As the gangs began to become politicized, they became 'al fresco' churches whose ministers brought the gospel [of Black Power] out into the streets."[19]

And in the late 1980s, as gang wars were raging across L.A., a mass of young black and Latino men gathered in Watts in broad daylight. Soup recalled, "Imagine seventy-five people standing in the street. Everybody thought it was a gang. All the Crips and Bloods were over there. It was funny. They're coming out with their guns thinking it was about to pop off and we're all there with our Bibles. Once they found out what it was they were tripping."[20] Another instance of holy hip hop misrecognition. Soup and his Nation were bangin' for a different cause, *fully armed* with Bibles instead of guns, scripture instead of bullets.

GETTING HAMMERED FROM ALL SIDES

While Soup was Raising a Nation That Will Obey, the Los Angeles Police Department, various local community organizations, and the black middle class responded to the prevalence of gang activities in Los Angeles in various ways. During the 1980s, the LAPD, led by Police Chief Daryl Gates, initiated a much more aggressive, stringent, and uncompromising attack on gang culture (*read* young black and brown youth) throughout the greater Los Angeles. Gates began such security policies during the 1984 Olympic Games held in L.A. with expanded gang sweeps, which were implemented across wide areas of the city but especially South Central and East Los Angeles. Between 1984 and 1989, citizen complaints against police brutality increased by 33 percent.

In 1987, the LAPD Community Resources Against Street Hoodlums (CRASH) initiative and antigang task force Operation HAMMER initiated one of the deadliest assaults on South Los Angeles. CRASH was an elite special operations unit of the LAPD established by Chief Gates in 1977 and tasked with combating gang-related crime. The influx of crack cocaine had dramatically increased gang violence throughout Los Angeles. Initially operating in the early 1970s as a unit of the 77th Street Division of the LAPD under the name TRASH—an acronym for Total Resources Against Street Hoodlums—the name was changed after activists argued that the name was harmful to the image of black and brown youth. By the 1980s, each of the LAPD's eighteen divisions had been assigned a CRASH unit, and under Operation HAMMER, CRASH officers conducted numerous raids that resulted in the mass arrest and imprisonment of black youth, some of whom were gang members, some of whom were just innocent residents.

On one such raid in 1988, droves of police officers descended on two apartment buildings at the corner of 39th Street and Dalton Avenue. A *Los Angeles Times* article reported:

> The police smashed furniture, punched holes in walls, destroyed family photos, ripped down cabinet doors, slashed sofas, shattered mirrors, hammered toilets to porcelain shards, doused clothing with bleach and emptied refrigerators. Some officers left their own graffiti: "LAPD Rules." "Rollin' 30s Die."[21]

The following year, Nancy Reagan accompanied Chief Gates during a drug bust of a "rock house" in what was then South Central. After the suspects were cuffed and arrested, he remarked: "These people are beyond the point of teaching and rehabilitating."[22] This view of innate black criminality began the philosophy behind the modus operandi of the LAPD. Specifically, the dominant discourse regarding young males and crime lumped youth offenders into two groups. White youth were generally considered "delinquents" in the restless and rebellious transition of adolescence who would eventually calm down in a more normative, law-abiding stage of life. Black youth, on the other hand, were considered juvenile criminals incapable of being rehabilitated into functioning, healthy members of society.

The seeds of these attitudes were planted under LAPD Chief William Parker, who was known for his racist commentary and policing tactics that in part fueled the 1965 Watts riots. Those who lived in L.A. in the 1940s and '50s remember this darker side of Parker, a man who was quoted calling black folks "monkeys" and referring to Latinos from the "wild tribes" of Mexico.[23] During this same time, Chief Parker railed against the activities of the Group Guidance Unit "because they 'gave status to gang activity' by treating gang members as socially transformable individuals."[24] By the late 1980s, the insidious nature of these attitudes had grown into a forest of thorns for black and brown youth in Los Angeles attempting to survive and navigate a cityscape of joblessness, dislocation, violence, and abandonment. Gaye Theresa Johnson has argued that "the militarization of urban space, anti-immigration policies, loss of assets, and disenfranchisement" all contributed to what she terms "spatial immobilization" among black and brown poor communities in Los Angeles.[25]

The successive criminalization of black and brown communities notably coincided with the rise of hip hop music and gangsta rap, especially in Los Angeles. The invocation of "black noise" and sonic terrorism often accompanies discussions about the spiritual poverty of the Hip Hop Generation. It is easy to see how hip hop culture and gang culture become aligned in these larger discourses linking to the "culture of poverty." While some gospel rappers were actually former gang members, almost all young black men on the streets of L.A. in the 1980s and '90s fell under the highly inclusive category of "suspected gang member" by the LAPD. One's religious beliefs don't always register in the eyes of racial profiling.

As Operation HAMMER subjected African American and Latino youth to increasingly harsh state laws, members of the black clergy and segments of the black middle class employed "God's Hammer"—the Bible—to further critique the moral depravity of inner-city youth in relation to God's law. (One is also reminded of the anti–hip hop pastor, G. Craige Lewis, sledge hammering and burning hip hop CDs in pulpits of megachurches).[26] Scholars have referred to this reaction by the black middle class as "black-lash," and thus, the LAPD's approach to crime can not only be considered an act of white backlash. Leaders in black communities across the Southland also supported the tactics and approaches of Chief Gates and Mayor Hahn.

In the late 1980s, the NAACP supported Mayor Hahn's attempt to impose martial law on the Playboy Gangster Crips, while the South Central Organizing Committee (SCOC), a church-supported local affiliate of the Industrial Areas Foundation (IAF), called for greater police deployment against street youth. Davis elaborates on the growing cross-generational tensions in African American communities:

> Black middle-class revulsion against youth criminality—indeed the perception that dealers and gangs threaten the very integrity of Black culture—is thus translated through such patriarchal bluster, into support for the extremist rhetoric of the gangbusters . . . How is it that inter-generational relations within the Black community have suddenly grown so grimly foreboding?[27]

Some of these internal polarizations began in the 1970s as African American public sector workers and professionals successfully integrated themselves into city business and the semi-skilled working classes in the private sector continued to suffer job losses due to factory closures and economic outsourcing.

Since the 1965 Watts riots, economic conditions in South Central had actually gotten worse, with unemployment rising from 5.6 to 8.6 percent.[28] Tensions between the LAPD and the South Central community reached an all-time high in 1992, resulting in the most lethal American riot of the century. Violence, looting, and arson exploded in the wake of the beating of a black motorist, Rodney King, by five LAPD officers and their subsequent acquittal by a jury composed mainly of white jurors. After five days of rioting, more than 50 Angelenos were dead, over

2,000 injured, and almost 17,000 arrested.[29] Property damages were estimated at $1 billion, and it took 20,000 police officers and National Guardsmen to return the city to some semblance of normal.

Not surprisingly, attempts to redevelop and reinvest in the riot area, such as Rebuild L.A., fell short. Ice Cube's third album, *The Predator*, which was released within months of the 1992 riots, featured "We Had to Tear This Muthafucka Up"—a song directed at the police officers acquitted in the trial. Cube, known for attacking Jews, police, and politicians alike in his lyrics, rapped the following over a jazzy upright bass line:

> Tearin' up shit with fire, shooters, looters
> Now I got a laptop computer
> I told you all what happened and you heard it, read it
> But all you could call me was anti-Semitic

Ice Cube went on to talk about how the inner city had to give President "Bush a push" and how his "National Guard ain't hard." He warned America that "You had to get Rodney to stop me," otherwise we would "have teared this muthafucka up." While Ice Cube was offering his controversial take on the riots, the West Coast Rap All-Stars—a collaboration of West Coast hip hop artists including Dr. Dre, Eazy-E, Tone-Loc, MC Hammer, and Shock G, among many others—had planted the seeds of reconciliation and togetherness through their 1990 hit single, "We're All in the Same Gang."

The story that received much less attention was the gang truce between the Bloods and the Crips that was brokered on April 28, 1992—a day before the riots broke out. Hundreds of black men gathered in Watts, once again, not with Bibles or guns but to declare a ceasefire between the two notorious black street gangs. The L.A. murder rate had just topped a thousand per year. Skip Townsend, a Rollin' 20 Blood from West Adams, commented, "I mean I couldn't even pump gas. I couldn't go to the grocery store. I couldn't do anything without interacting with someone who would want to hurt me or I'd have to hurt them."[30] Another young man there that evening of the truce in front of the Nickerson Gardens housing project was Aqeela Sherrills. Sherrills, a former Grape Street Crip, remarked, "*The Autobiography of Malcolm X*, James Baldwin's *The Evidence of Things Not Seen*. These things challenged me. They politicized me and they also gave me courage and language to begin to speak with folks in the neighborhood about what was happening."[31] Those who brokered the truce used the 1949 ceasefire agreement between Israel and Egypt as a blueprint for a formal written peace accord in 1994, revealing how these local geographies of violence and attempts at amity were implicated in global struggles for peace. While the truce lasted ten years with crime rates in Watts dropping significantly in the subsequent years, gang shootings continued. Sherrills lost a son in 2004.

SPIRITUALIZING SELF-HELP

Beyond the highly critiqued Rebuild L.A. initiative, black communities in Los Angeles responded to the riots and ongoing violence in a number of ways. Black churches and local community organizations engaged in religiously driven responses to help "troubled" youth. Social programs such as Amer-I-Can, Homeboy Industries, and Gangsters Anonymous have been premised on helping people change their attitudes and behaviors as opposed to just locking them up. Many of these services and self-help programs were anchored in Christian beliefs and spiritual ideals as well as self-help ideologies. Gangsters Anonymous attempted to help gangsters recover from pathologies of gangsterism and crime. Like Alcoholics Anonymous or Narcotics Anonymous, it followed a twelve-step program that outlines a course of action for recovery from addiction, compulsion, or other behavioral problems through accepting a greater power (i.e., God).[32]

Kenny Mitchell, an African American longshoreman and Inglewood native now in his late forties, founded Gangsters Anonymous in Los Angeles. He actually came up with the idea for the new society while in Alcoholics Anonymous. He recalled in a *Los Angeles Times* interview:

> One day, I was doing my fourth step with my sponsor, who was also a gangster. We got to the part about being powerless, and I said to him, "We need this for us!" If I'd had someone tell me this long ago, I wouldn't live wanting to control everything around me … Years later, I sat down with the blue book (the handbook of Alcoholics Anonymous) and I almost rewrote every page. Our first meeting was in 2001 at a barbershop on Western. The police came and accosted the gangsters who came! … We saw a need to recover as gangsters, and to show the world we can recover. We have been meeting ever since.[33]

The LAPD was certainly not convinced that "gangsters" were capable of recovery, whether it was in the form of religious conversion, imprisonment, or programs focused on behavioral modification. Not all African Americans have wholeheartedly supported programs like Gangsters Anonymous and the Community in Support of the Gang Truce (CSGT). Alluding to black-lash in a different context, sociologist Joao Vargas argues:

> Gang prevention groups, while able to draw support and sympathy from progressive social groups and movements, are not able to gain widespread acceptance among various social sectors of inner-city residents. A considerable number of Blacks, especially the relatively well-off, openly nurture a strong aversion to all that is related to gangs—and they remain aloof to both the market-oriented, individualistic wishes of success, and the claims for social justice that are part of CSGT's programs. Without recognition and support, the gang truce and the significant results it has achieved are at risk. The peace movement runs against the grain of both contemporary politics, determined in great measure by the public-sanctioned necessity of ever-expanding law-enforcement apparatuses, and widespread perceptions about

the social and racial components of poverty and social deviance. In this worldview, gangbangers will always be gangbangers, irrespective of their allegiance to the values and practices of the wider society: gangbangers are prisoners of their immanent social and racial essence.[34]

The worldview that posited gangbangers as "prisoners of their immanent social and racial essence" was certainly an incarcerating view of black and brown youth that revealed the ways in which gangbangers and former gangbangers were trapped by and in various racialized discourses of criminality throughout the last couple decades of the twentieth century.[35] This sense of being trapped and confined manifested in the literal caging of iron prison bars, handcuffing during street-side interrogations, exclusion from certain labor markets and jobs, and spatial segregation into particular areas and neighborhoods in the city.[36] Statistics in the early part of the twenty-first century showed that in Los Angeles County, one in three African American men between the ages of twenty and twenty-nine is under the supervision of the criminal justice system, either in prison or in jail, or on probation or parole. This situation was often attributed to alleged deficiencies in the character and morality of inner-city dwellers, but, as Vargas asserts, "it illustrates the reduced opportunities Black youngsters have in the formal economy and suggests orchestrated institutional efforts to maintain social exclusion."[37] Working within these incarcerating realities and discourses, young African Americans found ways to move and maneuver within myriad constraints and confinements. The dialectic of entrapment and setting free was even present in the language of juvenile delinquency. As Khanchuz told me one afternoon, sitting in his office at a Group Home facility that houses and treats youth with criminal records, "a juvenile youth achieves 'emancipation' and is released if he or she successfully completes the entire program."[38]

The next section will explore how gospel rappers navigated these carceral cartographies—terrains of upheaval and discipline—in relation to their religious conversions. The conversion narratives of Khanchuz, B-Love, and Cue show how many holy hip hoppers disrupted and exceeded many of the expectations of those *hammering* from all sides.

NARRATIVES OF CONVERSION

Those seeking a change from gangster and gangbanging lifestyles went a number of routes. Holy hip hoppers found their "emancipation" through religious conversion; they used hip hop music to mend and transform the environmental and social chaos surrounding them. For them, religious conversion not only initiated a spiritual *rite of passage* but also granted certain *rights of passage*—a route moving beyond incarcerating tropes and traps of "black criminality" as well as passageways into a wider array of public spaces, arenas of professional opportunity and cultural production, and fields of possibility. The making of spiritual moves, musical moves, and spatial moves were all deeply enmeshed. The allied movements of holy hip hoppers were not done outside of authoritative structures or in an effort to necessarily free themselves completely of such formations. Rather, the submission to certain higher powers and forms of control accorded them specific freedoms and flexibilities.

The varied and intersecting responses of the state (e.g., the LAPD), the church, and social programs constituted the nexus of structures, practices, and assumptions that shaped the everyday possibilities and constraints of holy hip hoppers from the 1980s to the early 2000s. The disciplining laws of these domains—court or state law, God's law, and social laws of proper conduct and communal well-being—comprised a complex terrain of subjectivation and governance. The exact laws that young African Americans chose to submit to in the pursuit of certain types of freedom and opportunity had specific emotional, physical, and musical consequences—consequences that then shaped how people understand their agentive capacity as well as God's influence.

Conversion is a particularly productive site through which to understand the bifurcated and sometimes contradictory nature of agency in religious hip hop practice.[39] Conversion, as a modality of agency, is a capacity for action that specific relations of subordination create and enable. Conversion is both inflicted upon the "believer" in a moment of profound faith and surrender *and* strategically enacted as a conscious position-taking in relation to a complex array of social variables. Like other devout religious followers, gospel rappers often displaced their own agential capacity, letting Jesus "take the reins" or "take the wheel," as they would often say. They attributed positive events in their lives to the divine intervention of Jesus and blamed the trickster Devil for unfortunate occurrences and stumbling blocks.[40] Their religious conversions posed a powerful challenge to anthropological theories of agency. As Talal Asad has argued, "Conversion is regarded by moderns as an 'irrational' event or process, but resort to the idea of agency renders it 'rational' and 'freely chosen.'"[41] And yet, to say that the moment of religious conversion owes something to cultural systems (as opposed to individual agency) is to intrude "culture" into a moment when it seems the most irrelevant and the hand of God the most palpable.

Taking into account the agency of the otherworldly means moving beyond valorizations of human control and accepting individual agency as a dialectic of action and passivity (to the will of God). Here, conversion defines a new set of choices rather than being "the result of an entirely 'free choice.'"[42] Moments of surrender, acquiescence, and discipline can actually enable opportunities for liberatory action and practices of freedom. Holy hip hoppers were entangled in a complex set of power relations that enabled conditions of both possibility and constraint; how they moved within laws of culture, nature, and the divine defined their agential field of action. In this way, their stories moved beyond the tales of victimization that pervade the "gang-book genre"—tales that depict black youth and especially black men as violent, uncontrolled predators whose behavior defined the social crisis of contemporary urban life.[43] Further, grassroots gospel MCs in Los Angeles were generally not in control of the dominant narratives circulating about holy hip hop.[44] In the face of multiple misrecognitions and stigmatizations from church leaders, the commercial music industry, the LAPD, and secular hip hop artists, it is not surprising that gospel hip hop artists were inclined to give their testimony or conversion narrative as a strategy of reauthorization. Testifying became an important practice of self-fashioning and means toward lived belief, especially in the face of demonizing discourses associated with the "culture of poverty." Through the repeated *seismic soundings* of conversion, gospel rappers authored their new religious selves into being.

How did the presence of hip hop in gospel rappers' lives disrupt the teleology of the conversion narrative that often glosses over long periods of resistance to organized religion as well as interactions with Islam and Rastafari? How did the performance of holy hip hop conversion narratives cloak other truths?[45] What were holy hip hoppers legitimating through their stories of conversion? What resources and networks did their conversions grant them access to? What histories of music, urban space, and racial formation were implicated in their narratives of salvation?

TRANSCENDENT TELECOMMUNICATIONS

Khanchuz's conversion story highlighted the imprisoning discourses of black criminality and incarceration even as it challenged them. Gang culture remained a central part of Khanchuz's life, even when he was working in the formal economy. After receiving his diploma from Associated Technical College, he began working in the telecommunications field as a network engineer. While he was making an annual salary of over $50,000, he remarked, "At the same time, I didn't have my life right with the Lord. So I was doing a lot of stuff that wasn't righteous, wasn't positive. I'm a network engineer but I'm a gangbanger too. Nine to five, I was a network engineer but I would come home at night and hit the streets of L.A. and I'm a straight gangbanger, drug dealer. Making good money but still selling drugs at the same time. How stupid is that?"[46] Khanchuz performed so well at his telecommunications job in fact, that his boss promoted him to run his own network site in Denver. With this relocation, new pay raise, and expanded professional responsibilities, he decided to quit gangbanging. Although with no one working under him in his plush tenth-floor office in downtown Denver with 360-degree views of the entire city, he quickly made the office his "party spot." He recalled, "So I literally used to be in my office, smoking weed. There was a liquor store across the street. I would walk across the street and get me forty ounces of beer. It was easy. Once you learn how to work that tandem switch there wasn't anything else to learn. If there was anything new to learn, they would come out and train me. It was real simple work—wiring, testing a circuit. So, I started making friends out there." Khanchuz's office became a site for all kinds of networking.

After a couple of years in Denver, Khanchuz fell in love with a Haitian woman. Her family was highly skeptical of his West Coast gangsta style and tried multiple times to stop their daughter from seeing him. After a few months, Khanchuz got into a confrontation with his girlfriend's brother about a cell phone that he had lent her. Upon hearing who the phone came from, her family promptly confiscated it. Khanchuz went over to her family's house to ask for it back and what began as a civil conversation eventually ended in Khanchuz's arrest for felony menacing. Khanchuz explained the altercation: "The brother comes to the front door and says, 'Get away from my mama's house, nigger, nigger.' It was the way he was saying it. They're from Haiti and they're black but they say, 'We ain't niggers 'cause we weren't slaves.' Saying this and that—whoop, whoop, whoop. That's their mentality. Now, if I had had the mentality I have now I would have called the police, told them what happened, and said, 'Meet me over there so I can get my stuff.' But no, I'm Mister-big-thug-gangbanger. I can handle this on my own." Here, in a confrontation between American and Haitian blackness, Khanchuz experienced a black-lash of a different kind. After the police ran his record in Los Angeles at the station, his previous offenses began to light up the computer screen. An invocation of ancestral enslavement resulted in a thirty-day jail sentence with a bail amount of $50,000. His story mapped out a carceral cartography that linked Africa, the Caribbean, and the United States, where chains became bars that gave birth to beats.

And this brings us to the jail cell in Colorado. Khanchuz was not yet "saved" or practicing Christianity at the time, but the gospel began to creep into his music.

> I wrote my first gospel rap when I was in jail, not even trying to write gospel. We made up a rap group of inmates called Eleven Able because that was the cell number we were in. Me, this dude, Law, this other guy, Wicked. He had a plastic spoon in his hand. He had long fingernails and I don't know how he would be making a beat that was out of this world. Just with that! It would sound like we had a stereo up in there. And we would be up in there writing rhymes, rapping, and entertaining the inmates and the guards. It was like a band. So Law said, "Let's try to write a spiritual song." That was the first gospel rap song I did. I wasn't even trying to write a gospel rap. I wasn't even trying to say, now I'm going to live my life for God now. That wasn't even a thought in my mind. We were in there saying when we get out of jail we're going to record a CD.[47]

While it took Khanchuz another year or so to actually weave his way to God, this experience catalyzed an awareness of spirituality through song. After further jail sentences, he decided to pack up all his belongings and return home to Los Angeles. His girlfriend, defying her parents' demands, joined him on his journey back west.

They arrived broke and in disarray, forced to live at Khanchuz's father's house, which was located at the geographic center of a major gang war, where Khanchuz had formerly banged as a member of the 51st Street Cat-Walk Neighborhood Crips (CWC). He explained the "home" he returned to in South Los Angeles:

> At the time in my neighborhood there was a gang war going on between these three gangs that all lived in the same community. I lived on 51st street so there was the 51 Trouble Gang (Gangsta Crips), then there was the 40's (the neighborhood Crips) and they don't get along with the Trouble gangs. Then there was a Blood gang called the BNG's. They were just killing each other off, man. Just shooting people in the streets and asking no questions. If you were walking anywhere in the neighborhood they just figured you weren't from that 'hood and would just shoot you no questions asked.[48]

Embarrassed by and frustrated with what he was able to offer his sweetheart in terms of "a life," Khanchuz reluctantly bought her a bus ticket back to Colorado, promising that he would call for her once he secured housing and a job. He never did end up seeing her again.

Returning to this hostile urban environment added to Khanchuz's confusion and despair. One hot afternoon under the blazing sun, he was walking down his block to the corner store to buy a beer and he saw an old friend, Michelle, sitting on her porch with two older women. Michelle called, "Hey Sleep, come here and let me give you a hug and kiss." He swaggered over to receive his warm greeting, but the other two women hit first with a question: "Why are you walking around here with all this stuff going on?" Khanchuz responded, "I'm not about to be a prisoner in my own home. I'm not for either one of these gangs." The women asked if they could pray for him before he continued on and he agreed. Holding hands in a circle, they prayed for God to protect him and grant him a safe passageway on these treacherous streets. Tired of being imprisoned in his own neighborhood, Khanchuz took a short walk through embattled grounds that ended up dramatically changing the course of his life, resulting in both a *rite of passage* and newfound *rights of passage*. One of the elderly women on the porch, Ramone, would later play a major role in Khanchuz's eventual conversion to Christianity. Historical sedimentations of race and place, intertwined social and economic conditions, and personal trials in Khanchuz's life had all broken him open to such a change, but it was one telephone conversation that encouraged him to "let God take the reins."

Khanchuz assumed Ramone was calling to help him find a job, but she had another agenda. "God had me call you for another reason," Ramone uttered softly. For the remainder of the telephone call, Khanchuz stood in silence and just listened:

> She started telling me about everything that I've been through, everything that I was thinking about. And she started getting so deep into my life that I was like, I'm scared. I started crying and my hands were shaking. Oh my goodness. I was just a

FIGURE 3. Khanchuz in his "old gang 'hood" on the block where his father lives in South L.A.

teary mess, snot running down my nose. And you know how people say they hear God speak. Well, I heard an audible voice as if someone was standing right over my shoulder yelling, "I sent her to you! She can see you right now! She can see you crying! Say something! Say something! Say something!" And I got so scared that I could hear this, that all I could say was "How do you know this about me?" She was so calm, she said, "Baby, God told me these things about you. That's how I know. Not only did God tell me about everything you've been through but he also told me about everything he wants to do for you. Do you know what God wants?" Then she started running off all these things I've ever wanted. It brought me so much joy because I had already realized that this was God, and to realize that God wants to give all these desires of my heart. There's no way somebody told her these things.[49]

By the time Khanchuz finished relaying this portion of his story to me, his dark eyes glossed over with tears and I felt as if he was transported back in time to this visceral and extraordinary moment of religious calling.

After his conversation with Ramone, Khanchuz decided he would "try God" and see what happened. Inspired by the example of Ramone's relationship with God as well as the felt presence of God during this exchange, he began to look for a church home and other Christians to fellowship with in his daily life. Despite being raised in the church, developing an authentic and adult relationship with God was new territory for Khanchuz. Up to this point, he had tried to find happiness through everything else but the Lord—"drugs, gangbanging, women"—but none of it worked. Now he was surrendering to Jesus in a moment of conversion that was crosscut by both divine and human intervention, during the fragile intimacy and profound aurality of a telephone call.

From the gospel rap reverberating from jail cell eleven to God's cry to "Say something!" echoing through the phone line, spirit, in Khanchuz's life, has always arrived through sound. As he moved deeper into his religious practice, he began to write rhymes about his new relationship with Christ. But it did not come easy. He explained: "So I tried to write about God back then and I couldn't. I could only write about what I felt and I was still in those streets. Something would happen on the streets and I would write about it and then bring it back to the homies the next day. They'd be like, 'Dang, man! You caught that whole scene, everything that went on. That's tight.'" Khanchuz then pleaded to God, "Let me write about you, Lord." He wanted to "pour" his new love for God into the vessel of his lyrics. Since that day, Khanchuz has not been able to write a secular rap. He described his new compositional process: "I can go to church now and hear a sermon that the pastor preach, go home and put it in a rap—just like I used to see what was going on in those streets. Something that deals with my spirituality—I can put it in my raps." The church, not the streets, served as the new territorial context for his lyrics. Spiritual practice, instead of gangbanging, became his ultimate subject matter. His brethren, rather than his homies, was his intended audience. One of his early gospel raps invokes multiple geographies and spatial metaphors—both sacred and profane:

> Glory be from the seed I was willed the one
> Oh woe is me so I plead Lord thy will be done
> And *kingdom* come, manifest, as it is in *heaven*
> Joy and peace with my brethren, not lusting worldly possessions
> But seeking peace intercessions and bangin *churches* as clicks
> No more Bloods and the Crips just like y'all didn't exist
> I know y'all going to be pissed to find out *heaven* ain't got no *ghettos*
> But I hope Pac was right about a *thug paradise*
> Not quite, see the light, get your life right with Christ
> Bang hard on the Devil, pray with all of your might[50]

Khanchuz's conversion was a challenging and ongoing process—a winding road filled with bumps and backslides. As he recalled, "I didn't drop everything in my life just to become a Christian. At that point, I was still smoking weed, still drinking. Eventually, I cleaned up my entire life." These early lyrics clearly revealed the prevalence and proximity of gang culture in Khanchuz's daily life. He and his holy hip hop crew, ADK, whose lyrics transposed the predatory impulse to annihilate rival gangs onto demons and the Devil, brought the fraternal solidarity and militant nature of gang culture to their musical projects and evangelism. References to black brotherhood, from political organizations to hyperviolent street gangs to religious bands of believers, infused his lyrics. Even in his outgoing message on his cell phone, he represented his fellow demon killers and offered a short spiritual instruction. During those years in L.A., when my calls to Khanchuz would go to voicemail, I looked forward to hearing his righteous message before the sound of the beep: "ADK. God bless. Any Demon Killa. Sorry I'm not available to take your call. If this is a state of spiritual emergency, hang up, fall on your knees, and call on Jesus." Then one of his gospel rap tracks—a spiritual and seismic beat with a gangsta rap feel—dropped in for another ten seconds. Although Khanchuz may not have been available to talk, he affirmed Jesus's capacity to answer the call of those in the midst of spiritual crisis. Khanchuz was a telecommunications expert after all. He, more than most, knew how the right call at the right time could make all the difference.

TRANSFORMATIVE TELEVANGELISM

Like Soup, B-Love heard God's call through the television. An African American mother of four children and gospel MC with the collective Hip Hopposite, she recalled, "I was tired of doing me."[51] B-Love began rapping at the age of eight while also attending Phillips Chapel—a Methodist church in Santa Monica—as a youth with her grandmother "'cause it was tradition." At various points in her life, she had forayed into what she deems the "New Age" health and spiritual world, Egyptology and "African American consciousness" communities, before she "got saved."

> I didn't pursue a relationship with Christ until I got into some trouble. I was about nineteen and started to be like, Lord, where are you? And you know, he got me out of a little trouble I was in. After that point, I still was doing my own thing and it really wasn't until 2000 when I really said OK, I'm gonna do this ... I was a single mother and in a toxic relationship with my children's father. I separated from him. I was going through a lot of stuff. I was sick of doing it on my own and doing it my way. I was still dating guys and looking for love in a sense. I was smoking weed and just getting high. You know, nothing too crazy, just kind of like, this is not it. And God just tapped me on the shoulder and said, "It's time to come to the faith."[52]

B-Love attributes the initial moment of her conversion to a television special featuring Bishop Noel Jones—born in Spanish Town, Jamaica, and brother to disco singer, actress, and model Grace Jones—who makes frequent appearances on Black Entertainment Television (BET) and the Church Channel (You can also watch his sermons on GodTube, the Christian counterpart to YouTube). B-Love eventually got saved in his church, Greater Bethany Community Church in Gardena, now renamed the City of Refuge Church and boasting over 17,000 members. Unhappy with the direction her life was heading, she collapsed on the floor of her bedroom to the bishop's moving, Pentecostal-inspired sermon. "I found out about him on TV and the Holy Ghost came and met me on the floor one morning."

As a young girl, B-Love was watching female hip hop acts such as Salt-n-Pepa and Roxanne Shanté on *Yo! MTV Raps,* attempting to recreate the bold and brazen styles of these MCs. It was again through the television that B-Love received a life-changing lesson. This time it was the gospel of black female empowerment through music. She was particularly drawn to Roxanne Shanté: "She was just tough. She had attitude. She was hardcore. Back then, the N.W.A. stuff was coming on the scene and she was like, 'I ain't taking no mess.' Run DMC, EPMD—all those guys really inspired me to do it." At night she would sit in her room, listen to the radio, and scribble down their rhymes so that she could rap them on her own. From there, she began writing her own lyrics and eventually formed the rap duo Diadora (taken from the shoe brand Diadora) with another female lyricist. Initially, she used a lot of profanity in her lyrics, but then "transitioned into a more conscious style" where issues of "community" and "standing up for the sisters" dominated her music. After B-Love "got saved," she struggled, like Soup and Khanchuz, to figure out how to express her relationship with God in her music. She recounted:

> There was no Christ in my lyrics but I remember this one song called "Paper Chase." It was about struggling and trying to be positive. It went like this, "Every single morning I get up to get my paper. Thank the lord for another day, he's the mover and the shaker." I was kind of on a Lauryn Hill tip before she came out, but they wasn't really feeling that tip. Lil Kim had just come out. But I just kept putting Him (God) in—in a bar there, or the chorus—and thinking about my blessings. I wasn't thinking about gospel rap, I was just like, "This is my life." I was still talking about other things. I think I had just one song that I dedicated to God, you know, like a lot of secular artists do. After so many doors slammed in my face, I said, "I'm good, I'm done." I was tired. I was a single mom at the time working full time and I would go to studios late at night. Meetings after meetings late at night and finally I said, "I'm cool, I'm done." And I prayed about it. God said, *"You have to use your gift."* I would literally wake up out of my sleep and have something to write on a piece of paper, like I gotta get this out. I blew it off but just kept doing it and finally I thought, all right, let me be obedient. I will keep a notebook by my bedstand.[53]

Gospel rap found B-Love on an AM radio station. The DJ was playing local holy hip hop artists I.D.O.L. King and Gospel Gangstaz. That was when B-Love began considering herself a gospel rapper. To deny this call on her life would be a greater sin than using popular music to worship Jesus. While her conversion was channeled through a television, she eventually saw her music as a *channel* through which God speaks. Invoking another technological metaphor, B-Love continued, "I'm taking my time with my music because I really don't want anything *micro-waved*. I really want God to just speak through me and rap about topics that He wants me to talk about. 'Cause you know I used to lady rap the blues but now I lady rap the gospel." Her hip hop music was for the glorification of God, but also for the empowerment of the women who first inspired her to rap.

BETWEEN MALCOLM AND MARTIN

Stephen "Cue" Jn-Marie, a former secular rapper turned gospel rapper, was born in Barbados and raised in the flood-prone and fault-ridden city of Baytown, Texas (a.k.a. Little Beirut), but would say he was baptized in the streets of L.A.'s Babylon. Since moving to Los Angeles, another geographically unstable region, in 1989, Cue has resided in a variety of places, including Long Beach, Inglewood, and Compton where he lived across the street from a notorious gangsta rap producer. He was one of the original members of the College Boyz, an early '90s West Coast rap group that included fellow Baytown-bread MC of Caribbean descent (and now actor) Romany Malco.[54] Known for their dynamic combination of gangsterism and Black Power politics, they were the first hip hop act to sign with Virgin Records. Their rookie album, *Radio Fusion Radio,* featured the 1992 hit singles "Hollywood Paradox" and "Victim of the Ghetto," the latter of which peaked at #68 on the Billboard Hot 100 and #1 on the Hot Rap Singles. Sharing stages with the likes of Tupac and DJ Quick, they also debuted on *The Arsenio Hall Show.*

Despite minimal success, Cue remembers this as a dark time. He was living in Compton during the 1992 riots. Images of storeowners on their roofs with guns still haunt him. "I remember the feeling when we heard the news that none of the officers involved in the beating of Rodney King were convicted: hopeless."[55] During this time, Cue was also hustling on the streets of Los Angeles. In 2008, over a coffee we had at Pann's Restaurant, the famed location of Samuel L. Jackson's dramatic monologue in the movie *Pulp Fiction,* his voice deepened with intensity and grit as he busted into a rap from those early days:

> My Chevy riding high so I can touch the sky
> I told y'all I was coming, run the streets
> Like Marion Jones at track meets
> You can't get me[56]

"Stuff like that," Cue explained. "And what I mean by "I run like Marion Jones" is that I run the streets, but I was in violation 'cause I was running dope, right? You got it? But you'd have to sit down and talk to me to get that." These statements illustrated how life facts are often secreted and embedded within metaphors, analogies, and rhyme. Cue also interpreted his conversion through the lens of hustling. In another conversation about six months later, Cue restated his decision to become a follower of Jesus Christ as a savvy business move: "I've been hustling all my life; I know a good deal when I see one."

Before choosing Christ, Cue wrestled with whether or not to become a Christian or a Muslim. It was the 1992 Spike Lee film, *Malcolm X*, which brought him closer to God:

> I went to watch the movie *Malcolm X* and I felt like God was saying something to me. There were two phrases that were really heavy on spirit because I was thinking about becoming a Muslim because I thought Christians were kind of soft. There were two phrases: "He died too soon" and "I want you to be like him." I felt like that's what God was saying to me. So it took me a little while to crystallize whatever God was calling me to do—to crystallize the call he put on my life . . . I heard about Jesus before and I was struggling with how can a man be God. At the point when I was watching the movie *Malcolm X*, I realized that even the Nation had set Malcolm up. You feel me? I felt like even Jesus was more pure than Mohammed. So I chose him. I believe it was God who showed me that. But how do I come with Malcolm and Martin at the same time?[57]

This attempt to fuse the spirit of Malcolm X and Martin Luther King, Jr. was at the core of Cue's music and activism. His politics as a local organizer embodied the philosophies of both black political leaders at different stages of his life. His hip hop music drew aesthetically from Muslim hip hop artists such as Rakim (affiliated with the Five Percent Nation) and Ice Cube. He was nurtured on the hard-hitting Black Power funk grooves that would become the musical bedrock for early hip hop in the late 1970s and early '80s, bringing with it a strong Black Nationalist current informed by Nation of Islam doctrines and rhetorical practices. Cue loved Public Enemy and became influenced by their Black Nationalist politics and social and stylistic militancy. Even now, as a gospel hip hop artist in his forties, he still talks about the profound effect Muslim rappers have had on his soul and his sound. In an interesting twist of fate and faith, it was Cue's walk with hip hop and Islam that routed him toward Jesus.[58] "I came to God in 1994," he told me—the same year as the major Los Angeles earthquake. "I realized that it was time to walk in his path."

Despite his relationship with Christianity, Cue has always felt a deep kinship with Malcolm X. Both were hustlers who underwent a religious conversion and became politicized. Before Malcolm found Allah in prison, he worked as a waiter at Small's Paradise while hustling inside the basement space. Ingratiating himself in the sordid Harlem underworld, he was eventually fired after referring an undercover military agent to a prostitute. Cue was also drawn to the black Muslim icon because like Malcolm, he too had roots in the West Indies. Cue commented, "The Gospel has always been reggae. I grew up listening to reggae—I'm more Dread than Christian. I'm a follower of Christ but ... I'm more of a Rastafarian in terms

FIGURE 4. Cue Jn-Marie and Flava Flav of Public Enemy at the Los Angeles Skid Row Hip Hop Summit in 2012. Photo courtesy of Michael R. Moore.

of culture."[59] Even in his early music with the College Boyz, he tried to infuse their West Coast rap sound with dancehall reggae aesthetics, sometimes even rapping with a distinct Jamaican accent. Cue had a particular penchant for mixture. His use of dancehall elements was typical in early hip hop music; it was the DJ-ing and MC-ing practices associated with mobile sound system culture in Jamaica that would inspire West Indian immigrants such as Afrika Bambaata, DJ Kool Herc, and Grandmaster Flash to create hip hop in the crucible of the Bronx. Dancehall music and Rastafarian culture have been central animating forces in hip hop music. And so Cue's holy hip hop practice, drawing from the spiritual energies already percolating in hip hop, merged multiple black religiosities—Christianity, Islam, and the Rastafarian movement—as it connected Jamaica, Barbados, Texas, New York, and California.

Initially, when Cue became a deacon at Faithful Central Bible Church housed in Inglewood's multipurpose indoor arena, The Forum, he didn't want anything to do with hip hop. There was a stigma attached to the music, especially among churchgoers, and he was already getting flack for not looking the part. He continued, "I was one of the first deacons who wore braids, and people couldn't even deal with that. They would look at me funny and things like that. That was 1994, 1995. And now you can see the difference between then and now because now everyone at Faithful Central wears braids."[60] Over time and after meeting a few gospel hip hop artists at Faithful Central, including Kirk Franklin, for whom he was a personal trainer in 1999, Cue began to see how he could reconcile his relationship with Jesus and hip hop. In particular, he wasn't very impressed by the gospel hip hop music he was hearing and felt that the beats and the lyricism were subpar to the secular hip hop that he was accustomed to performing and listening to. Taking matters into his own hands, he started a record label and began to make sense of what it would mean to do gospel hip hop on his own terms. He stated:

> The only thing I'm merging is Jesus . . . I don't even want to bring in the religious . . . There's nothing wrong with religion but I don't want to bring the religious aspect to our music. I just want Jesus. That's it. I want to take Jesus and just dump him in the hip hop world like nobody has ever heard of in church before . . . the sense of who he is, 'cause that's what's going to change people. . . . For us, it's becoming easier and easier to do gospel hip hop because we understand the hardness of Jesus. He was a lion and lamb at the same time. We understand that. The challenge is not to be condemning our own youth. We focus on mostly praising and worshipping God but in our context.[61]

Cue felt much more comfortable participating in gospel hip hop after making the distinction between "religious" hip hop and merging hip hop with Jesus. For Cue, reconciling Jesus's manhood with his own was a critical aspect of his conversion. Jesus accompanies him wherever he goes, as illustrated in the statement, "You'll notice I walk on this line that looks like I'm gonna fall off and that's because I know Jesus is right here."[62] Holding the tension of opposites in his music and everyday practices was a key part of Cue's dynamism and success as a street evangelist and hip hop musician.

GOSPEL GANGWAYS

The lives of gospel rappers, set against ecologies of fear and apocalypse, demonstrated the highly moralized and spiritualized nature of discourses about urban life and urban decay in Los Angeles in the latter part of the twentieth century. We must then question the common assumption that urbanization necessarily leads to both secularization and the decreased relevancy of Christianity in the lives of African Americans. On the contrary, it appears that modern individualism, ideologies of self-help, and the freedom to choose one's own religious (or nonreligious) path may in certain circumstances produce even more devoutly religious subjects, in turn strengthening the symbolic power of organized religion.

Gospel rap practitioners were *hip hoppifying* Christianity and *Christianizing* hip hop simultaneously in ways that cross-cut, enhanced, and sometimes disrupted both processes. Hip hop, in particular, was the musical practice through which they made sense of complicated and sometimes messy religious conversions (conversions that were ongoing), as well as one of the essential threads that linked holy hip hoppers' pasts and presents. Hip hop was the beat they bounced to as they walked with God. It was how they made sense of where they had been so they could figure out where they were going. Gospel rap became a means through which Christian rappers aestheticized and inculcated their new spiritual selfhood. Gospel rap became *earthquake music*. These *seismic soundings* that emerged from the environmental and social chaos of Los Angeles in the 1980s and '90s also generated moments of urban rapture. As hip hoppers converted to Christianity they utilized gospel rap to fashion their newfound religious identities in ways that did not exclude their previous cultural affiliations and musical affinities.[63] While gospel rap appeared to be a natural outcome of their life paths, oftentimes it was initially an uncomfortable practice and mode of identification. At the same time, it appeared to be a profound expressive arena for working out and wrestling with their new religious selves.

One theme that threads these holy hip hop conversion experiences together is the experience of freedom in and through the act of submission to God, once again evoking the relationship between black religion and black liberation. As relayed here, conversion was one way to pave a *passage* through L.A.'s uneven grounds—one response to the ways that black bodies and hip hop bodies were (and continue to be) discursively marked, segregated, and disciplined in contemporary urban landscapes. Coincidentally, the word *gang* originates from the Old English word *gong*, meaning a journey, a way, or a passage. Gangster, then, signifies someone who makes a way or a passage. The gangster and the convert, then, may share more than meets the eye and the ear. Or, perhaps, the road to Jesus is the gospel rapper's gangway (i.e., passageway). Holy hip hoppers banged for Christ within and in spite of intersecting laws of the state, nature, culture, and God. Constrained by these various disciplining and uneven terrains of power, moments of freedom were enacted.

Hip Hop Church L.A.

Shifting Grounds in Inglewood

We just praising the lord, we just doing our thing
God don't mind if I bring along my tambourine
Beat it on my hand, beat it on my hip, but I use hip hop as my instrument
—CELAH OF HIP HOPPOSITE (GOSPEL RAPPER), *"TAMBOURINE" (2005)*

When I heard the choir at Kurtis Blow's Hip Hop Church service in Harlem sing a sacred rendition of LL Cool J's 1996 hit, "Loungin' (Who Do You Love?)"—a steamy remix that featured the velvety vocals of R&B girl group Total as well as the unforgettable lyric, "Hot sex on a platter"—I was feeling a sense of cognitive dissonance. While I had attended numerous gospel hip hop shows at festivals and local music venues, this was first time I had witnessed the inclusion of rap music in a church service, and I was surprised to hear this sultry hip hop club classic in the sanctuary. But then again, Kurtis Blow could never completely divorce himself from the secular hip hop industry from whence he came.

Kurtis Blow was one of the first commercially successful rappers to emerge in New York's burgeoning hip hop scene in the late 1970s and early '80s and the first to sign with a major label. His 1980 hit song, "The Breaks," which he performed bare-chested under a white blazer on *Soul Train,* was the first certified gold rap song. He was the first rapper to tour the United States and Europe (with the Commodores), the first to record a national commercial (Sprite), and the first to be featured in a soap opera (*One Life to Live*). Many also consider him one of rap's original producers, winning rap's producer of the year in 1983 and 1985. To top off this list of "firsts," Kurtis Blow was also the first rap millionaire, even before the rise of hip hop moguls such as P-Diddy, Jay Z, and Master P. A key figure in the initial commercial elevation of hip hop into corporate music circles, Kurtis then became "born again" in 1996. The pop-icon-gone-gospel founded the Hip Hop Church ministry at Harlem's Greater Hood Memorial AME Zion Church in 2005 and began leading Thursday night services featuring rap music. Soon after, Kurtis teamed up with Holy Trinity ELCA (Evangelical Lutheran Church of America) in Inglewood to create the Hip Hop Church L.A.—an evening ministry that also put secular hip hop hits to work in the name of Jesus.

At one such service I attended at Holy Trinity in 2006, a small, motley youth choir sang soaring harmonies over an instrumental version of Snoop Dogg and Pharrell's 2002 hit track "Beautiful," changing the lyrics from "Beautiful, I just want you to know, you're my favorite girl" to "Beautiful, I just want you to know, you're my favorite God." This was one of many instances of *flippin' the script(ure)* that took place at the Hip Hop Church L.A. The original video for the song featured a bevy of Brazilian women in barely-there bikinis while Snoop rapped, "Don't fool with the playa with the cool whip." As if to preemptively address those who might throw stones at such a provocative song selection, Kurtis Blow, clad in baggy jeans, an oversized jersey, and silver cross necklace, offered the firm disclaimer: "This is not entertainment; this is not a show. This is ministry." When he called for an "Amen," the congregation responded with a resounding "Word!"—a common affirmation in hip hop parlance that is linked to the Islam-derived Five Percent Nation aphorism, "Word is Bond."[1] Kurtis Blow's hip hop churches welcomed and fused many seemingly contradictory aspects of hip hop culture.

Youth rose from the pews, one by one, to recite biblical passages over hip hop backbeats while Kurtis Blow provided musical transitions on two turntables.[2] The traditional Hymn of Praise was converted into a Rap of Praise, with lyrics that spoke of both divine supplications and worldly temptations. Kurtis's sermon, entitled "Holler at Ya Boy!" interpreted a passage from the book of Mark where Bartimaeus, blind and downtrodden, calls out to Jesus in faith for a divine blessing. Performing a uniquely hip hop exegesis of the passage, Kurtis Blow interpreted Bartimaeus's call to Jesus as "hollering at his boy," transforming the slang term "holla" into a call of faith, and ultimately, equating the act of hollering to praying. He assured the youth that they could use their own language—the language of hip hop—to communicate with God. His sermon suggested that when your homies fail you, when your family fails you, when your teachers and city leaders fail you, even when your church fails you—when all else fails—then "Holla at ya boy, Jesus! He'll meet you wherever you're at."

RACIAL, RELIGIOUS, AND MUSICAL FAULT LINES

The formation of hip hop ministries in Los Angeles in the early twenty-first century, often housed in predominantly black churches, brought together diverse and sometimes unlikely individuals, practices, and politics.[3] They became contested sites for negotiating the role of religion and popular culture in public discourses of racial uplift and the changing lives of African Americans. Different practitioners of holy hip hop, from gospel rap artists to clergy, pastors, urban youth workers, church musicians, hip hop fans, and congregants, young and old, mediated hip hop and Christianity in related but sometimes oppositional ways.

Hip hop ministries were not always well received by clergy and congregants. Sometimes they were vilified for their use of hip hop music as worship, intensifying experiences of urban marginality for black Americans who participated in such religious and musical practices. While the culture wars permeating hip hop culture have generally been characterized through the hyperracialized and polarized optic of black and white, sociologist Loïc Wacquant argues: "Urban marginality is not everywhere woven of the same cloth."[4] The hip hop ministries I attended in Los Angeles were of course enmeshed in histories of white and black hostility, territorial segregation, and social inequality, but they were also connected to waves of Latino immigration and internal tensions within black Christian communities. Specifically, the challenges and successes of the Hip Hop Church L.A. at Inglewood's Holy Trinity Church—a church whose congregation was predominantly African American and middle class—aggravated subtle fault lines along class, gender, and race in this historically black, but now very mixed neighborhood.

While race remains a dominant fault line or "axis of oppression" in the everyday experiences of African Americans throughout the greater Los Angeles, anthropologist João H. Costa Vargas, in his work on South L.A., argues:

> [E]xclusive focus on race can obscure how racial identities are inflected by and permeated with other identities, associations, and experiences . . . In attending to the inescapably racial dimensions of their experience, black communities run the risk of allowing blackness to occlude other axes of oppression and suppression like class, gender, sexuality, and citizenship.[5]

For holy hip hoppers, the merging of popular music and religious practice opened up fields of creative, economic, and spiritual possibility. But music and religion also served as alternate "axes of oppression" that shaped the opportunities and constraints of their daily lives. This chapter focuses on the religious and musical dimensions of urban marginalization *and* projects of urban renewal in relation to the changing significance of race and class in African American Christian communities.

Inglewood was a particularly apt place to explore these dynamics as it was once hailed as a model city of black uplift—a symbol of racial pride and possibility. Originally a white city until the arrival of African Americans in the 1960s, Inglewood has undergone many of the social and economic transformations that have challenged South Los Angeles communities: white flight (especially after the Watts riots in 1965), an influx of drugs, poor city management, new arrivals from Latin America and Asia, and subsequent black flight. While it is a city known for its many houses of worship—churches, mosques, and temples—it is also home to a proliferation of liquor stores and by-the-hour motels. Holy Trinity Church, in fact,

FIGURE 5. Holy Trinity Evangelical Lutheran Church in Inglewood, home to the Hip Hop Church L.A.

shares a block of Crenshaw Boulevard with three motels, revealing how Inglewood remains fraught with social and spatial contradictions.[6]

Churches, in addition to providing salvation, guidance, and community, have served as terrains of power and authority, inclusion and exclusion, through which people have wielded influence over others and, at times, prohibited certain individuals and groups from specific arenas of social and economic capital. In many African American Christian communities, critiques about the use of certain musical forms in religious worship have been deployed as foils for fears and discriminations based on age, ethnicity, gender, class, and place of residence. The alienation and marginality that holy hip hop practitioners and supporters experienced at Holy Trinity was located at the edges of religious tolerance; exclusions were enacted when the hegemonic norms and hierarchical structures of institutional Christianity were threatened by emergent and unorthodox voices and practices. In particular, the transgressive nature of hip hop was an affront to the notion of respectability politics espoused by many traditionally minded black churches, highlighting the limits of what is deemed appropriate musical expression. Sharon Collins-Heads, director of the Hip Hop Church L.A., commented:

The problem I have is when one Christian group talks about the way another Christian group worships. How do you expect non-believers to want to come to Christ when you're all talking about each other and the way they worship? Unless that group is preaching heresy, why do you get on people that like holy hip hop? And what people tend to forget, when the new gospel music came in, people didn't like it.[7]

FIGURE 6. Three motels adjacent to Holy Trinity Church near the corner of Arbor Vitae Street and Crenshaw Boulevard in Inglewood.

In the years I frequented hip hop services throughout Los Angeles, gospel hip hop remained mired in ongoing debates about the fault lines between the sacred and the profane, good and evil, youth culture and "the old ways." Gospel rap was, for young black Angelenos, *both* a means of coping with the multiple assaults on their physical and spiritual well-being *and* an instrument through which they were being challenged and stigmatized by certain members of their own communities, church leaders, local police, and commercial music networks. As Vargas's ethnography keenly reminds us, "We must be aware of the political, social, cultural, and generational chasms within the communities that bear the disproportionate brunt of structural inequalities and racist policies."[8] While holy hip hop provided practices through which young black Christians uplifted themselves spiritually and economically, these same practices were also highly contested, policed, experimental, and often ambiguous.

AND THEN THERE WAS HIP HOP CHURCH

Sean Heads, an African American male churchgoer and Inglewood native, was working as a security guard for the Urban Music Conference in Palm Springs in 2005 when he first met Kurtis "Blow" Walker. Well aware of the rap star's turn toward Christianity, the then teenager introduced himself and invited Kurtis to address the youth at his church home—Holy Trinity. Kurtis informed Sean about his two hip hop churches on the East Coast and his vision to bring a sister church to Los Angeles. Sean recounted his serendipitous encounter with Kurtis to his mother, Sharon Collins-Heads, who then brought the idea of a West Coast hip hop church to her dear friend, Carol Scott—an African American woman in her late forties, associate pastor at Holy Trinity, and longtime resident of Inglewood (since 1968).

Considered an "activist pastor," Carol Scott began preaching the gospel at nine years old in her backyard. She seemed destined for a life of pastorship. After the 1992 riots, she and other local activists and residents organized an annual "mock funeral" procession to bring attention to the high rate of homicide in L.A.'s black and brown communities. The event featured a multicar funeral procession in which hearses and other vehicles made a slow, sepulchral crawl down the streets of Inglewood, Lennox, and South Angeles. Bullhorns blasted from car windows, calling the community to action. The procession ended with a mock burial in Inglewood's Darby Park, over which Pastor Scott presided. Handguns were placed in a baby blue-hued coffin, symbolizing the death of violence.

Always looking for ways to bring the community into the church and the gospel to the streets, Pastor Scott called Kurtis Blow immediately. After a meeting one morning at Denny's that also included Sharon and Kurtis's friend, Mike Green, the Hip Hop Church L.A. was born. Pastor Scott explained:

> I connected with Kurtis and as we began to talk, as I heard his vision unfold, we had the same vision. And the vision that we both had was that while the *traditional* church, which has always been in place, speaks to some, God is bigger than that. And so there are other ways and avenues that I felt like we could use. And hip hop is such a big influence—the music, the dress. I have fifty-year-old men wearing pants that are hanging down . . . we weren't thinking about Christian rap or holy hip hop. We were thinking about using socially conscious hip hop. That was the initial idea. Kurtis wanted to strengthen the youth, which was also my mission. So his idea was

to come to this church and plant the seed of Hip Hop Church L.A. He wanted to teach the youth the traditional hymns but he also wanted some of the newer hip hop and holy hip hop songs to show them that you don't have to say certain words and use negative images . . . that you can honor God with hip hop . . . Because when Christian rock first came out, it wasn't happening. Nobody was listening. Even when gospel rap first came out, nobody was feeling it. That's because basically they take a few words and they say Jesus. You can't fool kids. But let's take a popular song and do it for the glory of God. And that's what the church should be all about—reaching out to the community. And I said, oh man, that's my vision too. So Kurtis and I went into partnership. What we didn't realize was the opposition.[9]

Carol Scott, as pastor of the Hip Hop Church L.A., and Sharon Collins-Heads, the appointed director of the ministry, worked diligently over the next year to implement the groundbreaking Friday night hip hop service. They were met with resistance. Congregants and leaders at Holy Trinity Church feared the stigma around the term "hip hop." Holy Trinity's head pastor, an older white man whom I will refer to as "Pastor Wallace," explained to me that most churches perceive hip hop as "evil" and "of the devil"—phrases that parallel many early critiques of blues and jazz music, especially as a medium of worship. Several Holy Trinity churchgoers expressed concern over having hip hop in the sanctuary, because, as Wallace once commented to me, "It can be next door in Parish Hall, but not in the sanctuary because the sanctuary is sacred."[10] Particularly in Los Angeles, hip hop and rap were often associated with the ungodly aspects of gangsta rap by artists such as Snoop Doggy Dog, Dr. Dre, Ice Cube, and more recently, The Game, Tyga, Nipsey Hussle, and Vince Staples, among others. Pastor Scott reflected:

> And really what people didn't understand is that hip hop is not gangsta rap. We weren't saying take gangsta rap and use it in the church. Gangsta rap is a totally different expression, a different experience, a different pain that needs to be heard. Things were happening that people were overlooking, so that voice needed to be heard. But that wasn't going to be a musical expression that the church needed to use. So, the leaders here were afraid that some of the old timers, when they saw that term, they would either leave or protest.[11]

During the initial conversations about the Hip Hop Church L.A., one of the older African American congregants of Holy Trinity brought in a video of G. Craige Lewis—a well-known speaker and church leader famous for his fierce polemics against hip hop and holy hip hop—in an effort to sway the church leadership from housing such an "immoral" ministry. Similar counterattacks further stalled the implementation of the hip hop church night. Pastor Wallace then lobbied to call the Hip Hop Church L.A. a "Youth Revival Blast," much to the amusement of the youth present at the organizing meeting. Pastor Scott pushed back, as she argued for the importance of being straightforward about the focus on hip hop music as worship. But Holy Trinity was not alone in its uneasiness toward broadcasting the inclusion of a hip hop ministry.

The Crenshaw Christian Center, a prominent Los Angeles megachurch that televises its traditional Sunday services, previously held a hip hop service every fifth Sunday led by Pastor Fred Price, Jr.—a preacher and gospel rap artist. Sharon and her son Sean attended one such "Hip Hop Sunday" that featured an array of hip hop performances before commencing with a traditional service. Sharon recalled, "That's what went on television; they didn't show any of the hip hop things that went on before because they were still kind of scared." Eventually, Pastor Price, Jr. would change the name from "Hip Hop Sunday" to "The Blueprint."

Watching this scenario unfold, Sharon began to understand that her struggle—the struggle of the Hip Hop Church—was perhaps not unique. After ongoing discussion and debate, Pastor Wallace finally agreed to hold the hip hop ministry every third Friday of the month. Although excited by the idea of attracting more youth to the church and developing culturally relevant church programs, he was also wary of the social baggage that often accompanies hip hop and wanted to make sure that the presence of a hip hop ministry in his church would not compromise its reputation. In a conversation we had in his office one afternoon, he offered a slightly different origin story for the Hip Hop Church—one that strategically focused more on efforts to draw in youth rather than valuing hip hop as a medium of worship. Wallace, who has served as head pastor of Holy Trinity since 1979, explained:

> The roots, as I see them, were started in 1996 when we called Randy Winston to be our youth minister here at Holy Trinity. His day job is working with high school students to get them into college. He was at Crenshaw High and Freemont High. He has been very successful getting youth from our community into college and getting them the financial support and aid that they need. We wanted to put more resources into youth and reaching them and their families . . . so that when we were approached in May 2005 by Kurtis Blow—you know, well, an old school rapper—wondering if we would want to do a holy hip hop worship, we said, "Well, yes, let's sit down and talk about it." So there was great openness to it and the possibilities of reaching deeper into our community because we know that there's a whole generation of young people right here in this community that won't come to church. And if parents aren't involved, they're not going to get involved and there's nothing that will bring them to church. The public school across the street, 71 percent of the students are in foster care. So, they're bringing all kinds of baggage to school with them. So to reach them at school over there, we've got to do something very radical.[12]

Pastor Wallace's interest in hip hop worship stemmed from his desire to bring more youth to Holy Trinity. As a pastor, he has used music to reach the communities he preaches in, and specifically, to engage younger folks and their families.

In the 1970s, before coming to Holy Trinity, Wallace was preaching to African American congregations in Harlem—another city long hailed as a Mecca of black culture and uplift. He often cited this piece of his personal history when talking about his efforts with the Hip Hop Church as way to authenticate his position of power and leadership within a black congregation. After arriving at Holy Trinity, he quickly changed the style of worship and the musical program of the church to reflect the tastes of Inglewood's African American communities. While still singing hymns from the traditional Lutheran hymnal, he began incorporating more gospel music. "In the African American tradition," Wallace explained, "there's a lot of talking back to the preacher and participation so we encourage that here." He has always taken great pride in having a "sense of what it means to serve in a community like this," even as he returns home every day to the safety and isolation of his gated community, "Briarwood"—a fortified sanctuary of brick townhouses, manicured landscaping, and tranquility hidden within Inglewood's somewhat less attractive urban sprawl that the *Los Angeles Times* once referred to as "the Beverly Hills and Bel-Air of Inglewood."[13] This fact would later add both a class dynamic and racialized tone to the tensions and misunderstandings brewing within the Hip Hop Church ministry.

Pastor Wallace viewed hip hop as a way to make Holy Trinity more culturally and stylistically relevant to the local community, and thus he privileged learning the languages of community members rather than forcing community members to learn the language of the church. He elaborated:

> There's a movie that came out some years ago called *Nell*, starring Jodie Foster, about a young woman who was discovered living far away from civilization in the woods of North Carolina. She had her own mysterious language. There was a psychologist that studied her. He concluded, 'She needs to learn our language for us to reach her.' But then another doctor said, 'No, we need to learn her language.' And that struck me that that's really what we need to be about if we want to attract young people to the church. We need to first learn their language and not expect them to learn ours initially. What I started to do in my sermons, in my preaching, was to include stories and examples that would connect with young people. And as I did that, young people started feeling very connected and then I started to do some rap. Yes, me, some old white guy.

That Pastor Wallace would fashion his mission strategy from the plotline of a Hollywood blockbuster starring a famous actress was strange and yet somehow fitting for a Los Angeles pastor. Christian hip hop artists often critiqued the church and other gospel rappers for being too "Hollywood"—that is, selling out to commercialism, pop spectacle, and the politics of ego and self-interest. While Wallace occasionally inserted short "raps" into his sermons—*converting* traditional hymns and scripture into simple rhyme—he rarely spoke about hip hop music or addressed topics of social relevance that are often articulated through hip hop music: racial injustice, poverty, gang culture, police brutality, incarceration, and other daily realities of inner-city existence. He also showed little enthusiasm for incorporating actual rap music and rap artists into the hip hop service.

Pastor Wallace's initial statement on the origins of the Hip Hop Church also foregrounded the efforts of Randy Winston over Carol Scott, a point of contention for Pastor Scott and Sharon that would give later struggles a gendered tone in addition to the growing dissonances of race and class between church leaders and members of the council and congregation. Pastor Scott often spoke of the entrenched patriarchy of the church—how certain male leaders continue to take issue with women becoming pastors and assuming positions of authority within the church. "I think that's probably one of the major downfalls of the church and hip hop," she lamented, and then continued:

> When they go to interview any religious leader, if you're female, they're not going to interview you. You're not seen as the leader. I've had Kurtis do several interviews where he would mention my name in terms of who was running the Hip Hop Church, but he was the authority in terms of what was happening here. It's a man-made issue. It's a power issue—an ego issue. It's a sin issue in my book. But that's not where my focus is. They'll see the fruits of our labor and then they can't say anything. That's where I'm at. Don't get angry too long. I work in a male-dominated arena and I'm looked over.[14]

Due to some of the more negative experiences associated with being a black female leader in the church, Pastor Scott and Sharon began to interpret roadblocks and challenges to the implementation of the Hip Hop Church through the lenses of race and gender.

INGLEWOOD FALLING THROUGH THE CRACKS

Pastor Wallace had an affinity for preaching to inner-city black communities. During the years I attended Holy Trinity's hip hop services, its highly intergenerational congregation was approximately 95 percent African American—the remaining 5 percent made up of white and Latino families.[15] Despite belonging to the Evangelical Lutheran Church in America, a very small minority of the congregation grew up Lutheran; most members were raised in various Protestant denominations. The church was located off Crenshaw Boulevard in the heart of Inglewood, around the corner from three notable L.A. landmarks: Hollywood Park and Casino, Inglewood Park Cemetery, and the Great Western Forum. Its geographical proximity to these places, as well as the fact that the city of Inglewood boasts more than one hundred churches, was not insignificant.

Examining *where* the politics and performances of religious hip hop are reworked and enunciated gives insight into the forces shaping the possible futures of hip hop ministries and holy hip hop. Interestingly, the Great Western Forum,

FIGURE 7. Welcome to Inglewood, "City of Champions." Street sign from 2008.

former home of the Los Angeles Lakers and Los Angeles Kings, has hosted "Battle Zone"—an annual hip hop dance competition that featured a street dance style known as krumping. Born in the neighborhoods of South Central, krumping, or clowning as it is sometimes called, is a hyperkinetic dance resembling street fighting, moshing, sanctified church spirit possession, and aerobic striptease. Every Sunday, the Forum holds the megachurch congregation of Faithful Central Bible Church, where hip hop–inspired gospel star Kirk Franklin formerly led the musical program on Sundays and hosted a biweekly hip hop "Take Over" service. In another sacred-secular twist, the Battle Zone competitions I attended began with a Christian prayer while youth at Franklin's "Take Over" often krump-danced during Christian rap interludes throughout the service. The arena continues to fuse elements of sport, competition, media, hip hop, and religion and is shaped by entanglements of culture, power, and space that are unique to Inglewood.

It was the earthquake of 1920 that originally put Inglewood on the map. Visitors flocked to see the damage caused by the 4.9 magnitude quake, and many ended up staying due to the inviting, temperate climate. Over the next five years, it was the fastest growing city in the United States. After the Olympic marathon ran through Inglewood in 1932, the former settlement became touted as the "City of Champions." Three Inglewood High School alumni were Olympics winners: Hector Dyer for track in the 4x100 meter relay, George Jefferson for the pole vault, and Frank Booth in water polo. The Hollywood Park Racetracks opened in 1938, where millions of dollars were handled and exchanged every week. Eight years later,

George Foster opened the first Fosters Freeze in Inglewood. Introducing the soft-serve cone and a line of soft-serve desserts, Fosters Freeze truly could be described as California's first fast-food chain. Constructed in the late 1960s as the city became racially integrated, the Forum attracted more crowds and commerce to the "City of Champions," hosting not only the World Champion Lakers basketball team and Kings hockey team but also championship boxing.

Inglewood's accessibility to major freeways and the Los Angeles International Airport (LAX) drew business investors as well as the expanding air freight industry. High-rise office and government buildings were erected, most recently the fourteen-story, $50 million Trizec building on La Cienega. As new buildings penetrated the skies, some notable individuals chose to be buried below ground in Inglewood Park Cemetery. Opened in 1905, it has served as the final resting place for civic leaders like Mayor Tom Bradley and Supervisor Kenneth Hahn and entertainers such as actor Cesar Romero, William "Buckwheat" Thomas of *Our Gang* fame, and vocal legend Ella Fitzgerald. Many of the stars who helped make Hollywood famous also now rest permanently in Inglewood.

All of these developments led to Inglewood receiving one of the All-America City Awards in 1989 by the National Civic League (and yet again recently in 2009 for its visible progress). But by the 1990s, the "City of Champions" also suffered some losses. Property values declined as air traffic steadily increased at nearby LAX. The Lakers and the Kings, long the saving grace of Inglewood, announced plans to move to downtown L.A., placing the Forum's formidable tax revenue in limbo. The "Landers" earthquake of 1992 (M7.3) and "Northridge" earthquake of 1994 (M6.7) further shook up matters. Roosevelt Dorn, who served as mayor of Inglewood from the late 1990s through his resignation in 2010 after pleading guilty to the misuse of public funds, was known for his bombastic prophecies for Inglewood's impending resurrection. *LA Weekly* journalist Eric Pape states:

> Out on Market Street, once the city's shopping nexus, struggling merchants find such optimism hard to fathom, highlighting the mayor's tendency to talk of far-fetched scenarios and unsigned deals. The commercial strip is today virtually lifeless, a line of desolate buildings, fortified jewelry and loan shops, 'For Lease' and 'For Sale' signs. Parking is far too easy . . . Yet Dorn speaks with zeal about Inglewood's incipient revival, his optimism staked in part on massive aid infusions and development projects he expects to bring online by the end of his term—Home Depot, Starbucks, car dealers, a new 16-to-20-screen theater and plenty of hotels. Add to that hundreds of millions of dollars for schools from a recently passed bond measure with state and federal matching funds, as well as massive neighborhood revitalization and other projects he claims are in the pipeline. In a couple of years, Dorn promises, "You won't recognize Inglewood."[16]

Mayor Dorn, in his persistent fervor for Inglewood's resurrection, used to begin council meetings with a prayer. But Inglewood was in need of much more than prayers. Columnist Erin Aubry Kaplan lamented that "Inglewood has always *fallen* through the media cracks . . . As a study in the great possibilities of urban renewal and the dismal failure of local, solidly middle-class government to enact them, Inglewood should be an endless source of stories."[17] What were the stories circulating about Inglewood?

As elaborated in previous chapters, these challenges of urban decay laid the groundwork for a cultural and political landscape in which multiple stories and narratives of salvation would intersect and strengthen one another. Vargas argues, "During the 1980s, the semantic connection between race and urbanity became fully accepted by a large proportion of the U.S. public. Dominant political discourses equated, on the one hand, the urban inner cities, and on the other, neighborhood deterioration, people of color—especially black—and purported amorality."[18] Influenced by these discourses as well as the growing moral panic over the content and messages within hip hop and especially gangsta rap, certain cultural critics and censorship advocates, such as Tipper Gore, spearheaded efforts to keep America's youth safe from the ills of inner-city life. They did not want their own children listening to the harsh tales of daily life in black American ghettos. This "purported amorality" was not only leveled at black youth by white middle- and upper-class Americans, but also by African Americans from various social strata (what I referred to in the previous chapter as "black-lash"), creating intracommunal and cross-generational tensions within predominantly African American neighborhoods. Such tensions would surface in the efforts to implement hip hop ministries in and around L.A., and particularly, at Holy Trinity. The nexus of discourses at work in equating amorality, blackness, hip hop, gang life, and the inner city also found parallels in narratives of Inglewood's failed urban renewal and therefore a place of *fallen*, unrealized glory for African Americans. In so doing, it has also *fallen* through the media cracks. Hip hop, black youth, and Inglewood, according to such accounts, were all in need of some serious *saving* and *salvation*. As Tupac raps on "California Love," the iconic 1996 hip hop collaboration, "Inglewood always up to no good."

Latino youth were not absent from this barrage of assaults by both local Angelenos and the national media. Increasing black and brown animosity and violence in Inglewood at the turn of the twenty-first century put further stress on the neighborhood. In the 2003 article "Gangster's Paradise Lost," Dennis Romero quoted three sources as saying that Hispanic gangsters in that year were moving to Inglewood as a result of higher rents, or "gentrification," and increased police presence in West Los Angeles districts where they had been living.[19] Inglewood became home to many displaced Latino Westside gang members as well as an influx of Central American gangs like MS 13, who were more brutal, CIA-trained killers than the local gangs.[20] The black presence in old-line black neighborhoods such as Watts, Compton, and Inglewood was receding, making the notion of a geographically delineated African American community an impossibility.[21]

These shifts in the geographical borders and concentrations of black neighbor-hoods produced a great deal of instability around issues and experiences of home, turf, and territory between blacks and Latinos and within African American com-munities of various class levels. The Hip Hop Church L.A. was one of the many efforts by local church leaders and organizations to reach both African American and Latino gang-involved youth in the musical vernacular of the times and address such "dislocations" and "fragmentations" on a spiritual plane. After the 1992 Los Angeles riots, Pastor Scott was particularly committed to ending the gang violence in her communities and creating spaces of positive intergenerational interaction. She had heard and seen the effects of this violence firsthand at the previously defunct Martin Luther King Jr.–Harbor Hospital (what used to be the main desti-nation for gunshot victims), where she volunteered as a chaplain.[22] During one of the mock funeral processions in 2005, she delivered a prayer, calling on "advocates and peacemakers to raise the consciousness of our community and show solidar-ity with families and friends who've lost sons and daughters in this continuing war against urban terrorism."[23] Her humble hope for the Hip Hop Church was to provide a sanctuary from this urban terror for gang members and those in the trenches of violence. She also hoped it would provide a space for intergenerational exchange as schisms between the black youth and elders, black working classes and black upper-middle classes, were growing wider and more entrenched.[24]

Pastor Scott and Sharon bemoaned the generational divides and differences that gave rise to misunderstanding and alienation at Holy Trinity Church and on the streets of Inglewood. While common critiques of this perceived generation gap have often scapegoated black youth or blamed the instability and irrespon-sibility of the black family, other historical factors have drastically altered intra-communal and intergenerational relations and resource-sharing within black and brown neighborhoods: the collapse of public institutions, state policies of urban abandonment, the uneven development of capitalist economies, and the punitive containment of the black underclass. Loïc Wacquant theorized about the shift in American cities during the twentieth century from the "communal ghetto"—a kind of urban existence that Pastor Scott romanticized as the days of old—to the "hyperghetto" of the last two decades:

> The historic shift from *communal ghetto* of the mid-twentieth century, a compact and sharply circumscribed sociospatial formation to which blacks of all classes were consigned and bound together by a broad complement of institutions specific to the group and its reserved space, to the fin-de-siecle *hyperghetto*, a novel, de-centered, territorial and organizational configuration characterized by conjugated segregation on the basis of race *and* class in the context of the double retrenchment of the labour market *and* welfare state from the urban core, necessitating and elic-iting the corresponding deployment of an intrusive and omnipresent police and penal apparatus.[25]

These forces of spatial and social division continued to pattern the conscious-ness and practices of urban residents, contributing to interactions of misunder-standing and hostility. Growing class inequalities manifested spatially and socially across historically black neighborhoods in Los Angeles. "And so the Crenshaw District stands divided," Aubry states, "with the modernized Baldwin Hills Cren-shaw Plaza serving as a kind of Berlin Wall where the two populations occasion-ally intersect in a food court or shoe store, but later retreat to their respective north-south camps."[26] African American residents in Los Angeles experienced and articulated class dynamics and geographic segregation in dichotomous terms. Among churchgoers, the rhetoric was often couched in religious images and ideas around sin and salvation and illustrated the way that territorial stigmatization and religious/moral stigmatization were enmeshed. And yet, Aubry's statement did not account for all the subtleties of socioeconomic instability and fluctuation across class levels. Nor did it account for the ways in which black residents moved across and around various "Berlin Walls" within the city, within the span of a day or a lifetime.

For instance, Sharon raised her two children—son Sean and daughter Sim-one—in the church in hopes of passing on the Christian tradition in her family. And yet, she may be unable to pass on aspects of the financial security that she has achieved in her life. Sharon came from a middle-class, well-educated black family. Her father, while never finishing high school, went on to get a master's degree and a law degree and was one of the first black council members in Ingle-wood. In those years, Sharon made a good salary teaching dance classes at South-west College, but between two costly reconstructive knee surgeries and rigorous physical therapy treatments as well as being a single mother, she did not have excess income to invest significantly in her children's future—what Vargas has referred to as "intergenerational status fall."[27] Within many African American middle- and working-class families, increased earnings still cannot compensate for a lack of inherited wealth, making it difficult for African American parents who acquire financial capital to pass it on to their children, thus providing them with certain life opportunities. And yet, her house—a property that has been in her family for years—is increasing in value due to the rising real estate prices in Inglewood. Massive houses and Mercedes-Benzes now line the blocks surround-ing her home.

Here, Aubry's portrayal of "two populations"—those who have prospered and those who have not—falls a bit short in its reductionism, as middle-class and up-per middle-class African American families are often subject to many of the same problems and constraints that lower- and working-class families face. Terms like "working class" and "middle class" do not even adequately capture the subtle-ties and intermediate classifications that are a part of the everyday lives of black Angelenos. Further, class distinctions often appear to have less to do with economic standing than "everyday matters of speech, style, labor, and leisure": how one moves, walks, and talks, where one resides, what and how one eats, and with whom one interacts and associates.[28] Social classes are fluid categories dependent on a wide range of factors and practices.

VICTORY IN DEFEAT?

One story about Inglewood that did receive some media attention was Wal-Mart's 2004 campaign to build a megastore near Hollywood Park. Despite the promise of an abundance of new jobs, local residents decided it was not in the neighborhood's best interests. In what was deemed a major civic victory, Inglewood inhabitants rallied together against the high-powered, high-financed efforts of Wal-Mart to successfully defeat the initiative.[29] Always an advocate of local politics, Pastor Scott also found herself at the center of the proliferating Wal-Mart debacle, which highlighted tensions between the interests of corporate America and communities of color, big business and local commerce.

After the Wal-Mart initiative, known as Measure 4A, was defeated, a story was published in *LA Weekly* about Annie Lee Martin—an elderly Inglewood resident and member of Holy Trinity Church who got "duped" into becoming the poster girl for the corporate giant Wal-Mart. Pastor Scott was surprised when she received a colorful mailer from Wal-Mart featuring a photo of Annie Lee Martin and a letter encouraging Inglewood residents to approve a ballot initiative allowing the company to build a supercenter—what Larry Aubry called an attempt to "put a folksy, African American face on an increasingly heated battle over the fate of development in Inglewood."[30] Pastor Scott was concerned because Holy Trinity had recently joined the fight against the Wal-Mart initiative, and the congregation had been holding discussions about the downsides of Measure 4A. Scott was not convinced that the mailer reflected Martin's actual views on the subject and decided to give her a call. Confirming her suspicions, Martin told Scott that Wal-Mart had tricked her into being their poster girl for a mailer that was central to their campaign. None of the words on the letter were hers. None of them were true. The letter said that the eighty-two-year-old Martin—a retired nurse who lived in a senior complex near Manchester Boulevard—had resided in Inglewood for fifty years, when in fact, she had only lived there for thirteen.

Martin was aggressively approached by Wal-Mart representatives in the parking lot of her local grocery store. They were snapping photos and asking if she supported the creation of new jobs for youth in her neighborhood. Tired of being harassed by young folks for "quarters," she quickly supported the idea of creating new jobs in her community, unaware of the potential negative impacts of certain measures laid out in the initiative. She was later asked to sign a blank piece of paper under the guise of a petition. Martin was dismayed by what she considered an invasion of privacy orchestrated by Wal-Mart and embarrassed that the public assumed she was a Wal-Mart spokesperson.

The fact that Martin belonged to Holy Trinity Church was critical in the eventual surfacing of her story. In 2004, the church became one of the newest members of L.A. Metro, essentially a local chapter of the national community-organizing group Industrial Areas Foundation (IAF). L.A. Metro is involved in a variety of progressive, grassroots campaigns, many of which promote workers and workers' rights. After catching wind of Martin's news, Pastor Scott, other L.A. Metro members, and several Inglewood officials and activists held a town-hall meeting at a packed Holy Trinity about the Wal-Mart initiative. Scott told the *Los Angeles Sentinel*, "Here's one of my seniors being used, and I'm angry. I see this as a church issue, and I'm going to take the gospel out to the people. We're not going to wait for it to happen."[31] Even though the Wal-Mart initiative was defeated, one of the more distressing outcomes of the campaign was Martin's refusal to support any causes in the future. Formerly a stalwart voter, she threatened to retreat from the democratic process altogether. But she also refused to shop at Wal-Mart, despite her constant need of low-priced goods for her children and grandchildren.

It was not always easy for Pastor Scott to connect the church with social services and advocacy in her local communities. Inglewood residents may have won the victory against a giant corporate entity, but ironically, Sharon and Pastor Scott sometimes found it more challenging to help individuals and provide them with the ongoing support and resources they need to make transformative changes in their lives. For example, at one of the Friday night hip hop services at Holy Trinity, a young man walked down the aisle and confessed, "I don't want to be in gangs anymore. I'm tired of being in gangs, but give me an alternative. What else can I do?" Sharon recalls how hearing this man's words broke her heart because she didn't have any resources to offer him. She asked him for his phone number so that she could keep talking with him about his situation. "Well, he was in transition," she explained, "so he didn't have a number we could reach him at." Sharon ran into him again a month later at a local gym where she pleaded with him to come back to the Hip Hop Church. He shrugged his shoulders as he walked across the parking lot, hunched over with his head down. Sharon remembers feeling helpless and despondent, as if she had "left somebody in the jungle to die."

Hip Hop Church services did not explicitly address the aforementioned structural and social conditions at work in the production and transformation of such inner-city realities—that is, the multiple effects of joblessness, gang involvement, the justice system, institutionalized racism, segregation, massive immigration into the inner city, and income and wealth concentration. Instead, Sharon and Pastor Scott attempted to address the social and spiritual alienation within the black inner city itself by opening the doors to people who felt unwelcome to sit in the pews. Through the many challenges these two women faced in implementing the Hip Hop Church and the general lack of support from the Holy Trinity congregation, they began to understand their work as a truly "grassroots deal"—something more about creating "community" than attending church. Pastor Scott proclaimed, "It's not about being in church. It's not about trying to get you to do anything. It's to bring in those that have really been hurt and are hurting but they're seeking comfort and they need a place where the music speaks to them." Hip Hop Church existed as a respite from the unpredictable conditions of urban existence, as a place to worship through gospel rap, and as a sacred forum to discuss the social issues that churches have not traditionally addressed.

HOLLYWOOD IN THE CHURCH

On a sweltering summer night in 2007, I attended what would be one of Carol Scott's last Hip Hop Church services. Due to her worsening health, she no longer mingled and socialized with folks before the Friday night worship. Instead, she would lie down on the couch in the Holy Trinity office to rest before taking the pulpit. Lymphoma was just one of the many battles Pastor Scott was fighting. While she rested, Revelation—a female gospel rapper and former stripper from Long Beach—stood in the aisle with a microphone as she completed her sound check.

Revelation was the CEO of RAP4GOD records and had released her first gospel rap album, *I'M REVELATION "Tha Boss Lady,"* two years earlier. In the midst of some technical difficulties, she turned to me and commented under her breath, "I'm a devout Christian, but churches have not been accepting of my gospel rap thing." The sound engineer struggled to adjust the levels of her prerecorded track so that her rhymes could be heard above the blaring music. Sporting tight white pants and a cropped denim jacket, she ad-libbed on the microphone: "It's hot. It's summertime, but we gonna praise Him anyway." With increased attitude, she rapped a few lines about the 2007 Don Imus comments, in which the radio host called the Rutgers University women's basketball team a bunch of "nappy-headed hoes." Revelation, enveloped by the rising heat of the church building and her loudening track, boldly proclaimed, "Every time it's hip hop that gets the fire and then the churches point fingers!"

This was the first night I met Sharon. She saw me sitting in the pews and walked over to introduce herself. Quickly identifying me as a confidant and supporter of her cause, she recounted the recent trials and tribulations of the Hip Hop Church. "It's a struggle," she lamented. "It's been an uphill battle with the church. People hear the word hip hop and just stop there. They don't know the history of hip hop. They think it's all bad." Above her head hung four signs. The two on the right bore the words, "New Exodus" and "In the City . . . † for Good." Sharon continued,

"But you know what, whether it's ten people or ten thousand people that show up, someone will get blessed." My eyes then moved to the two signs in the left corner of the room: "It Takes a Village" and "Love in Action."

Hip Hop Church attendees began to arrive, scattering themselves throughout the pews. One young man got a call on his cell phone and answered, "Excuse me, I'm in church," and then quickly apologized to Sharon and me for the disturbance. A cluster of teenagers a few rows behind him talked loudly and casually about a friend of theirs who recently got shot—someone in a gang—as if this was a common occurrence.

A middle-aged African American woman rose from the first pew to lead the congregation in praise and worship, encouraging the congregants to "Praise Him how you want!" In a more traditional twist, she then belted out the gospel music classics "Eye on the Sparrow" and "To God Be the Glory" with impressive melismatic runs. Certain concessions to the traditional order of worship were made in order to give congregants something familiar to cling to. And yet Pastor Carol Scott continued to make openings for the individuality of worship and worshipful expression through her preaching: "We hear your voice this way, Lord—as spirit calling in the language of each person." Intentionally expanding her preaching practices to the hip hop community, she admitted, "Sometimes I don't even say that I'm a Christian, because if you do, they think you ain't hip and you don't know what's what. I just say, 'I'm a follower of the way.' For me, hip hop is just a freer way to reach those who are seeking."[32] During the Hip Hop Church services, Pastor Scott's preaching style "moved beyond the box," as Sharon used to say. Scott reflected one afternoon, "I had to really let loose and I had to also understand that I really wasn't their age. So I couldn't come in dressing their age. I had to know some of the language but I still had to be me."[33] Young people responded well to the balance she struck between addressing older and younger generations and her organic integration of hip hop into her own personal style.

A young spoken word artist then delivered a portion of his testimony—how he grew up on the streets of Los Angeles and ran with gangs before turning to Christ. His first rhymed poem repeated the line "Don't put me in boxes." Performing a cappella, he reminded the church: "[It] ain't about the tracks. It's about the Word"—a sentiment often expressed by gospel rappers.[34] Not surprisingly, many of the gospel rap artists delivered their rhymes unaccompanied when performing in churches in order to further highlight their lyrical message.

Kenny Z, an African American man in his forties who hosted a "Gospel Hip Hop Praise" television show on an L.A. public access station, strutted up to the pulpit. The youth generally appreciated the content of his lyrics, but felt that his music and style of delivery were sometimes "corny" and therefore too humorous to be taken seriously. The black pinstriped suit and polished pointy shoes he donned that night were at odds with the more casual attire of the youth in attendance. Bouncing his head to the beat of his track, he pointed at individuals in the congregation as he rapped in a slow style about the dangers of "Hollywood in the church"—a statement that alluded to the tendency of certain churches, preachers, and churchgoers to prioritize celebrity, status, and flashiness over piety, worship, and humility. A heavy-set man stood behind him, crooning the chorus, "Hollywood, church up to no good," in a floating falsetto over a laid-back hip hop groove. Kenny Z shouted, "Hollywood has no concern for souls" as his wife, Rozzie, danced in her seat from the first pew, clearly pleased with her husband's performance.

Listening to Kenny Z's rhymes, I was reminded of the ways in which Hollywood has already *been* in Inglewood: Rick Famuyiwa's 1999 film *The Wood* depicted three young black men growing up in Inglewood and their intertwining journeys from boys to men; scenes of "inner city" life from *Boyz in the Hood* (1991) and *Training Day* (2001) were shot in Inglewood; and the infamous scene from *Pulp Fiction* (1994) with Samuel L. Jackson took place at Pann's Restaurant—a long-standing 1950s diner just down the road from Holy Trinity Church (at which I conducted one of my interviews with gospel rapper Cue). These cinematic representations, along with the rap music references—"Inglewood, always up to no good"—and Inglewood's worsening public image in the press made the city a less desirable point of destination for people beyond its borders. For instance, Pastor Scott tried to get several Lutheran churches from the Valley to visit the Hip Hop Church, but they never showed up. She claimed, "They got scared of Inglewood." Sharon recently told me about another damaging Hollywood misrepresentation of the city: "That movie, *Grand Canyon* [1991], really gave folks the wrong idea about Inglewood. They have Kevin Kline leaving a Lakers game at the Forum and suddenly he's in this crime-ridden ghetto with graffiti and gangs and barbed wire. That's a lie. That's not the Inglewood I know. People ask me, 'Aren't you scared to be there?' No! Dentists and doctors live here. They got it all wrong."[35]

One would also think that Kurtis Blow's star-studded status and involvement with the Hip Hop Church L.A. would attract financial resources and notoriety to the ministry. Although Kurtis gave occasional monetary gifts to keep the ministry afloat, he was rarely present at the Los Angeles services due to his touring schedule and involvement with his East Coast hip hop ministries. But as Sharon used to say, "One monkey don't stop the show. So whether he's here or not, we want the service to go on . . . he's from the East Coast and what you have is the East Coast–West Coast thing. Not everybody remembers him because he hasn't done music in many years. People out here don't always feel him." Due to generational and geographical distance, Kurtis Blow's name did not hold as much clout and capital in Los Angeles with a younger generation as it did in his native Harlem. His ties to the Hip Hop Church would wear even thinner as Pastor Scott's health worsened.

The Hip Hop Church L.A. did not receive any economic and organizational support from Holy Trinity. In fact, aside from housing the Friday night hip hop services and offering some file space in one of the church offices, Holy Trinity did not contribute any funds to the production of the Hip Hop Church. The monthly hip hop ministry was able to function on an extremely limited budget, cobbling together minimal compensation for the performing artists—what Sharon referred to as a "love offering"—and the usual post-service meal of hot dogs, potato chips, fruit punch, and chocolate chip cookies. The money collected from the offering at hip hop services was modest as attendees had often already contributed to the offering at regular Sunday services. Many of the gospel rappers and spoken word artists offered to perform without pay, but Sharon—a dancer and performer herself—was adamant that artists should receive proper compensation for their time and talents. Sharon and Pastor Scott also wanted the Hip Hop Church to be a place where, if a homeless person walked in the front doors, they could offer them a bed or connect them with a transition house. "Jesus didn't just preach the word," Sharon used to say. "He also fed and healed." Beyond directing people to the motels down the block from Holy Trinity, they were able to offer people little more than some canned and packaged foods from the church pantry.

FROM HOLY TRINITY TO MOBILE MINISTRY

Months after I started attending Hip Hop Church services, I received a call from Sharon informing me that Pastor Carol Scott had lost her battle with lymphoma and passed away. My heart sank. The *Los Angeles Times* obituary stated that she was known for her hip hop ministry, her "activist in-the-streets form of theology," "her campaign to bring peace to violent neighborhoods," and her desire for Christians to "take off the veil of elitism."[36] Sharon was in tears as she told me the details of Pastor Scott's passing, distraught that her best friend was gone, concerned about the three children she left behind, and worried for the future of the Hip Hop Church L.A. The loss of Pastor Scott at just fifty years old, along with the death of her cousin and two reconstructive knee surgeries, served as catalysts for many changes in Sharon's life. In particular, these events crystallized her vision for and commitment to hip hop ministry, even as she had to walk around on crutches for the many months that we worked together. Pastor Scott's death also unveiled the divergent interests and investments in the Hip Hop Church that eventually led to Sharon's exclusion from Holy Trinity and the splintering of the ministry into two factions. The controversies that followed also made visible the patriarchal forces at work even in an alternative hip hop Christian imaginary.

Shortly after Pastor Scott's passing, Sharon, her son Sean, and Candace Jordan— a young African American woman who helped plan and produce the Hip Hop Church services—met with the Holy Trinity council. After Pastor Carol Scott's memorial service, the council wanted to put the Hip Hop Church on a four-month "hiatus," allegedly needing time to find a pastor to replace Carol Scott. Sharon rebutted, "You don't just stop church services when someone dies." She was skeptical of the proposed "hiatus," arguing that it was a way for Holy Trinity to shut down the Hip Hop Church in order to implement a "tamer" youth service that didn't spotlight hip hop so overtly. Pastor Wallace was hoping to supplant the Hip Hop Church with his "Youth Revival Blast." His subtle discomfort with the ministry had become clear through the scant marketing of the hip hop Friday night service: the Hip Hop Church sign went up on Friday morning and came down promptly at 9 p.m. on Friday night after the service finished. During hip hop services, Pastor Wallace began sitting in the back pew of the church instead of his normal seat in the third pew, sometimes even leaving the service early through the back entrance.

Then came a litany of complaints. The youth minister grumbled that the Hip Hop Church never started on time, with Pastor Wallace adding that the service started an hour and a half late. Other council members complained that the Hip Hop Church lacked organization and that the gospel rap artists "come and perform" but "are not ministering." To back up their accusations, members of council were picking up Bibles and quoting scripture. Pastor Wallace and the council often talked down to Sharon and other female leaders of the Hip Hop Church as if they were disobedient daughters rather than equal believers in the ministry. Sharon later told me, "The hits just keep on coming, so we know we're on the right track. It's just so difficult. Even before we had that male domination thing going on, it was still women doing the work. And they don't want to give us the credit." Pastor Wallace had wanted Sharon removed as director of the Hip Hop Church well before this particular encounter in order to create "a hip hop ministry without hip hop," as she put it.

Aside from growing tensions between Sharon and Pastor Wallace, the main issue of concern was whether the Hip Hop Church belonged to Holy Trinity or existed as a separate ministry under the direction of Kurtis Blow. Sharon began making plans to leave Holy Trinity and transform the Hip Hop Church L.A. into a mobile ministry.[37] "I'm tired of walking into meetings and getting ambushed. We're going to take the Hip Hop Church elsewhere because it doesn't belong to them. Now they don't have to worry about outsiders at their church anymore. This pariah doesn't have to be here." Pastor Carol Scott's memorial service would be the last time Sharon would attend Holy Trinity as a member of that church.

Sharon then called an emergency meeting among Hip Hop Church faithfuls in the hope of trying to develop a new vision for the hip hop ministry. I got the call the next day: "We're meeting this Saturday. Ten a.m. at the Starbucks in the Inglewood Hollywood Park shopping center. I need positive people there."[38]

When I arrived at the Starbucks on Century Boulevard and Crenshaw in Inglewood, Sharon was visibly upset, still shaking with the twin emotions of anger and grief. Kenny Z, Candace, and Sean were all present, along with Mike—a friend of Kurtis Blow who had helped organize some of the first Hip Hop Church L.A. services. Everyone agreed to hold Carol Scott's memorial at Holy Trinity during the Friday night hip hop service. Then the ministry would go mobile. "A three-month hiatus will kill the Hip Hop Church," Sharon warned, "We gotta keep it going, otherwise souls may be lost." Pastor Scott's initial dream was to take the Hip Hop Church to the people—in group homes, rehab centers, and juvenile halls—instead of making folks come to the church. Furthermore, everyone was wary of trying to find another church home for the hip hop ministry after the frustrations they experienced at Holy Trinity. Mike warned that most churches would want all of them to become members and that there would always be some opposition from certain council or congregation members who wanted to put limits or restrictions on what kinds of music and performers were allowed. Candace chimed in, "And whatever church we go to needs to know that the youth come as they are. They wear hats, baggy pants . . . At the last hip hop service some older folk walked away from the service because people were wearing hats."

Mike then called Kurtis Blow on his cell phone to get his opinion on the matter of the Hip Hop Church. Kurtis, now on speakerphone, confirmed that the Hip Hop Church L.A. was an offshoot of Hip Hop Church America—not under the ownership of Holy Trinity—and added definitively, "Sharon is the only one who can run the Hip Hop Church." After all the tasks for the upcoming memorial service were divvied out, we held hands in a circle and prayed in the middle of Starbucks while Stevie Wonder's "Love's in Need of Love Today" graced the airwaves.

As the Hip Hop Church was planning their mobile ministry to various local churches, prisons, and festivals in Long Beach and Inglewood, Pastor Wallace and members of Holy Trinity's council began to develop a new vision of hip hop worship—the "Hip Hop Youth Revival." Proudly sitting behind his large wooden desk in his office at Holy Trinity, he explained the council's reevaluation and replacement of the Hip Hop Church in the wake of Carol Scott's passing:

> We agreed that we still wanted to follow the purpose of bringing in youth, but we felt that we were not doing that. Now within that group, there was disagreement. Some said, "Oh, yes we are." With that disagreement, there were a couple leaders who left us because they said, "We want it to remain as is. We are doing this and that's the way it should be." One thing that we say is that we can agree to disagree, but because you disagree does not mean that your view will dominate, even if you speak loud, you know, and try to dominate. So a couple leaders left and that was painful. And then in the midst of this, as you know, we lost Pastor Carol. So, because she had been, for that congregation, the primary leader, that created a huge vacuum. And so we decided, we cannot replace her so let's not try. Let's instead try to restructure the leadership and try to expand the leadership of the Hip Hop Church.[39]

Pastor Wallace eventually appointed Pastor Scott Fritz to coordinate their Hip Hop Worship Task Force and enlisted one of the younger men of the church to preach, in addition to an adult pastor.[40] While this new hip hop night better honored the purpose of involving and engaging youth, hip hop music was largely absent from the service. Wallace invited a guest youth choir, a dance ministry, and a saxophonist to perform at the Hip Hop Youth Revival night, but no hip hop artists or gospel rappers were included during those first few services.

PASTOR SCOTT'S DREAM

I heard the hip hop–styled sounds of drums and organ spilling out into the sun-baked parking lot of Holy Trinity Church as I strolled up Crenshaw Boulevard. It was the night of Carol Scott's memorial service—Friday, October 5, 2007. Sharon, Candace, Kenny Z, and Sean crafted an impeccably organized and dynamic program. The service started on time with Kenny Z calling Pastor Wallace down from his high perch on the church balcony to come and participate in the service. In a gracious and diplomatic gesture, Kenny made a subtle appeal for forgiveness and the uniting of the hip hop church and traditional church in his prayer. "We have to know where we come from," he encouraged, "and stay the course of tradition. The word of God does not change even though we are in the hip hop generation." A large photo of Pastor Scott hung behind him, smiling down on the congregation.

The service opened with a small group of conga drummers—Sharon and her Cuban drum teacher among them. Dressed in all white and donning bright blue eye shadow on this special occasion, Sharon hit the conga with authority and attitude. She sought closure, connection, and catharsis. As the last hit of the drums echoed through the sanctuary, Big Preacha rose regally to the microphone. "Got to be bold! Got to be bold in the spirit," he barked. As a gospel rapper walking the streets of Inglewood, Watts, and the Crenshaw district, he was known for approaching strangers and asking them if they wanted to pray with him. "I used to *be* on the streets," he told the congregation, which is a common way that gospel rap artists refer to their previous lifestyles of sin, a secular state of mind, or the time before converting to Christianity. Big Preacha articulated this territorialization of experience: "After I was saved, all *home turf* here. You can hip hop for Jesus and be free. It's cool serving Jesus. I wish I would have known that ten years ago."

Speaking of the people still living the life of the streets, Big Preacha continued, "They need something to chip away the stone around their hearts and give them hearts of flesh." With this phrase, Big Preacha's "stone hearts" conjured the concrete of the streets—a mythic and all too real world of cold, brutal, stone-faced and stone-hearted men and woman. For Big Preacha, hip hopping for Jesus, instead of worldly things, initiated a process of humanizing the heart into flesh. His performance of the track "Bow Down" *cemented* his point. The song title referenced a well-known Snoop Dogg line demanding people to bow to his gangsta prowess, but Big Preacha's rap spoke about surrendering one's life to Jesus.

Then Sharon danced. Dressed up like an old and haggard homeless woman, draped in threadbare rags and hunched over a wooden cane, she danced like a woman dancing her last dance, overextending her limbs in motions both swooping and jagged. She conveyed the bitter ache of aged bones and the hardening inflexibility of poverty. Her cane seemed to be an appendage, an extended finger perhaps pointing blame or twirling invisible smiles into the air. She danced for her dear friend and mentor, Carol Scott. She danced for their shared vision of the Hip Hop Church.

Sean concluded the service, reminding the congregation, "This was her dream! We love you, Pastor Scott!" Summoning Pastor Scott's teenage daughter, Lauren, to join him in the pulpit, he put his arm around her and called everyone in the church to stand and clap as loudly and fiercely as they could for the life and spirit of Pastor Scott. The congregation rose to its feet, applauding, stomping, cheering, and hollering—raising praise for this brave, committed, and visionary woman. In this moment of embodied, emotional eruption, a tear fell from Lauren's eye as her heart filled with the enormous spirit of her mother's life—a life of beautiful struggle. The memorial was a performance of legitimation for the Hip Hop Church L.A., an emotional release, an unspoken standoff between the traditional church and the hip hop ministry—a night of endings and new beginnings.

Food and fellowship commenced in the adjacent gymnasium after the service. After fueling on hot dogs, the youth swarmed the dance floor as the DJ played "Crank That (Soulja Boy)." While the song contains controversial lyrics suggestive of certain demeaning sexual behaviors toward women, these young people seemed to find a deep sense of "church" upon hearing this *Billboard* top 100 hit. Soon, many of them were lined up in rows to dance the *electric slide*. Pastor Scott would have enjoyed this jubilant hip hop scene.

· · ·

Since discontinuing their partnership with Holy Trinity, the Hip Hop Church L.A. has persevered as a mobile outreach ministry that hosts services wherever it is welcome. They also hold an ongoing hip hop service every third Sunday at Inglewood's Faith Lutheran Church as well as an annual Rap & Praise Awards. Hip hop ministries continue to emerge in Los Angeles, as well as places like Harlem, Chicago, and Atlanta, among others—cities that traditionally have boasted a strong black middle class but continue to experience the fragmenting and segregating effects of urbanization and gentrification. The merging of Christianity and hip hop—two of the biggest cultural forces at work in African American communities—has created a matrix of power dynamics fraught with competing religious and commercial interests across multiple fields of social and financial capital. These dynamics and debates are really nothing new, just dressed up in modern attire with more flashes of pop culture commercialism amidst the increasing constraints of life in urban America.

The trials and triumphs of the Hip Hop Church L.A. illustrate and sound out several important realities in hip hop ministry. First, the importance of telling this tale is to account for the diverse practitioners of holy hip hop who were often eclipsed by the commonly seen face of the male gospel MC. Mothers of adolescents, white pastors, black female pastors, ex-hip hop stars, female rap artists, young hip hop fans, and youth ministers, among others, were all crucial laborers in the daily toil of hip hop ministry and street evangelism.[41] Oftentimes, their work went unseen, but they were all carving out pathways, however contested, for the merging of Christianity and hip hop.

Second, musical performance remained a contested terrain among church congregations and communities, as music was often deployed strategically as a platform to introduce new ideas, people, ministries, and practices into the church. Styles of musical worship, how much music is played during a service, and compensation for church musicians are just a few of the specific challenges regarding musical practice in African American Christian communities.[42] These issues may seem merely musical, but in fact are involved in complex struggles around race, gender, class, social status, territory, and age. In the cultural politics of hip hop churches, music *matters*.

Change to the existing norms of musical worship in churches does not come easily. Often, it is the enormous and enduring effort of a few courageous and committed pastors.[43] As seen with the emergence and acceptance of gospel music in 1930 and '40s, change in religious worship is more effectively initiated from positions of authority within the church.[44] Thus, we see more and more gospel rappers becoming pastors and preachers. While some might expect Pentecostal or Holiness churches to be more open to the emotive expressivity of hip hop music, denominational characteristics actually appear to have little to do with whether or not a church and its congregation will allow hip hop in the pulpit. Rather, the trust a congregation has in its pastors and the ability of the leadership to find musicians who, while pushing the boundaries of musical worship, present this musical change in an accessible and palatable manner prove to be more important factors in the process of changing traditional practices. Despite personal squabbles and misunderstandings among those working with the Hip Hop Church, both Pastor Scott and Pastor Wallace exhibited great openness to possibilities of a hip hop ministry and a profound commitment to the presence of youth at Holy Trinity.

The politics of respectability in expressions of African American Christianity, as well as conflicts over who is allowed entry into the realms of power and authority within black churches, often play out in ideological struggles over what constitutes appropriate music and language in the pulpit. Internal policings within black religious communities reveal the costs and benefits of citizenship in black churches as well as how religious, spatial, and aesthetic boundaries in predominantly black communities are both highly fixed and endlessly flexible. The manner in which Sharon, Sean, Pastor Scott, Pastor Wallace, the council members, and the gospel rap artists who performed at Holy Trinity navigated the shifting grounds of the *hip* and the *holy,* illustrated how complicated negotiations of the sacred and secular can activate social fault lines within churches and congregations. Ultimately, Los Angeles gospel rappers would have to take their music beyond the church walls.

3

———

Beyond Babylon

Geographies of Conversion

*As a radical standpoint, perspective, position, "the politics of location" neces-
sarily calls those of us who would participate in the formation of counter-
hegemonic cultural practice to identify the spaces where we begin the process
of re-vision.*

– BELL HOOKS

*With music, mek we chant down Babylon
This music, mek we chant down Babylon
This music, come we chant down Babylon*

—BOB MARLEY, "CHANT DOWN BABYLON"

I heard Khanchuz before I saw him—his most recent gangsta-inspired Any Demon
Killa beats accosting my ears through his car windows, alerting me to his imminent
arrival. He parked, locked the doors of his metallic beige Cadillac, and swaggered
slowly up Degnan Boulevard in Leimert Park Village—a historic black arts district
in Los Angeles that continues to struggle against the twin forces of urban abandonment and encroaching gentrification. Standing at the opposite end of the block,
I caught a glimpse of his faux diamond cross swinging gently across his chest—
a pendulum of light against the dark night as he passed a colorful mural bearing
the words: "At the crossroads, a vision is shaped." Khanchuz greeted me with a hug
before we turned the corner onto 43rd Place. Another sonic curiosity beckoned.
This time inside Sonny's Spot—a small cavernous music club that hosted the long-
standing "Poets Jazz House" and where the local Artists for Justice and Liberation
collective previously held action meetings to "Save Leimert Park." The interior walls,
tagged with layers of writing and adorned with various jazz memorabilia, provided
our backrest as an elderly African American pianist improvised to the tune "Nina's
Dream." Overhead, King Oliver's Creole Jazz Band gazed down at his dancing fingers from a washed-out black and white photograph across the room.

Our night crawl continued as we passed the vaudeville era and then boarded-up Vision Theater—a neighborhood movie palace originally known as Leimert Theater that was *converted* into a Jehovah's Witness church under the name The Watchtower. Purchased and renamed the Vision Theater by actress Marla Gibbs in 1990, the property was foreclosed on and the city took ownership in 2000. One storefront down, we reached our destination: KAOS Network, a cultural center that was home to the infamous weekly underground hip hop open mic, Project Blowed, that gave rise to MCs and rap groups such as Aceyalone, Freestyle Fellowship, Medusa, and Jurassic Five. But on that balmy fall evening, KAOS Network was hosting a different brand of hip hop—a religious open-mic called Klub Zyon where local gospel rappers gathered every month to "chant down Babylon" through biblically inspired rhymes. Zyon, the open mic's founders explained to me, was where we were going—the ultimate place, a spiritual homeland for wandering travelers.

Before Khanchuz got saved, he was at Project Blowed rapping about gangbangin', both on stage and in the freestyle battles that would spill out onto the street corner and linger into the break of day. As we walked through the scattered dreams, memories, and visions of Leimert Park and finally came face to face with the front door of KAOS Network, Khanchuz stepped back in silent wonder as he reflected on the conversion of both his soul and this place.

CONVERSION AS SPATIAL PRACTICE

Holy hip hop practitioners, through their musical practices and discourses, worked with and on what I refer to as the "living architecture" of the city to create sites of gospel rap production. Gospel rap artists perceived and performed *place* as a converting body and a site for the potential conversion of religious subjects; they also experienced and enacted *conversion* as both a spiritual transformation and a spatial practice. Their spatial practices constituted the manifold ways in which holy hip hoppers moved through, used, altered, and made meaning out of space.[1] Their spatial practices were especially critical in L.A.'s terrains and conditions of uncertainty.

As previously argued, Los Angeles in the late 1980s and 1990s was wrought with social and environmental volatility.[2] The Southland's morphing geography was in part due to the extent to which the deindustrialization of L.A., strict land ordinances and housing covenants, and inner-city neglect led to a lack of consolidating apparatuses that delineated regularities of territory in the city. Renovations and restructuring in the wake of the Watts riots and the 1992 riots along with the changing nature of Los Angeles churches, specifically the rise of megachurches, further complicated the city's shape-shifting landscapes. This instability was, at times, managed and manipulated by state bureaucracies and apparatuses to implement certain reforms. As Elana Zilberg argues, policing practices in L.A., such as gang injunctions, constituted a "technology of spatial legislation," creating certain segregations, marginalities, and foreclosures.[3] And yet instability also provided the conditions of possibility for city dwellers to radically re-vision and transform the existing urban milieu. Holy hip hop practices formed a technology of spatial improvisation that produced new kinds of sacred space in the city— what I call geographies of conversion.

During the five years I lived in Los Angeles (2003–8), holy hip hop comprised a highly complex field of practices that included music labels, local scenes, ministries, radio programs, award shows, and musical collectives that functioned in an astonishing variety of buildings and locations deemed both religious and non-religious. And yet, their unique expressions were not always perceived positively by church communities or secular hip hop fans and artists. Existing oftentimes *in between* the club, the church, and the streets, gospel rap artists struggled to locate receptive audiences and find a true dwelling place—to find "Zyon." In fact, holy hip hop was one of the few black Christian musical practices where the church— often referred to as the Body of Christ by both Catholics and Protestants—was not the primary location of power and performance.[4] While many church leaders and congregants were condemning holy hip hop, many African American youth perceived the church as a "negative asylum."[5] Holy hip hoppers often sought refuge from its constraints, but nightclubs were not necessarily welcoming of Jesus-centered hip hop either. Female gospel MC B-Love cleared the dance floor after she performed holy hip hop at her sister's birthday party at a local club. "The party was dead after I got up there. People didn't want to hear about the healing power of Christ while they were drinking and partying. But maybe someone got touched."[6] So where did holy hip hoppers find a sense of belonging?

This chapter explores some of the "key sites" of gospel rap fellowship and performance.[7] Three holy hip hop–inspired events in Los Angeles aimed to welcome and integrate diverse subjects and beliefs: The Row, a street corner in downtown L.A.'s Skid Row *converted* into an "airborne" church service; Klub Zyon, a hip hop–based cultural center *converted* into a place of musical worship and religious fellowship; and Club Judah, a church sanctuary *converted* into a holy hip hop "club." These geographies of conversion, as they intersected with holy hip hoppers' own biographies of conversion, underscored music's role in the mutual construction of both the changing body of the city and the changing bodies inhabiting it. How did the space of a church, street corner, or club, reworked by the practices of gospel rap, serve as a site for the creation of new kinds of places of activity and interaction as well as new kinds of religious subjects? How did the lived and imagined geographies of holy hip hoppers in Los Angeles inform, define, and disrupt the socially constructed and policed boundaries between the sacred and the profane, Christianity and hip hop, ministry and entertainment, the church and the streets?

What holy hip hoppers did physically and performatively to their urban surroundings through the cultural production of gospel rap was always in relation to the sedimented meanings and histories of specific places. Holy hip hop was actualized in the practices of creating and converting places not traditionally used for either hip hop or religious expression into locations that could house the interface of diverse social actors and sacred, secular, and profane elements.[8] And yet, where gospel rap was performed and actualized mattered. Specific places (as always and already constituted by an arrangement of social relations, spatial imaginaries, and grounded, material realities) also affected the holy hip hoppers that sought to use, shape, and inhabit them. The embodied musical practices, spiritual practices, and spatial practices of holy hip hoppers were deeply enmeshed, acting as allied modalities of agency fleshing out different bodies of the city.

MAPPING BLACK L.A.

The history of black music in Los Angeles is one charged with race and religion, marked by extreme contrasts of both inter- and intracommunal integration and segregation, and inextricably embedded in the geopolitics of the ever-expanding and converting body of the city. Los Angeles is often articulated as a city of racial, class-based, and territorial divisions on the one hand, and cultural assimilation and multiculturalism on the other. Both narratives enunciate the entanglement of realities *and* myths of the city. Jacqueline DjeDje and Eddie Meadows, in their introduction to *California Soul* (1998), highlight the intersecting histories of migration to Los Angeles, dating as far back as the 1929 stock market crash, which resulted in policies (e.g., restrictive housing covenants) and obstacles that forced African Americans into segregated communities, affecting the possibilities of musical expression and exchange within the city.[9] Los Angeles nightclubs have historically been one of the battlegrounds of such enduring patterns of racial discrimination and exclusion precisely because of the possibilities for mixing they can offer and inspire. Conversely, the church has often served as a haven of interracial, intergenerational encounter and a cultural resource in both everyday practice and scholarly discourse—a place that nurtured the artistic development and professionalism of black sacred music (i.e., gospel music).

Mark Anthony Neal argues that the church and the jook-joint (i.e., club) have historically been the two main centers of black life.[10] In the holy hip hop scene, certain pastors, church members, community members, and hip hop artists articulated a separation between sacred and secular spaces, and specifically, between the church and the streets. The streets often represented the constitutive outside or immoral other against which certain church members defined the sanctity of the Christian church. "The street becomes a religious trope," writes Omar McRoberts in his ethnography of Chicago African American churches, "alternately embodying notions of irredeemable evil and combatable sin."[11] But clubs and churches have not always been clearly delineated spatial entities, and in fact, have often occupied the very same buildings.

In the face of such geographic segregations and exclusions from the larger public space, black Angelenos utilized city buildings in a variety of ways—ways that planners, builders, and owners may not have intended. Clubs, in mid-twentieth-century Los Angeles, as places where people of various racial and ethnic backgrounds could dance together and intermingle, were the target of systematic shutdowns and discriminatory policing tactics based on fears of interracial mixing. Ralph Eastman explains how after-hours black nightclubs in L.A., often referred to as "breakfast clubs," sprang up in "storefronts, back rooms, and second floors" as alternative places of music making, dancing, drinking, and socializing outside the legal reach of the racially charged policies structuring nightlife in Los Angeles.[12] These clubs, Eastman argues, were where black musicians could partake in "unselfconscious experimentation" with "openness to new forms."[13]

Similar spatial practices were enacted in the block parties and schoolyard battles of early hip hop in the Bronx, where African American and Latino youth hooked up turntables, speakers, and microphones to street lampposts to party and purge on public grounds. Thus, a superficial or surface-level mapping of black musical locations does not account for the multiple uses and conversions of urban space that (have had to) occur behind walls, after hours, and therefore, out of sight. Eastman argues that Los Angeles's African American musical heritage has been "ignored and forgotten," referring to this absence as an "entrenched critical myopia."[14] This lack of a particular kind of critical sight has rendered invisible certain key sites of black musical performance. The tendency of black music studies to both represent the church and the club (or the church and the streets) as a social binary of African American cultural life *and* to avoid examinations of nontraditional uses of space has led to a spatial bias that excludes valuable forms of music making in black communities. While academic and public discourses separate these sites, music *sounds* their entanglement, giving voice to lived spatial resonances. The blurring of spatial categories is constitutive of holy hip hop's geographies of conversion.

BABYLON'S RACIAL AND SPIRITUAL CARTOGRAPHIES

Place holds prominence in hip hop, from the territorial and regional affiliations of rap artists to the mythologizing of the "ghetto" in hip hop lyrics and in the greater public imagination. As Eithne Quinn writes in his seminal text on Los Angeles gangsta rap, "rappers responded to the uprooting of their communities by redoubling their claims on the 'hood."[15] Murray Forman's work has brought a critical spatial awareness to the study of hip hop cultures. Forman argues that hip hop has been in a process of "going local" where representations of and contestations around turf, territory, and 'hood are inextricably enmeshed in the cultural production of the music.[16] His examination unpacks the analytical categories of race, space, and place as they relate to the shifting scales of spatial discourses in rap music. Less examined are the everyday spatial practices of hip hop practitioners. However, he does open up possibilities for the exploration of specific hip hop cartographies that account for "fictive" or imagined mappings of the city (often through music and lyrics) as well as "actual" spatial practices in and across the city. Here, the meaning(s) people make from particular spaces are critical and contingent on a variety of linked social realities, including race, religion, class, and gender. Moving the focus from the Hip Hop Nation as a historical construct to hip hop as a "geo-cultural amalgamation of personages and practices that are spatially dispersed"[17] allows us to interrogate the various geographies that hip hop practitioners—as "alternative cartographers"—reimagine and remap.[18] If gangsta rap assembles "geographies of gangsta," as Quinn suggests, holy hip hop's geographies of conversion constitute one of many diverse and intersecting hip hop geographies.[19]

As musical and spiritual cartographers, gospel rap artists sound out multilevel mappings of the city. On the surfaces of Los Angeles's church-laden streets, Khanchuz once mapped for me a cityscape of separation: "There is an aura of spiritual division here. There are so many churches and yet each church is separate from the next. L.A. is made up of churches, motels, and liquor stores. In Inglewood, you have church, motel, liquor store, church, motel, liquor store, liquor store."[20] Mike Davis confirms, "Black small businesses have withered for lack of credit or attention from the city, leaving behind only liquor stores and churches."[21] The topography of Inglewood articulated by Khanchuz, which is repeated in many other historically black neighborhoods throughout Los Angeles, reveals the proximity of "sacred" and "secular" spaces but occludes certain alliances, integrations, and manipulations of space that are socially and relationally produced by city inhabitants.[22] In other words, what did this particular mapping conceal or leave out? Gospel rap soundings amplify other spaces and cartographies of black L.A.

And yet, Khanchuz's mapping forces us to consider the connotations of race, gender, and class that particular kinds of places evoke, where churches, motels, and liquor stores connote black religiosity, prostitution/promiscuity, alcoholism, and criminality. Michael Keith argues, "There is a racist discourse of depravity that draws its provenance from a racialised construction of a black urban Babylon."[23] How we language our environment *matters*. "As vocabulary maps the city, it creates cartographies of the social."[24] Whereas early L.A. gangsta rappers, such as N.W.A., sonically and visually mapped frenetic inner-city territories of poverty, policing, and violence—Compton, Watts, and Long Beach—gospel rappers remapped those same racialized territories using biblical metaphors and narratives of spiritual rebirth, most notably Babylon and Zion.[25] Similarly, in the 1980s, East

Coast Muslim MCs created a new spiritual geography of New York (or what was sometimes referred to by hip hop heads as Zoo York). The city was "rechristened via Islam's holiest sites, with Harlem becoming Mecca and Brooklyn becoming Medina"—another instance revealing the entanglement of hip hop, religiosity, and geography.[26]

Los Angeles, with Hollywood at its cultural and commercial center, was often imagined through holy hip hop lyrics and everyday speech as the biblical city of Babylon—a city of excessive luxury, sensuality, vice, and corruption. The Bible portrayed Babylon as a place of captivity or exile for the Jews after the ancient empire of Babylonia conquered Israel in sixth century B.C.E. The exilic experience of holy hip hoppers navigating and traversing religious, musical, and physical borderlands of Los Angeles's Babylon paralleled and remapped this ancient narrative of displacement. In *American Babylon,* Robert O. Self argues, "Babylon as both place and concept passed into the lexicon of radical black politics in the late 1960s, borrowed from African American religious traditions as well as from the Jamaican Rastafarians for whom Babylon denoted Western capitalism and imperialism."[27] As the metaphor of Babylon connotes cynicism, it also articulates a hopeful belief in rebirth and recreation. In the 1979 reggae classic "Steppin' Out of Babylon," Marcia Griffiths sang, "I've got no alternative, in a Babylon, but I know, yes I know, there's a Mount Zion." Paul Gilroy, in a chapter that shares the same title as Griffiths' hit, further elaborates that Rastas adhere to a worldview that "identifies the present state of oppression as a cohesive human creation—Babylon system—but simultaneously acknowledges the potential power of working people to transform it."[28] Holy hip hoppers followed in this spiritual and musical diasporic tradition of transformation—of building Zyon in Babylon.

Getting beyond myopic mappings and instead "under the skin of the city," as Keith states, is in part a task of unmasking the "hidden racialized genealogies" that structure our ways of analyzing the city.[29] It also involves *tuning in* to spatial practices—how holy hip hoppers sonically produced and spatially enacted geographies of conversion.

SKID ROW AND THE "AIRBORNE CHURCH"

Many gospel hip hop artists preferred not to perform in churches, not only because of their evangelical impulse to preach to the "unsaved" but also because they felt artistically limited and monitored inside church walls. At times, the performance of gospel hip hop came across as a particular kind of indirect resistance to or critique of the traditional church and its "outdated" and exclusionary practices. Gospel rappers also felt performatively restrained, which was ironic considering the emotive, expressive, and physical intensity of most African American religious worship. B-Love, a female gospel hip hop artist with the Los Angeles collective

Hip Hopposite, felt that she always had to warn the congregation ahead of time, beseeching them to try to listen past their assumptions about hip hop to the spiritual message within her rhymes. She once rapped to me over the phone: "The four walls ain't the only way to reach a soul that's got outta the box. That's why I hip hop, and it don't stop, don't stop." She also grew weary of being the musical aberration of a given church service—the hip hop element that felt outside of, rather than welcome within, an overarching gospel aesthetic. Other artists spoke about the physical constraints and challenges of performing hip hop in churches, depending on the size of the pulpit area, where congregation members sit in relation to them, and the quality and capability of the church's sound system.

Those who have attempted to bring hip hop into the church have encountered other institutional and aesthetic challenges. As illustrated in the previous chapter on the Hip Hop Church L.A., the development of hip hop ministries housed within traditional churches engenders a complex web of power relations between proponents and critics of holy hip hop. In the song "Tambourine," Celah of Hip Hopposite states: "Every year, man, in L.A. holy hip hop and gospel MCs get so much opposition from the church." Further, numerous hip hop ministry leaders explained to me that they felt unwelcome, monitored, and surveyed as leaders of the "traditional" church would often "drop in," conspicuously and inconspicuously, during hip hop services to "check up" on their activities.[30] At hip hop services I attended, the leaders of the traditional church would sometimes walk in late, sit in the back pews, and often portray a stoicism and sternness at odds with the playful and lively nature of the hip hop service. But Celah also critiqued the growing trend of hip hop ministries and churches:

> I'm about to be very honest. Hip hop churches to me are very very corny. That's as corny as they get. I know they trying to reach people that need to be reached. I believe the Word reaches people. The Crossover Church in Florida in the one real hip hop church. There's Christian graffiti. The pulpit is a big spray paint can and they got turntables and all this stuff. They actually converted it and made it hip hop.[31]

In one of the harsher critiques of the Christian church, Cue, self-titled "Pastorfarian" and now a member of the Christian rap group Asylumz, stated,

> So the church has become more like a negative asylum and I wouldn't say all churches, but most of them, they've become like a prison. They're supposed to be like a place that you can go to get help and be rehabilitated. That's why we call our group Asylumz. So I don't feel like I'm going to church just because I went to the church building, I feel like I'm going to church when I sit down face to face with somebody in the context of where they are, wherever they are . . . So we still have to deal with the stigma, especially in the urban church, that goes with hip hop and gospel hip hop. You still have to go to bat with some heads—people preaching that it's the devil's music and all that. But I tell gospel hip hoppers, you know, why people haven't been

responding, because you're all so busy trying to get the church to accept you instead of . . . Hip hop is made for the streets. We should be out in the streets reaching people. The church will come because the church always follows the movement. So why should we sit there and get the church to accept us? We don't need the church to accept us.[32]

In the spirit of this assessment, Cue, along with members of the New Song church (of which he is also a member) and his gospel hip hop group, began holding an outdoor church service every Friday night on the streets of Skid Row in downtown Los Angeles where sidewalks are lined with cardboard boxes, shopping cars, and makeshift tents. The blocks that comprise Skid Row, formerly agricultural lands until the 1870s with the advent of railroad lines in Los Angeles, have been home to a diverse and ever-changing assemblage of low-level offenders, alcoholics and drug addicts, migrants, veterans, mentally ill and handicapped patients who have been "dumped" there by local hospitals, and folks just down on their luck.[33] Cue has been committed to working with these urban communities as "evangelicals miss what's going on in the streets."[34]

While dangers and temptations pervade Skid Row, it is a place that also offers help and services in the form of food, counseling, and spiritual support. Cue's open-air church meets at the corner of Wall and Winston Streets—an intersection in the heart of Skid Row and rife with various forms of hustling due to the curved nature of the streets, preventing one from being able to see down to the other end of the block. Rain or shine, Cue often preaches from a black music stand under a street lamp surrounded by barricaded storefronts. Some people stand. Others sit in fold-up chairs that have been brought by volunteers.

With a population of almost twenty thousand—one of the largest stable populations of homeless in the United States—it is difficult to predict who might show up or what might occur during Friday night services. Recently, a homeless man burst into spontaneous song. Another woman gave her life to Christ from the balcony of a nearby building. "The gospel is airborne," as Cue once remarked. "You never know where it's going to land."[35] For certain hip hop–loving Skid Row residents, the gospel landed in 2012 when renowned rap group Public Enemy visited Skid Row on the weekend of Martin Luther King Jr.'s birthday and just twenty years after the riots, performing their Nation of Islam–inspired hip hop for local residents in an effort to spotlight the political and economic plight of Los Angeles's homeless. Cue continues to advocate on behalf of homeless populations and was an invited speaker at the 2016 homeless awareness rally at the University of Southern California.

The concept of an "airborne church" is really nothing new. The early religious gatherings of enslaved Africans in brush harbors—often referred to as the "invisible church"—provide an early example of creating church in the open air.[36] Cue elaborated:

FIGURE 8. Cue Jn-Marie preaching at The Row ("The Church Without Walls") on Los Angeles's Skid Row, c. 2016. Photo courtesy of Ariel Blandford for the Center for Religion and Civic Culture at the University of Southern California.

We call it The Row. It's not a building but we call it the church without walls—the church moving. The street that we preach at on Skid Row is a major crack vein—drug vein. There's no real format to it. We preach the word and sometimes we'll do a song or someone from the street will just sing a gospel song. It's crazy the way it happens. After the Word we feed the people and eat with them because we want to be a part of their community as well. We don't just want to make them our project. People are not projects. We have a community of people now. If we would love people, then the church would go airborne, no matter where you are, there would be church. So that's what Asylumz is; it's a place of refuge. So even the name is deep in meaning.[37]

The Row illustrates the way that certain gospel rappers collapse *people* and *place*. Cue's statement asserts that it is *people* who are an embodiment of the church and that Asylumz—a group of people—is actually a *place* of refuge. Gospel hip hop artists perform a conscious expansion of the sacred beyond the church walls to other social arenas in both their discourses and practices; they spatialize holy hip hop in clubs, schoolyards, living rooms, street corners, cyberspace, radio airwaves, and public access TV shows. The Row, as a church without walls, holds certain implications for experiencing the city as a constantly converting body and the manner in which gospel hip hop artists hold out the same potential for the conversion of space as they do for the conversion of souls.

FIGURE 9. The view down Winston Street from the corner where The Row takes place every Friday night on Skid Row. Photo courtesy of Ariel Blandford for the Center for Religion and Civic Culture at the University of Southern California.

During the several years that I attended holy hip hop events, gospel rap artists generally preferred "mixed" events that embodied heterogeneity and promoted an individual's process of *becoming* in both a musical and religious sense.[38] Although, this was not always what was actualized at these events, and the outcomes of such gatherings sometimes served to strengthen the very discursive, musical, spatial, and imagined borders they were trying to dismantle. I now turn to two ongoing events or provisional sites of holy hip hop music: Klub Zyon and Club Judah. They both exist at the intersections of multiple fields of power, juxtaposing and integrating hip hop space, church space, and city space in experimental and ever-changing ways.

KLUB ZYON CROSSROADS

Klub Zyon, as previously mentioned, was a monthly open mic that took place on every third Friday at KAOS Network—a cultural center established in 1984 in Leimert Park by filmmaker and activist Ben Caldwell. Cue founded the event in 2006 through his nonprofit organization the S.H.A.W. (sports, health, arts, and well-being) Community Transformation Corporation in the Crenshaw community of Los Angeles with the mission to provide an artistic meeting ground for different bodies and beliefs in the city. This vision of encounter and integration was realized and experienced in certain moments, however brief; other times, it stood as a spatial and social metaphor of holy hip hop politics. Online promotional materials for the event read: "Zyon is more than just an open mic. It is a place that offers a safe place for expression to artists, to the community, to activists, to those who are ready to see things change and are ready to make that happen." Avoiding any explicit links to Christianity in marketing and promotion, Cue's primary hope was to attract a range of diverse participants. Occasionally, some very unlikely artists took the mic. John Serrins (a.k.a. Johnny Cash), a white man in his twenties and member of Asylumz, wrote the following on a homemade flyer for the event: "Zyon is an open space for free expression, all who grab the mic are entitled to spit whatever they would like. All who grab the mic can speak their mind freely. No censorship. Klub Zyon does not share or promote ideas expressed by those who grab the mic. Klub Zyon is an event that is open to all, regardless of race, religion, gender, sexual orientation, socio-economical standing, style of clothing, and/or eye color."

Biblically speaking, Zion is known as the historic land of Israel symbolizing the Jewish people. More specifically, it is the Canaanite hill fortress in Jerusalem referred to in the Bible as the "City of David" and used to symbolize the city as a religious center. In a metaphoric light, it represents heaven as the final gathering place of true believers or any idealized, harmonious community—a utopia. Klub Zyon's name, therefore, acts as a symbol and promise of this biblical geography of spiritual home. Here, Zion is not the Garveyite's Africa or even the Rasta's Ethiopia; it is a feeling of oneness and homecoming that was created in a cultural center in one of L.A.'s most iconic black neighborhoods—a neighborhood that has attracted such residents as Ray Charles and Ella Fitzgerald.

Leimert Park was not always a black Mecca. The area bound by Rodeo Road on the north, 4th Avenue and Roxton Avenue on the east, Vernon Avenue on the south, and Crenshaw Boulevard on the west, was once home to soybean fields known as Rancho Ciénega o Paso de la Tijera[39] until it was developed by Walter H. Leimert in the late 1920s. Considered a model of urban planning with Spanish Colonial Revival homes and tree-lined streets, the village was originally inhabited by white families. After the Supreme Court officially ended racially restricting housing covenants in Los Angeles in the early 1950s, the effects of white flight—the loss of jobs, capital, and local businesses—afflicted many burgeoning black communities. Leimert Park suffered less than Watts, Willowbrook, and other South L.A. communities as a stronghold of successful African American professionals organized under the banner of Crenshaw Neighbors to help slow the inevitable process of white flight. Despite its image of black success, Josh Sides argues:

> Leimert Park was not immune to the roiling changes of the 1970s and 1980s, decades in which African American poverty skyrocketed nationwide because of the disappearance of industrial work; in which gangs exploited idled young men; and in which highly-addictive and dangerous drugs hit the streets. And Leimert Park residents also faced the challenge of maintaining community cohesion, as the most prosperous residents moved up into Baldwin Hills. But the commitment of remaining residents to keep Leimert Park special never died. In 1967, brothers Alonzo and Dale Davis opened the Brockman Gallery, "the premier venue for exhibiting black art in the city," according to historian Daniel Widener, and the hub of a citywide black arts movement. Residents led clean-up committees to erase graffiti, blocked efforts to add liquor stores to the area, and organized political action committees.[40]

Black arts continued to thrive in Leimert Park with the addition of the World Stage performance center in 1989, a joint effort between jazz drummer Billy Higgins and activist Kamau Daáood. The Zambezi Bazaar, an African-themed arts and crafts store, opened in 1992 and in the same year, former Skid Row resident and African American veteran Richard Fulton opened Fifth Street Dick's Coffee House—a haven for music, chess, poetry, and comedy alike and where I conducted several interviews with gospel rappers. Caldwell's KAOS Network was among several burgeoning arts spaces in the area, and in 1997, Babe's and Ricky's Inn—a blues club originally housed on Central Avenue—moved in next door. Across the road, Leimert Park Plaza has housed an array of black-themed celebrations from Kwaanza to Malcolm X and Martin Luther King Day festivals.

The iconography adorning KAOS Network reflects Leimert Park's diasporic cosmos of art, community, and racial struggle. A large black and white photograph of Malcolm X and Muhammad Ali hangs in the storefront, consecrating the space as a cultural Mecca. Upon entering the small, intimate venue, three regal figures hold court: a painting of Nigerian musical and political legend Fela Kuti, a poster of bebop master Charlie Parker, and the image of a sphinx-like head bordered by

FIGURE 10. KAOS Network storefront in Leimert Park featuring a photograph of Malcolm X and Muhammad Ali. KAOS Network was home to both the underground hip hop freestyle event, Project Blowed, and the gospel hip hop open mic, Klub Zyon.

different hieroglyphs and figurines rendered in an Egyptian aesthetic. The interior décor paints a black Atlantic scene that links specific places and genres—Los Angeles, hip hop, Nigeria, afrobeat, Egypt, and bebop—across both real and imagined terrains of local and transnational crossing. During nights that I attended Klub Zyon, nothing was physically altered in the space except the sounds and bodies inhabiting it; the social, musical, and religious dimensions of Klub Zyon were what defined the event as distinct from its secular counterpart, Project Blowed. Although the majority of the performers were young African American males, I was always struck by the consistent diversity of the crowd, which included people of various socioeconomic classes, ages, sexual orientations, and religious, racial, and ethnic backgrounds, hailing from various Southland neighborhoods, and exhibiting a wide array of urban apparel and fashion—from understated in a T-shirt and jeans to what some may consider a Christian "ghetto fabulous" style.

Sonically, gospel hip hop artists subjected KAOS Network to the rhythms and sensibilities of hip hop music, rapping, freestyle, testimony, and prayer. DJ Heat, another member of Hip Hopposite and Christian rap radio DJ on Headz Up FM, would spin both secular hip hop beats and gospel rap songs throughout the evening—a curious choice given that many gospel rap artists avoid secular hip hop altogether. When playing secular hip hop tracks, he would only play the instrumental versions. But most crowd members were familiar with the lyrics of these well-known hits (e.g., Nas's "Whose World Is This?" or Outkast's "Player's Ball") and traces of their somewhat unsavory associations sometimes seemed to linger in the room. DJ Heat never showed much emotion or energy while spinning records, projecting a stoicism often seen in church musicians who steadily and dutifully provide music to encourage congregants to catch the spirit.

An evening at Klub Zyon was divided into three distinct sections. Initially, after the host MC welcomed everybody with a short prayer, rappers took to the stage to freestyle (improvise rhymes) over hip hop beats of DJ Heat's choosing. Those who signed up early for the open mic were allowed to perform one or two "writtens" (precomposed rhymes or songs) either a cappella or over pre-recorded tracks that they generally brought in on CDs or iPods. The night concluded with a featured performance set by a local gospel hip hop artist or group. This format mimicked a typical church service found in many mainline denominations: a lively and participatory "Praise and Worship" section, followed by gospel music performances or praise dance, and ending with the main event of the sermon. The host closed the night with another short prayer before participants poured out onto the street corner for more fellowship and freestyling.

"THIS AIN'T YOUR DADDY'S MUSIC"

On a cool and clear November night in 2007 at Klub Zyon, Johnny Cash introduced TripLL-H (a member of the holy hip hop crew G-Boy Union) as the host MC for the night. Khanchuz quickly reminded me that, in holy hip hop, MC stands for "Minister of Christ," not "Master of Ceremonies" or "Microphone Controller," before he and Gandhi—an MC of small stature and South Asian descent—were summoned to the stage. Over a mix of hip hop beats curated by DJ Heat, Khanchuz delivered his rhymes with ferocity, kicking his leg up in the air and wearing a righteous scowl. His whole body compressed with conviction, his stomach becoming the fulcrum from which his chest and legs contracted. His flow was clear and well annunciated over a quintessential L.A. gangsta rap beat as he rapped, "Preaching heat in the streets like a ghetto apostle." Gandhi, surprisingly for his size, commanded a huge presence. His flow was sporadic, sometimes landing words right on the beat, other times falling just off it. Eventually, he lost his voice while rapping over his own prerecorded track. With a definitive head nod, TripLL-H confirmed: "This is how we do it for Jesus. We lose our voices for Jesus."

Statements like this were part of a larger effort to sacralize the space and inscribe a sacred meaning on the activities that shaped Klub Zyon, however secular they appeared. They also undergirded the desire and willingness to offer up one's body for the glorification of Jesus and the edification of the Body of Christ, even if one was ultimately rendered voiceless. In a similar manner, Young Chozen, a young black MC in his late teens, later shouted into the mic, "How many of you glad you got butts to shake? God is good." In one verbal move he celebrated both body and spirit, calling for butt-shaking as praise as he praised God for butts that shake. These were the unique body politics of Klub Zyon. Young Chozen, in particular, demonstrated an ability to intertwine religious and secular themes, thus appealing to both religious and secular audiences. His friendship with Wes Nile, another young male MC who frequented Klub Zyon, resulted in Wes Nile's eventual conversion to Christianity.

Many young folks of all backgrounds were "touched" by the music that took place at Klub Zyon. They felt blessed and inspired by the testimonies that gospel MCs delivered through their music. It gave them a new way to understand themselves as believers who could also participate in the cultural movement and musical language they knew so well: hip hop. This music gave young hip hop heads seeking God a way to belong as well as a way to become themselves amidst the radical upheavals and instability that permeated their everyday lives in Los Angeles.

Later in the evening, as it approached the midnight hour, Asylumz—the featured group consisting of six men in their twenties and thirties, hailing from Nigeria, Barbados, and the United States—brought house-wrecking contagion to KAOS Network with their original brand of "Worsh-Hop."[41] A term used to represent Asylumz's unique sound, "worsh-hop" was a raw and embodied mixture of "praise and worship" music *and* hip hop.[42] It was hip hop that intentionally glorified God, releasing transformative and ecstatic energies through the friction of the sacred and the profane. Following King David's triumphant assertion of his willingness to humiliate himself for the sake of his God, Asylumz claims they are willing to become "even more undignified" in their worshipping.

Raucously dancing across the stage, the members of Asylumz slammed into each other's bodies in praise. Their joyful, hyperkinetic energy was accompanied by a hard, masculine edge that matched the ear-splitting volume of the music. The instrumentals featured heavy-handed snare hits and pulsing high-pitched electronic notes over a dark synthesized bass drone. A chorus of men chanted militantly on the track, "Ay! Ay! Ay! Aaaaaaaay!" As the performance reached a crescendo, they jumped from the stage to the dance floor, colliding into audience members who also began chanting the song's hook: "This ain't your daddy's music! This ain't your mama's music! This is how I praise! This is how we praise! I'm a stomp and snap then whip that Cadillac. I know the Lord felt it cuz he didn't send it back."

Audience members—especially those who had been in the holy hip hop scene for a while—bobbed their heads and threw their hands in the air, clearly reveling in the opportunity to praise Jesus through hip hop beats, lyrics, and movements. This "Worsh-Hop" felt natural to them—a dynamic merging of their musical and religious sensibilities—and lifted them up not just in belief, but in community. But after the performance, Khanchuz explained to me: "I wasn't really feeling them tonight. I'm not gonna lie, it was entertaining, but I couldn't hear a word they were saying. For all I know, it could have been secular rap." For many gospel rappers, the message is the main factor that distinguishes holy hip hop from secular hip hop. Thus, sound levels, as they relate to the relative volumes of lyrics and beats, are a contested terrain in gospel hip hop. PK 1000's, a twenty-two-year-old African American male who frequents Klub Zyon, would often tell DJ Heat to turn his track down so that the audience could hear his lyrics. Once, I heard the sound engineer tell DJ Heat to drop the track out intermittently to highlight what the MCs were saying. Given these negotiations of musical dynamics, it is not surprising that interested passersby not familiar with the mission of Klub Zyon or the Christian orientation of its founders often mistook the sounds emanating from KAOS Network as secular, commercial, or even gangsta rap as opposed to holy hip hop. Such aural assumptions and misrecognitions were often what produced spontaneous, unexpected, and experimental moments of encounter—between gangsta rappers and gospel rappers, Muslims and Christians, prostitutes and pastors.

One such instance took place when an Asian American woman, Magita Passion, decided to take the stage at Klub Zyon. Her long, straight, and striking black hair was streaked with bleached blond and hot pink highlights. A short tattered pink shirt revealed her slightly bulbous belly—smooth and unashamed—as well as a large Chinese character tattoo that hovered just above black and white pinstriped pants belted by a red dragon-print satin ribbon. Her eyelids sparkled with burnt orange shadow while the stage lights reflected off her fuchsia patent-leather platforms. The crowd was unsure of what to expect from her. Magita, familiar with the location as the home of Project Blowed but unaware of Klub Zyon's Christian underpinnings, began a spoken word piece that revealed herself as a sex worker and advocate of sex worker rights (including the decriminalization of sex workers and the legalization of prostitution) to an audience comprised mainly of Christian hip hoppers. She further explained that, historically, people have been supporting themselves with the money they earn from sex work—in her words, "getting paid for making love"—but they have been marginalized and stigmatized by a society with double standards.

As Magita uttered the final words of her performance, a deafening silence swallowed the room. TripLL-H walked over and put his arm around her, then said ruefully, "We're going to pray for you." A Christian woman from the audience approached the stage, attempting to befriend her as members of the crowd shouted, "Plant that seed!" As Magita began to realize the spiritual nature of the event, she rolled her eyes in annoyance, retorting, "I don't need your prayers." Sensing that

TripLL-H's "call to prayer" may not have been the most sensitive or affective response to her poem, the crowd began to encourage Magita to perform another song, hoping to restore Klub Zyon's environment of openness and tolerance. Deciding that she wasn't in the mood anymore, she left with the apology: "Sorry for crashing your *church*." Magita didn't want pity or prayers; she had just wanted to share her story through rhyme.

Despite the appearance of failure in terms of achieving Klub Zyon's vision for an all-inclusive space, this was just the kind of interaction that Cue was attempting to facilitate—for a non-Christian to walk into the mix, stir things up, and trouble the waters. This was the kind of productive *trouble* Cue was trying to get into during nights at Zyon. After Magita Passion left, Cue asked Mercy, another MC from Asylumz, to lead everyone in a prayer for her. He spoke of many things, but most strikingly, he prayed, "We ask for forgiveness, Lord, yours and hers, if we've offended her in any way. She is one of us. We are all the same. What I like about her, Lord, is that she is bold. Jesus needs bold people in the kingdom." Through this humble self-reflection, something was restored. Although TripLL-H and others' methods for bridging a religious divide did not prove to be successful in that moment, both the real and imagined geographies of Klub Zyon were remembered and re-visioned through this collective prayer and apology. The gospel rap that followed was less worshipful than it was healing. Again, holy hip hop became *earthquake music*. The rhythmic prayers and performances helped to navigate the shifting grounds of Klub Zyon—grounds wrought with moral and musical tensions as well as racial and religious fissures, grounds that many have struggled to transform into Meccas and Zions.

The stories relayed here highlight moments of interaction and transformation between diverse hip hop subjects and expose crosscutting interests and investments (e.g., artistic, political, religious, etc.) enacted in sites of holy hip hop. The walls of the building had less to do with the lived geography of Klub Zyon than the dynamic of musical interrelations that the event produced between diverse spatial bodies, human bodies, and anatomies of belief. That said, the fact that Klub Zyon took place in a well-respected location for "underground" hip hop battles gave credibility and accessibility to the event.

At Klub Zyon, unexpected brushes with the profane and brushes with the sacred suggested a contested yet ecological relationship between church bodies, club bodies, and the arteries of the streets.[43] What *happened* in this time and place was less defined by the event producers than it was by the participants, audience, and passersby, thus broadening our conceptions of what we consider to be gospel rap and who we consider to be participants and cultural shapers of the scene. What can we draw from the relationship between the biographies and geographies of holy hip hoppers is that the very actualization of these sites was capable of diverting temporal itineraries and life courses, thus illustrating how for holy hip hoppers in Los Angeles a walk *with* God was in many senses a walk *through* the city. And along that walk, the *seismic soundings* of gospel rap moved the ground they walked on.

CLUB JUDAH ALCHEMIES

Club Judah was a weekly holy hip hop night housed at the Love and Faith Christian Center near Western and Manchester Avenues on the outskirts of Inglewood—the area where Mayor Bradley declared the first sunset-to-sunrise curfew on the second day of the 1992 riots. On Saturday nights, Pastor Colette Cruz and other Club Judah leaders rolled the pews to the outer edges of the room, set up large circular tables with black tablecloths, and dimmed the lights to create a clublike atmosphere for young people to experience God in a more hip, relaxed environment. Historically, black churches have been used for a number of sacred and secular activities. Historian Evelyn Brooks Higginbotham notes:

> By law, blacks were denied access to public space such as parks, libraries, restaurants, meeting halls, and other public accommodations. In time the Black church—open to both secular and religious groups in the community—came to signify public space. It housed a diversity of programs including schools, circulating libraries, concerts, restaurants, insurance companies, vocational training, [and] athletic clubs—all catering to a population much broader than the membership of individual churches. The church served as meeting hall for virtually every large gathering. It held political rallies, clubwomen's conferences, and school graduations.[44]

Similarly, Pastor Colette Cruz made the Love and Faith Christian Center a gathering place for a wide range of activities. She initially created Club Judah for her adolescent daughter, who is a fan of hip hop music. The church's website reads:

> "We're Spittin' Holy Fire! Club Judah began as a club for teens, a Christian alternative to what the world offers them on the weekends. Though teens are still the focus of Club Judah, it has expanded into much more. Each week now, Gospel Hip Hop artists from all over Southern California, and even some from out of state, come in to minister through heavy beats and even heavier Word based lyrics. The audience is not only entertained but also, and more importantly, edified by the Word of God."[45] The event was free, because as Pastor Colette always said, "Jesus has already paid the cost."

Club Judah represented and enacted both historical and ongoing geographies of conversion. The spatial transformations that took place every Saturday night entailed a physical *conversion* of the church sanctuary into a club. While Club Judah was in session, the room remained very dark. The stage, which served as the pulpit area during regular church services, featured colored lights against a maroon curtain. The interior space, like the exterior of the building, was stark, unadorned, and boxy. At the end of the night, everyone present helped to dismantle and convert

FIGURE 11. Love and Faith Christian Center at the corner of Manchester and Western Avenues. The church was home to the weekly hip hop praise night, Club Judah.

the club back into a church space for Sunday morning service. The fluorescent lights flickered on; those present folded up the tables and chairs and stacked them neatly in rows against the walls. Witnessing and partaking in the temporary, fleeting nature of the "club" space was surreal at times. The youth who were invited there in the hopes of religious conversion were also a part of the spatial conversion of the evening.

The Love and Faith Christian Center was formerly the site of a Western Surplus (gun store) before the building was looted and burned during the 1992 riots, the carcass then renovated into a place of worship. Undergoing a kind of urban alchemy, the plain, unassuming white façade of the building now reads "House of Judah." In the Bible, "Judah" is known as the fourth son of Jacob and Leah and the forebear of one of the tribes of Israel. The name originated in Leah's words of praise to the Lord on account of Judah's birth: "Now will I praise Jehovah, and she called his name Yehudah"[46] and is now known to mean "praised" or "praise."[47] Therefore, Club Judah quite literally means Club Praise—a club where one praises instead of parties and gets high on Christ instead of drugs or alcohol. In another diasporic twist, the building's backside features a mosaic-tiled mural featuring a lion. Multicolored bodies hold hands on either side of it. The Lion of Judah, while

FIGURE 12. The Lion of Judah at the center of a mosaic-tiled mural on the side of the Love and Faith Christian Center.

sometimes a symbol of Jesus in the Christian tradition, is also a potent image for the Rastafarian movement and often depicted as golden and crowned. Dancehall reggae-inspired hip hop grooves, over which gospel rappers were "Spittin' Holy Fire," often graced the stage of Club Judah, further forging sonic and spiritual connections between black Atlantic religious cultures. Some of the holy hip hoppers in attendance participated in the rioting on those very same grounds fifteen years earlier before they were "saved." These were the everyday gospel rap alchemies that transformed gun metal into lion's gold. This was *earthquake music* in action, wherein within destruction also lies the possibility for creation.

Club Judah served as the location for many holy hip hop record release parties and anniversary events, as well as the destination for gospel hip hop artists visiting from outside the Los Angeles area. Attendees, mainly composed of African American families with children ranging from two to eighteen years old, often arrived early to hang out, play monopoly, basketball, or video games, shoot pool, and fellowship. Moving through these various stages and spaces of the evening was integral to the family-friendly experience of Club Judah—a space which at times functioned like a Boys and Girls Club.

For the year and a half that I frequented the event, Pastor Graham of Hood Ministries and Khanchuz hosted the evening program and often performed alongside other invited gospel hip hop artists. With tattoos and silver chains, both of these men embodied an aesthetic and an intimate knowledge of the streets. They often donned baggy camouflage pants, bandannas, and oversized hoodies.

At first glance, they appeared more "gangsta" than "gospel," adding to their credibility among the youth. Khanchuz and Pastor Graham led attendees in a church/concert hybrid, interspersed with prayer, musical performance, a short sermon, announcements, collective dance, and a final altar call. While they spit rhymes over their gospel rap tracks, little kids wandered onto the stage, danced freely, and bounced around waving church fans. The hard-edged, heavily synthesized beats brought in the unforgiving nature of the streets while the rhythmically rapped lyrics spoke of the Lord's grace in the midst of urban instability. That a church sanctuary could bring together and integrate these seemingly incongruous experiences for young people was powerful. The music seemed to both bring them into their pain and provide the cure for it.

I witnessed several youth give their life to Christ at Love and Faith Christian Center, undergoing a religious conversion in the nightclub-like space of Club Judah. In many ways, this was the penultimate expression of Pastor Graham's *earthquake music*—young folks so shaken and moved by the lyrics, beats, and righteous delivery of gospel rap that they would give their lives over to Jesus. But in the spring of 2008, for undisclosed reasons, Pastor Graham decided he could no longer remain the host of Club Judah. Khanchuz stayed on for a while longer as a promise to the youth to maintain a consistent weekly space for them to congregate.

In 2008, on a sweltering summer night in Los Angeles, I strolled up to the blacktop parking lot in the back of the church. Young guys were playing basketball at the far end under the fluorescent street lamps. A group of young girls, Khanchuz's daughter Jaysha among them, locked my arms with theirs, forming a line of about five or six of us. They buzzed across the pavement like a swarm of bees, talking over each other and erupting with laughter. "Hey cousin, come on, follow us. We'll take you in," Jaysha reassured me, before yelling at the boys playing basketball to stop their dribbling and shooting so that we could pass in peace. Balls whizzed around us but my young escorts guided us through the cool light of the parking lot, parting the band of boys like the Red Sea. Once I was situated in the green room with Khanchuz, they made a quick dash back outside to continue their blacktop revelry. Having just woken from a nap, Khanchuz slowly dished up some fruit salad and water. I could tell that a long week of working two jobs had taken its toll on him. Like his name's transformation suggests—from Sleep to Khanchuz—he did not get much rest anymore. There was something a little gloomy about his energy and the building that night. It was the first time I had been to Club Judah since Pastor Graham had stepped down from his co-hosting duties.

Khanchuz confirmed that the space felt a bit depressing and heavy, partly because of Pastor Graham's absence and partly because of the weight that he feels the building carries. Quite literally, this site used to "pack a lot of weight" as it is weighted by sedimentations of racial discrimination and physical violence. Hindrances to the conversion of space, and perhaps souls, were attributed to unseen spiritual forces (e.g., the felt presence of the Devil), but also shaped by matrices of history, memory, and power. When holy hip hoppers created places of activity, those activities changed buildings just as the buildings carried meanings that molded the subjects within them.

"BORN AGAIN" BODIES OF THE CITY

Holy hip hop's geographies of conversion made visible certain "off the map" or "below the radar" activities and life stories of people living in predominantly black communities in Los Angeles as they sounded subterranean levels of urban existence and history that were concealed by the current topography of "church, motel, liquor store." The spatial practices of holy hip hoppers were not accounted for in conventional mappings of black L.A. Instead, they revealed the existence of multiple black L.A.'s that were much more complex and diverse than certain popular urban vocabularies articulated. This was the often invisible but audible city that holy hip hop sounded out.

Klub Zyon and Club Judah were not always clearly defined or physically permanent locations, but instead temporary, provisional, and overlapping social embodiments produced through a confluence of musical practices, evangelical methods, and spatial tactics. These events gave holy hip hoppers a way to belong, demonstrating that the power of gospel rap was oftentimes more about providing a sense of cultural and spiritual belonging than it was about reaffirming belief. But they also gave rap evangelists a way to interact with a wide range of city inhabitants at the crossroads of sacred and profane urban spaces.

During these nights of hip hop rapture, both the city and human soul were understood as "living architectures" capable of being rebuilt and reformed. Conversion was both undergone and enacted spiritually *and* spatially as holy hip hoppers converted street corners into airborne churches, houses of worship into hip hop clubs, and Babylons into Zyons. The forming of these rare urban configurations exposed the unfinished business of spiritual maturation as well as the unfinished geographies of Los Angeles—the bodies of the city "born again"—that at specific moments allowed for the creation of new kinds of social arrangements, subjects, and spaces. These sites were fleeting and, at times, blighted by their indefinite nature, but also provided the grounds for envisioning and embodying potential futures of racially, religiously, and intergenerationally integrated space.

Once again, conversion emerged as both a spiritual transformation and a multimodal practice of possibility within limitations. These holy hip hoppers realized it was possible to do something different on and with the bodies of the city than was specified by certain structures of power.[48] At the same time, the territorial uncertainty of the Southland was also capitalized on by the state to enact and obfuscate the systematic displacement of certain city inhabitants, practices, and enterprises.

The Zambezi Bazaar, often deemed the soul of the Leimert village, was purchased and closed in 2014 after the MTA (Metropolitan Transportation Authority) voted to put a rail stop in the village along its Crenshaw-LAX line. The Vision Theater is undergoing a multimillion-dollar renovation and fundraising campaign. While The Row—"The Church Without Walls"—still takes place every Friday night on a corner in Skid Row, Club Judah hosts events on a less regular basis.[49] In 2016, Club Judah's church home—the Love and Faith Christian Center—relocated to a storefront on 54th Street near Crenshaw Boulevard, where the gospel hip hop event will hopefully re-emerge on new grounds. Klub Zyon, however, ceased holding open mics in 2009 due to lack of funds and communal support. These are the paradoxes of possibility and foreclosure that continue to permeate black L.A.

4

The Evangelical Hustle

Selling Music, Saving Souls

"I must be about my Father's business."
—PASTOR OF REDEMPTION (HIP HOP PASTOR)

As gospel rappers crisscrossed the varied landscapes of the Southland, converting urban spaces into airborne churches, they endeavored to spread the Gospel to the far reaches of the city. They ran their evangelical game in devout street teams—the G-Boy Union, Hip Hopposite, Hood Ministries, ADK (Any Demon Killa), The Nameless Fellowship, Freedom of Soul, Tunnel Rats, Preachers in Disguise, Gospel Gangstaz, and the list goes on. Wielding both hip hop technologies and biblical mythologies, they enacted their business mission of simultaneously *selling* music and *saving* souls—a mission that took into account their immediate spiritual and economic needs as well as the temporal horizon of the Promised Land.

In this chapter, I examine how gospel rappers' religious beliefs interacted with their everyday struggles to balance the need for a paycheck with winning the big payback of life everlasting. Drawing from the title of Canton Jones's well-known Christian rap trilogy, I argue that holy hip hoppers engaged in a kind of *Kingdom Business*—ultimately working for the glorification of God.[1] Following the three releases of *Kingdom Business*, Canton Jones then released *Dominionaire*, which also played on themes of money, power, and authority. Writer Kellus Hill comments, "just as a millionaire or billionaire is rich due to their money, a Dominionaire is rich due to the Lord's position of authority that will never run dry or lose value."[2] In holy hip hop's spiritual economy, Jesus functioned as the kingpin, CEO, or "Lord of the Underground." Gospel rappers referred to themselves as His foot soldiers, street disciples, and indigenous missionaries. They pushed holy hip hop CDs in His name and hustled to get the Word out, all the while steadily "bangin' for Christ."

Automatically dismissed by mainstream rap labels or relegated to a niche category within a major gospel division, gospel hip hop has never been considered big business. Prominent holy hip hop artists struggled to find performance venues both in and out of the church. Christian music labels were often hesitant to sign gospel rap acts due to the profane associations of hip hop. In the absence of mainstream distribution and marketing, L.A. gospel rappers often produced and promoted their albums independently and locally.[3] While many of these MCs would have welcomed economic success (especially if it meant exposure for the glory of God), monetary gain was certainly not the primary focus. Gospel rappers engaged in the twin projects of musical missionizing and marketing often negotiated an embattled nexus of religious morals, sentiments, and affiliations that complicated purely economic notions of success and visibility. How did holy hip hop function as a spiritual, social, and economic resource in the lives of gospel rap artists?[4] How did gospel MCs earn authenticity and credibility as they managed the seemingly incommensurable logics of capitalism, Christianity, and hip hop?[5] Gospel rap presented new challenges, complexities, and confines in hip hop's ongoing call to "realness." Competing cults of authenticity (i.e., race, class, gender, and now religion) shaped how holy hip hoppers walked, talked, and made music, but also how they evangelized, sold, and consumed cultural practices.[6]

The larger economic cosmos of holy hip hop can be conceived of as a relational dynamic between overlapping spheres of activity on different scales: the national networks of the gospel music industry, independent labels, the institutional level of Christian churches and organizations, and the street-level interactions of gospel hip hoppers. This chapter focuses mainly on the everyday, small-scale, street-level business practices involved in the cultural production of gospel rap across the fractured, postindustrial cityscape of Los Angeles—a constantly shifting terrain of encounter marked not only by the circulation of money but also by networks of social exchange. Taking into account the political economies inherently embedded within their daily practices as a point of entry, I analyze the ways in which gospel rappers assembled relations of reciprocity and set their financial exchanges to a sacred pitch through strategic performance, musical and linguistic play, differential pricing, biblical metaphor, and audacious acts of faith.

The indeterminate and intertextual practices of gospel rappers—both visionary and pragmatic—enabled the performative transposition between the realms of hip hop, evangelism, and the economic market, which these MCs experienced as deeply enmeshed in their daily lives. Ultimately what emerged was an unforeseen transposability of techniques, ethics, and modes of capital between overlapping social terrains, as well as the unlikely uses and outcomes of turning expressive culture into things it may not have been initially intended for. Managing these fields amid continued economic restructuring, massive unemployment, and draconian policing tactics, Los Angeles–based holy hip hoppers provided an example of what people do when neither secure wage labor nor the illicit economy is readily available or acceptable.

Gospel hip hop in L.A. existed in a multidimensional configuration of social space, where the everyday activities of art, commerce, and spirituality often overlapped, opening up possibilities for the *creation* and *conversion* of new kinds of subjects.[7] Here, the hegemony and pervasiveness of the commodity form in late capitalism did not necessarily produce sameness or absolute social reproduction; instead, it allowed for a heterogeneity of outcomes and contradictions, and perhaps, a more realistic understanding of the global economy on the ground—the ways it moved (and was moved by) people in particular places at specific times. Gospel rappers' everyday practices demonstrated the costs and benefits of bringing religious expressions into certain cultural markets and, at the same time, unveiled the ways the market has always already been a part of Christianity.

A significant portion of the literature that addresses the relationship between religion, media, and the marketplace examines how Christian booksellers juggle the institutional logics of religion and the capitalist market through three main strategies: (1) "resistance" to the modern secular world; (2) "accommodation" to the modern secular world; and (3) "sacralization," a fusion between Christianity and capitalism.[8] Holy hip hop presented a significant variation from these booksellers in that these artist-missionaries were not just selling the Word, they were also selling their artistic and musical gifts. Gospel hip hop artists battled the dichotomy of selling something that is supposedly free—salvation, where the grace of God has no cost—and selling something that we generally expect to pay for—skilled artistic expression. As creative agents, gospel MCs were not only reconciling money and faith, but were also juggling the added layers of artistic creativity and critiques of racial and spiritual authenticity in relation to their marketing and missionizing methods. Therefore, sacralization is not an adequate concept to encapsulate the multiple, performative, and flexible negotiations of gospel hip hop artists. Gospel hip hop artists were instead involved in an *evangelical hustle*—a practice that accounted for the creativity of artists as well as other nonfinancial and nonspiritual rewards and resources that gospel hip hop practice yielded and generated. It was this dance between various fields that allowed artists to manage the polyvalent power relations, moral codes, and structures of legitimacy with which they were faced.

HOLY HUSTLING

Former secular rappers turned born-again Christians, many (but not all) of whom were previously employed in illicit economies, occupied a particular "guru position" in holy hip hop circles because they were seen as authentic street soldiers who had paid their dues in the secular world—a rite of passage—before (re)turning to Christ. These streetwise Christian gurus commanded the respect and attention of their younger street disciples, owing to their intimate knowledge and lived experiences in the 'hood, and, more importantly, their hands-on experience with hip hop music.[9] For instance, Kurtis Blow, old school hip hop's King of Rap *gone gospel,* exercised a certain spiritual authority by virtue of both the material and symbolic capital he accumulated in mainstream hip hop, as well as on "the street."

For many gangsta rappers turned gospel rappers, their previous lines of work included pushing various forms of "product"—that is, gangbanging, pimping, prostitution, and, more generally, *hustling* to make ends meet. After dedicating their lives to Christ, many of them described the challenges of shifting into more formalized work that did not compromise their religious beliefs. And, most took pay cuts at the expense of worshipping at the altar of Jesus instead of the almighty dollar.[10] Christian hip hop leaders, while streetwise, were also well versed in biblical scripture and the ritual prescriptions of black Christianity, modeling ways to behave appropriately with youth and "old heads" alike, while skillfully navigating multiple community and corporate spaces. In the masculinized world of gospel rap, holy hip hoppers walked tightly scripted, heavily policed lines between expectations of hardness, realness, and righteousness among hip hop music markets, audiences, and congregations. As Richard A. Peterson states, "authenticity is a claim that is made by or for someone, thing, or performance and either accepted or rejected by relevant others."[11] Indeed, holy hip hoppers carefully managed their own daily performances in relation to how "relevant others" would perceive them. Authenticity became a cultural, ethical, and even disciplinary technology within these sacred and secular borderlands, and was often a precondition for the twin goals of *selling* music and *saving* souls.[12]

In interviews, gospel hip hop artists often spoke of their musical ministry as a hustle, recontextualizing language from their previous informal business practices into a spiritual realm. They "grind for Christ," "roll with Christ," "get their evangelic game tight for Christ," "get their hustle on for Christ," "get their Christian lean back on," "ride or die for Christ," and "bang for Christ." These phrases refer to a transposition of the hustler's *ambition* and *creativity* into the overlapping terrains of hip hop and evangelism. As one female gospel MC explained, "I was tired of doing me, so now I do everything in His name."

Cue, as previous chapters have elaborated, was a former member of the secular rap group the College Boyz and founder of the monthly Christian-oriented, hip hop open mic, Klub Zyon. Klub Zyon was housed at KAOS Network, also home to the infamous weekly underground hip hop open mic, Project Blowed.[13] Cue sacrificed the coherence and success the night would achieve if it were billed as either Christian or secular in favor of a diverse, mixed crowd with a range of religious orientations. In an interview in 2008, Cue explained his evangelical practices as a hustle:

> First of all, I don't care who you are. You got to get your *hustle.* I don't care if you're a believer or not. And Jesus tells you, if you don't get your hustle on, you shouldn't eat.

He tells you that in Thessalonians, when Paul talks about, "Hey if the guy is lazy, why should he eat?" So we have to work it. Paul was a tent maker; he was a hustler. So, it depends on how you translating hustle.[14]

Cue was not alone in repurposing his hustle to do God's work. A look into the etymological underpinnings of the word hustle reveals the different ways that this word has been employed. According to the *Oxford English Dictionary*, "hustle" derives from the Dutch *husselen/hutselen*, "to shake, to toss," from the Middle Dutch *hutselen*, meaning "to shake the money in the game of hustle-cap" ("hustle-cap" explained later in this chapter). This early definition has clear connections to the metaphor and the practice of *earthquake music*. By the eighteenth century it meant "to push or knock a person about roughly or unceremoniously," and by 1821 "to move hastily, to hurry, to bustle; to work busily." In the mid-nineteenth century, especially in the United States, it was "to obtain, produce or serve by hustle or pushing activity." More recently, hustle has also become a popular term in American sports vernacular referring to athletes who play with scrappiness and urgency.

In much of the sociological literature on urban black neighborhoods, the hustle or hustling is generally viewed as strictly illicit or informal activities occurring in the street (not generally associated with the sacred), something one is forced into, and linked to a "culture of poverty."[15] But gospel rappers had a very different vision of the hustle. Soup the Chemist explained:

> In some way, we are all hustlers, when it comes to getting that money, and the church is no exception. They tell you to give money to meet their needs, or wants, and you will be blessed. Therefore, I do not hate the hustle, but I do hate it when the hustlers, record companies, radio stations and rappers label the positive, conscious legit hustle, as something or someone who is "weak." When in actuality the weak one takes the quick route; hiding behind his gun, his negative mind state, and his dirty money.[16]

For gospel rappers, the hustle did not always refer to "getting that money." Transposed into the realm of holy hip hop, the hustle was the deployment and practice of certain embodied capacities (i.e., lyricism, fast moves, improvisation, rhetorical abilities, scriptural knowledge, a flair for both marketing and missionizing), motivations (i.e., artistic, evangelical, financial), and sacred and profane literacies (i.e., hip hop, street-life, the Bible).

When I asked Cue what everyday activities and practices constituted his evangelical hustle, he answered:

> Well, one of them would be music, right? The other one would be networking. Really and truly, almost anything is a hustle. Jesus was hustling for his Father. Doing the work of my Father is my food. That's my hustle. That's how I get paid. That's how I get fed. That's how I get nourished. Hustle can be good and it can be bad. Reading my word, studying about God. I want to know him. I want to be more intimate with God. That's part of what I do.[17]

From these statements and the meanings at play around the word hustle, the term *evangelical hustle* was ultimately a kind of musical bootstrap evangelism that was close to the streets, compelled by both a hustler's *ambition* and a missionary's *zeal,* done in the name of Christ as opposed to in the service of cash.

MONEY, MORALITY, AND MUSIC

Gospel rappers negotiated money, morality, and music in myriad ways. Grass-roots gospel rappers in Los Angeles believed that holy hip hop was a sacred calling in their lives. Though they were not against making money through their musical ministries, touching people's lives by delivering the Gospel was their primary goal. As the gospel MC Street Pastor rapped at a Hip Hop Church L.A. service, "I ain't trying to sell records. I am trying to kill sin." In particular, holy hip hoppers were deeply skeptical of those who earned exceptionally large profits from gospel rap, and often articulated and performed a forceful disavowal of commercial intention in their recordings and live performances. The romance of both Christianity and underground, grassroots hip hop as commercial-free zones produced a double disavowal of commercialism in gospel rap culture, which was in part due to a generalized disgust toward the excesses and hypermaterialism venerated in mainstream hip hop, as well as the controversial financial gains of those churches and pastors subscribing to Prosperity Theology.[18] As Erin Aubry Kaplan warned in an *LA Weekly* article about Los Angeles's Crenshaw district, "Churches have always been the most consistently prosperous of black businesses, though their prosperity has little trickle-down in the aging neighborhoods where they tend to be located."[19]

The growing presence of Prosperity Theology among rap stars is what historian Joseph Sorett has referred to as hip hop's "gospel of Bling." He argues that "the version of Christianity most frequently visualised is an idiom largely made accessible over the airwaves by televangelists and marketed by megachurch pastors. It often also includes the celebration of a gospel of 'Bling' evidenced in the affinity of many rappers for prosperity preachers."[20] Pastor Creflo Dollar, perhaps the most popular black prosperity preacher, has made cameo appearances in rap music videos and is even mentioned in verses by rappers Mase and 50 Cent. Sorrett continues, "Pastor Dollar, for whom wealth is indeed a core spiritual value, seems to embody for many rappers the essence of *hip hop's hustle doused in holy water.*"[21] His World Changers Church has offices in South Africa, Australia, Nigeria, the United Kingdom and New York, while his Atlanta megachurch, the World Dome, houses 8,500 congregants. Usually clad in flashy pinstriped suits and alligator shoes, Dollar preaches religious devotion as a way to get out of debt—as a route toward financial prosperity. Moreover, he promises his followers that if they give an offering to the church, they can expect a bountiful return on their investment. This is spiritually sound business, Pastor Dollar often reassures his audiences, because he works for the King of Kings.

In particular, Southland gospel rappers were highly critical of celebrity preachers like Creflo Dollar and others. Cue recalled, "When I came into the church, I looked at the pastor and I thought, yeah, these cats are pimps. They wanna blow up. They got the whole star mentality. The same mentality I have. I can't say they worse than me. We're all dirty, but I recognize it." Beyond money and material possessions, Los Angeles gospel MCs also explicitly questioned the concepts of stardom and celebrity in both their lyrics and performance practices as they were cognizant of the continued pairing of religion and power in both the church and popular culture. MC TripLL-H, who called his Los Angeles–based Christian rap crew the G-Boy Union a "Holy cartel, banging for Christ," rapped one night at Klub Zyon about being in the "holy trenches," exclaiming, "No limelight, just make sure my walk's right."[22] Well-known Christian rapper Trip Lee put these concerns to rhyme on the track "Cash or Christ," erecting a fierce opposition between two arenas that commercial hip hop tends to blur together. He raps:

> Forget the cash and chains, that stuff will pass away
> And you can't take it with you to your after days

The stigmatization of money and materialism in holy hip hop extended to how people acquired and spent money, making it either benevolent capital or dirty money.[23] For instance, storefront preachers, who have historically committed themselves to working with those at the margins, have been critiqued for taking donations from gang members and securing resources for their outreach through informal or underground economies. Based on the multiple levels of stigmatization, how did gospel rappers contend with the tensions that emerge in the conflicting desires for ministry, business, and music making? What were the costs and benefits of selling the sacred?

BIG MONEY JESUS

Nothing seemed to epitomize how Los Angeles gospel rappers felt about the ostentatious displays of wealth by commercial hip hop artists more than the name of the gospel rap group Hip Hopposite. As their moniker suggests, these rappers, beat makers, and DJs saw themselves in direct opposition to the hip hop industry's celebration of hypercommercialism and bling. The five core members—Celah (say-lah), DJ Heat, B-Love, Sound Doctrine, and Crossfire—were all doing their own thing in rap music in the 1990s—an era that witnessed the catastrophic effects of natural disaster, gang violence, police brutality, riots, and mass incarceration—before coming together officially as a collective in early 2000s. Sound Doctrine, a Compton native who was raised in the church but drawn to the sounds of commercial hip hop he heard on the local radio station KDAY, formed a Christian rap

FIGURE 13. Gospel rap group Hip Hopposite, c. 2007. Left to right: Sound Doctrine, DJ Heat, Celah, B-Love, and Crossfire. Photo courtesy of Eric Drake.

group called The Fishermen. Celah and Crossfire, who actually attended the same high school together and later crossed paths again while rapping on the gospel hip hop circuit, asked Sound Doctrine to "give them some beats." They then brought in DJ Heat and female MC B-Love to round out their sound. Their vision was for a collective of highly talented artists who each was capable of releasing their own solo project—something along the lines of the Wu-Tang Clan. They gathered weekly at Sound Doctrine's Compton home to fellowship, share music, and record tracks. The home studio was humble, equipped with a computer, small mixing board, and turntables. They recorded their vocal tracks in a small closet with a desk lamp on the floor for light.

I met Celah, the lead MC of the collective, along with Slack of I.D.O.L. King, at Westside Bible Church in South Los Angeles. Celah is a Hebrew word commonly found in the book of Psalms that the Bible translates as "pause, and think of that," or as Celah explained, "a stop in the music." It gives the listener an opportunity to digest and reflect on what has just been said. Celah believed that "holy hip hop MCs shouldn't strive to be marketable, but should rather strive to leave their mark." His online presence was almost nonexistent and his marketing tactics were always very grassroots. He once dialed Verizon 411 to ask for the telephone number for Pizza Hut and, upon hearing a song by Christian rapper Lecrae in the background, exchanged emails with the Verizon operator. Celah sent the operator some of the free online Hip Hopposite mixtapes, who in turn ended up attending several of their live shows. Musical marketing for Celah was a product of happenstance and spontaneous connection. He developed his networks and notoriety through building relationships with people.

While Celah despised the materialism and bling of the commercial hip hop industry, he had an equally harsh critique of "big money" churches and pastors. Hip Hopposite's *Big Money Jesus* mixtape (2005) was in many ways a response to the rise of Prosperity Theology in Los Angeles and many other megachurches across the country. "The Prosperity Gospel thing on the West Coast was out of control," Celah lamented. "Prosperity Gospel teachings are just scriptures out of context."[24] On "Church Spirit," a track from the 2005 *Big Money Jesus* mixtape that features a sped-up sample of Aretha Franklin's hit "Spirit in the Dark," Celah critiqued this exact church practice:

> I'm through with playing church
> I'm about my Father's business
> These fake churches, man, I hate it there, I hate it there
> Just to get a blessing gotta pay a fare, pay a fare

The mixtape also features game show skits between each musical track that satirize the celebration of financial wealth and fame in Christianity.

> Game Show Host: We're back with our second round. Here's the question. According to Deuteronomy 8, God gives us the power to?
>
> Ziomarah: Get wealth, you know a little bling . . . a nice spot in Beverly Hills.
>
> *Ka-ching!*
>
> Game Show Host: Oh, Durante sounds the buzzer for the challenge.
>
> Diante: It's pronounced Diante. Deuteronomy 8 is talking about something altogether different—talking about the Israelites and how they was obedient to God and his mercy and his goodness toward them. Why you guys always gotta focus on power and wealth? What's going on?
>
> Game Show Host: Well, let's see what the panel says. Judges?
>
> Judges: Wrong!
>
> Game Show Host: I'm sorry, Dante, it looks like your challenge has been rejected.

In a subsequent skit, Curtis, another contestant, answers the following question after winning the *Big Money Jesus* game show:

> Game Show Host: According to Romans 4:17, who can call those things which do not exist as though they do?

Curtis: That's anybody that got enough fame.

Game Show Host: Curtis, You're our winner! You're going to get a chance to open the windows of heaven!

The host then explains to Curtis that he has won an all-expenses paid trip to the Word of Prosperity Harvest Conference held at an arena in Boca Raton, FL. If Curtis is able to answer one more question, he can win a grand prize. In this game show scenario, opening the windows of heaven entails riding home in a Cadillac Escalade and a chance to win $100,000. With *The Price Is Right* music cheerfully chirping in the background and the audience applauding feverishly, the host tells the winner that they want to send him home in style: "Remember, Curtis, you're the head and not the tail." But as Celah once reminded me, in Matthew 19, Jesus says that it is more difficult for a rich man to enter the gates of heaven than for a camel to pass through the eye of a needle. Creflo Dollar would vehemently disagree.

"DON'T PROSTITUTE YOUR GIFT"

One way that gospel rappers avoided navigating the boundaries between mission-izing and marketing was by the separation of their musical ministry from their material livelihood. Most of them had "day jobs" as youth counselors, secretaries, teachers, bankers, and electricians, as their holy hip hop practice generally did not provide enough to live on. "I don't really do this for money anyway," Sound Doctrine once remarked to me. "If I did, I would be broke." Earning income from other kinds of work in the formal sector liberated them from the moral and financial challenges of making their musical ministry their main source of income. Instead, the evangelical business of gospel hip hop was something they hustled to do in their free time.

In order to maintain the moral and artistic integrity of their music and keep their hip hop "opposite" from the commercial hip hop world, each Hip Hopposite member worked another "day job" in addition to their involvement in gospel rap. When he wasn't making gospel hip hop beats, Sound Doctrine worked for Los Angeles Water and Power as a meter reader. DJ Heat did part-time grocery delivery in addition to his paid DJ gig for Klub Zyon. Celah was a customer relations specialist and B-Love was a secretary at a high school in Santa Monica. Both were in business school as well. Crossfire worked at a nonprofit where he taught at-risk youth job training skills. Their jobs allowed them to make music without the burden of financial gain, but more importantly, it allowed them to put their religious messages front and center. As Celah used to caution his fellow gospel rappers, "you should get a job so you don't prostitute your gift."

Even if gospel rappers relied on jobs outside of holy hip hop for their daily livelihood, money, however minimal, still came into play in their everyday interactions around rapping the Gospel: audiences and congregations still expected to pay for holy hip hop CDs; artists received donations and offerings for their performances; portions of the offerings collected on hip hop ministry nights were sometimes disbursed back to gospel rappers who performed on those nights; and events like Klub Zyon often suggested (though did not demand) a cover donation at the door. Crossfire explained how he and Celah approached the issue of selling Hip Hopposite CDs:

> The business side was something that me and him [Celah] had to tackle when we were getting into this. We were just thinking, we'll just go and do this John the Baptist style—just talk and rap and do what we love and just let it be what it is. Or, we can really try and get it to a lot more people. And that's when we were like, we gotta tackle this whole business thing 'cause we felt like, the music is free. The doctrine is free. But that CD that it takes to get to you is not free. And we felt like there was a lot more ministry going on while listening to people's CDs as opposed to seeing them at different concerts. Concerts are wonderful but I wasn't expecting everyone in the crowd to run up and get saved. So I felt myself growing as I was listening to gospel hip hop music. You know, listening to Ambassador or Lecrae—this is really where I'm getting fed when I get to repetitively listen. So the CD! CDs really cost money. The rapping didn't cost and the gospel didn't cost, but to get that CD to you, that costs. That's why it's a business, because we want to get this to everybody the same way Public Enemy did it, the same way Pac and them did.[25]

But Hip Hopposite didn't always charge the same amount for their CDs. Differential pricing tactics and sliding scales were common in gospel hip hop exchanges. Sound Doctrine described his practice around charging people for his beats:

> See, people like to come over here and record and make beats stuff . . . and what I'll do is I base it on the relationship that I have . . . if I know you really well and I see you around, you know, I won't give you no out there price. I'll give you a price, and you say, oh man, I really can't do that, c'mon. I'll try to work with that. If you say, I'll give it to you in six weeks, then I say okay, give it to me in six weeks. I have a set price but I just kind of feel off the person.[26]

A lot of these interactions were "off the books" and yet still had to be in accordance with the teachings of the good Book. Within these moments of exchange, when did holy hip hoppers bracket off their morality or religious beliefs in order to reach certain people? When did they completely invest in their faith at the expense of financial gain? How did music complicate and/or enable these negotiations?

GAMES OF CHANCE AND LEAPS OF FAITH

Hustle's original association with the game of "hustle-cap" provides a symbolic link to the ways in which contemporary gospel rappers approach their musical ministry. The *Oxford English Dictionary* defines hustle-cap as "a form of pitch-and-toss,

FIGURE 14. Khanchuz during the filming of his music video, "What the Bible Say," in 2016 in the Western Mojave Desert. Photo courtesy of Prophet X and Prophecy Records.

in which the coins were 'hustled' or shaken together in a cap before being tossed." Pitch-and-toss is a general term for games of chance, in which bets are placed in relation to the ways coins will fall (heads or tails) after being tossed into a designated area. (Shooting dice could be considered a modern-day correlate.) Similarly, gospel rappers engaged in games of chance concerning their finances in order to adhere to their religious beliefs, sometimes even displaying a resistance to rational, profit-driven business practices.

Khanchuz, who resided in Inglewood, entered into what could be deemed financial games of chance when he hustled to book and perform church gigs. In the years I was hanging out with Khanchuz, he rapped for Christ at every opportunity, in between working his two jobs: one as a youth counselor for a group home near the Crenshaw Mall and the other as a drug test administrant in Long Beach. He would often don two silver chains—one with a medallion of Jesus and the other a faux-diamond encrusted microphone. The image of these two symbols clinking together across his chest gives an inkling of the unpredictable, contradictory, and mystifying ways that money, hip hop, and religion operated within his evangelical hustle. Eventually, he switched to two silver chains with crosses.

Church gigs generally gave rap artists a modest "love offering," but according to many gospel rappers, churches were also notorious for expecting them to perform for free because they were seen as Christians doing good works for Christ. DJ Heat recounted one such instance:

There were five of us in the group at this particular time and we were invited out to a big conference in Ontario—some big Southern California Gospel getdown where they had everybody from Bishop Tutu to Kirk Franklin. Of course they had a budget. That's what they always say, "we have a budget." They already knew that certain artists were gonna get paid and certain artists weren't. So we fell into the category of those that weren't. So they wanted us to jump off from Los Angeles, all five of us, and go down to Ontario. And I'm thinking, well at least can they just give us some gas money. And these people, they can't even afford that. We already know the game, we know what's going on. If you're taking money for tickets, there's going to be some overhead. You're going to be able to pay people. We said OK, that's fine, we're probably not going to make it to Ontario.[27]

Khanchuz was invited to perform one song for "no pay" at a church service twenty miles away from his home in Inglewood. His bank account was at zero, his gas tank was half-full, and it would be a week until his next paycheck. His twelve-year-old daughter, Jaysha, had asked to stay with him that weekend, but he told her he did not have the financial means to take care of her. Missing her father, she decided to come stay with him anyway. Khanchuz, despite the unfeasibility of this evangelical endeavor, chose to perform for the service in the hopes that serving God might reap unknown and spiritual rewards. One might consider driving miles and miles to perform for free in churches, especially in light of Khanchuz's tenuous financial situation and increasing fuel prices, an *unsound* business practice.

Called by God to minister through his music, Khanchuz fervently believed that the reward for this musical service, whether financial or spiritual, was hidden and yet waiting to be revealed. When he arrived, one of the other artists scheduled to perform that day cancelled and Khanchuz got to perform a few more songs in his place. When the pastor approached him at the end of the service, Khanchuz thought he was going to get chewed out for looking "too thug" or "too gangster". Instead, the pastor told him he wanted to support his future work with a small donation and slid a check into his hand. Khanchuz just folded it, and, without looking at it, slipped it in his pocket. Later, while he was driving home he unfolded the check and saw that it was for two hundred dollars. He and Jaysha were able to eat heartily for the rest of the week. Khanchuz felt he had not only earned a little bread, but also helped bolster the spiritual worth of gospel hip hop among a new congregation.

Other gospel hip hop artists and groups gave up potential celebrity and economic success in favor of maintaining and honoring their Christian commitments. L.A. Symphony, a less explicitly Christian rap group, turned down a record deal with a secular label because they felt they would be pressured to water down the religious nature of their message. This decision led to financial struggle for the group. To compensate, they ramped up their hustle to book church gigs as one of their main sources of livelihood. Khanchuz and groups like L.A. Symphony often exhibited a kind of "God's Got My Back" strategy in their financial practices around gospel rap (giving away many copies of their own CDs, performing for free, making substantial offerings to churches, etc.), trusting that if they kept serving God's will, they would be blessed in return. These were two examples among many in which gospel rappers defied financial logic in favor of a faith-based conviction in the (re)circulation of money, gifts, and blessings. Sometimes financial rewards were reaped, other times gospel rappers came away empty handed. This was not a clear-cut system of exchange. What was critical here was that benevolent and fortuitous events were then interpreted as rewards for doing God's work and continuing to be in His service. As Slack of I.D.O.L. King told the members of Hip Hopposite one night in Compton at Sound Doctrine's house:

> What are you really in it for? You gotta be willing to do it even if you don't get anything. There will be times when you get a lot and there will be times when you get very little. There will be times when you say, I just wanna come and you just sense it. I need to be there. I'm gonna come if I gotta pay myself, and then all of a sudden somebody will call you while you there or down the street and you get two thousand dollars and good lord, where did that come from? It's cause that's what God had in store for you.[28]

MILK BEFORE MEAT

Constitutive of each gospel rappers' holy hustle was a dance between their creative agency, Christian morals, and the market. Certain gospel rappers found loopholes in morality in order to achieve greater circulation potential for their music, and therefore, the Gospel. Circulating the Good News was a core concern for many of them, and each gospel rapper deployed a different evangelical method for achieving it. Gospel MCs marketed their music in order to missionize—they leveraged hip hop to win souls for the Kingdom. Many of them evoked the metaphor of fishing to refer to their musical evangelism—fishing for lost souls with all the appropriate *bait* and *hooks.* This practice was not necessarily dissimilar to the commercial hip hop tactic of using catchy and often sung *hooks* or choruses to capture listeners.

Weary of scaring potential listeners and believers away with dogmatic scripture and explicit religious titles, artists often eschewed the name Christian rap in favor of other more ambiguous, less overtly religious monikers for their music. In an interview, Cue stated, "In black music, we have never been scared to talk about God, but as soon as you put the Christian cloak on it, it becomes something else. You don't want people to be blinded by the Christian cloak." Therefore, when selling and giving away CDs, it was common to hear a gospel rapper explain their music as truth music, *earthquake music,* worsh-hop, hip-hope, just plain ol' good music, or simply hip hop.[29] This (mis)labeling practice was challenged by a common axiom flowing through gospel hip hop communities in L.A.: "Christians need to come out of the closet"—a phrase I often heard throughout my fieldwork. But gospel rappers'

FIGURE 15. Cue Jn-Marie's "secular" hip hop group, Slum Peasants, c. 2008. Left to right: Elden, Mercy, and Cue. Photo courtesy of Phat Efx.

desire to reach people—to get even just one hook in—often trumped this moral imperative to disrobe and make one's religious standing public.

Cue's evangelical outreach involved a two-pronged approach to fishing for souls. He led and rapped in two different hip hop groups: one named Asylumz, a group he marketed as explicitly Christian rap dealing with overt Christian themes; and

FIGURE 16. Cue Jn-Marie's gospel hip hop group, Asylumz, also featuring Mercy.

Slum Peasants, one he marketed as a secular rap group. While they occasionally made lyrical references to God, Slum Peasants presented other social and political issues in their music and even used profanity on a very selective and strategic basis. Winning souls was a byproduct, not a strategic intention, of this particular project. Interestingly, both groups were mostly composed of the same members, all of whom were Christian men. Cue explained, "For Asylumz, if you've been so extreme in the depths of evil, you need a refuge. That refuge is only for believers. For Slum Peasants, the brush with the devil is still really close so you can't hide behind the religion." He saw these two groups as speaking to two different kinds of audiences. Asylumz was edification for believers. Slum Peasants was for the unsaved streets.

The music videos of Slum Peasants and Asylumz exposed the divergent ways the two groups highlighted and prioritized different agendas. In the Slum Peasants video, "All the Love Is Gone," Cue and Mercy ride solemnly in a blue convertible through the streets of Los Angeles—down deserted alleyways, through the slums of skid row, under freeway overpasses—offering a reportage of L.A.'s urban underbelly. Mercy sings the chorus with a rich velvety vibrato over a slow syncopated hip hop groove. The only references to religion are the crosses hanging around their necks. This grim urban reality reveals truth, but lacks love. As Cue would say, "Truth without love is like doing surgery on someone without numbing the pain. The goal is crazy love." Asylumz's video for "Crazy Prayze" provides the antidote to the hauntingly despondent scene depicted by Slum Peasants. Footage of people passionately praising the Lord with frenzied histrionics and spontaneously catching the Holy Ghost in various religious contexts (church services, baptisms, wedding ceremonies, etc.) is juxtaposed with live footage of Asylumz giving a hyperkinetic, raucous performance at Klub Zyon in Leimert Park. The MCs of Asylumz rap with ferocious speed, conveying a sense of spiritual urgency and frenzy. And yet, there is a satirical tone permeating the video; the outrageousness of some of these outbursts of crazy praise is really a call for that crazy love that Cue was speaking about—a love that says "I'm ready to die for my faith."

The juxtaposition of the two groups' musical styles, lyrics, and performance practices raised questions around the evangelical currency and efficacy of the groups. Cue's greater evangelical philosophy behind this was epitomized by the biblical expression "milk before meat," a metaphor for an individual's process of spiritual maturation.[30] He explained:

> You gotta give them milk before meat. You gotta give 'em something they like to give 'em something they need. For me, in order for gospel hip hop to engage the world on a more significant level we have to be able to feed them milk. Most gospel hip hop, it's not meat that I would call it, but it's meat for the world. They're not there yet. Slum Peasants is going right into where we are. We're not coming and trying to make anybody be anything. We're just saying, hey, this who we are and if you wanna roll, then let's roll.[31]

Cue elaborated on this philosophy in an anecdote about a young gospel MC that he mentored. When Cue first met this MC, he was "rhyming with the Word." Cue asked him what he wanted to be and the young MC retorted, "Well, I want to reach the world for Jesus." Cue assured him that he wasn't going to reach the world just putting scripture into rhyme, and told him, "That's too religious." The tension between blinding potential converts with the Christian cloak or hiding Christianity behind the cloak of hip hop was at work in Cue's evangelical hustle to gain credibility as both an authentic hip hop artist and sincere disciple of Jesus. This latter credibility—being seen and heard as a true and sincere Christian—was critical as many of Cue's musical projects were in part funded by his church home, the New Song Church.

Similarly, Majesty, a female gospel rapper from Inglewood, warned, "We got kids on the street prostituting. Hit 'em where they at! You can't hit 'em with the word. Hit 'em where they at and then reel them in like you going fishing. You fishing! Throw your hook in. Go to them where they at. And then you reel them in slowly."[32] She explained her plans to drop an underground album for the streets called *Heaven and Hell* before dropping one for the believers, explaining, "I'm feeling to hit with some secular before I hit 'em with some Christian rap. It's gotta all be mixed in but we gotta get out there secular. They [Christian rappers] don't want me to say that. They don't want me to do that. Still, God is still with me throughout the whole thing but I went through something and I can't ignore that." She viewed dropping a secular album not only as a smart mission strategy, but also as a necessary, inseparable, and authentic part of her life journey, her conversion story, and, therefore, her musical expression. Her strategies to gain access and credibility coincided with her artistic self-fashioning. Her creative agency allowed her to hold the secular/sacred tension of her marketing and missionizing strategy, and to express what many see as a contradiction as an integrated wholeness.

Compton Virtue, a Christian rapper and spoken word poet from Compton, talked about her use of secular hip hop beats:

> I realized that if you're going to be a fisher, you gotta have some bait. So, I would take urban hip hop beats that are popular on the radio that young people are listening to, because that is what is infectious . . . People that are not Christians don't listen to holy hip hop. People that are already Christian listen to it. How are we gonna get these people that need the message to hear it? Spit the gospel of Jesus Christ on beats they know.[33]

Both Majesty and Compton Virtue invoked the metaphor of fishing for souls—a biblical idea that comes from Mark 1:17, where Jesus tells his disciples, "Come ye after me, and I will make you fishers of men."

Hip Hopposite sometimes employed the strategy of spitting the gospel over well-known commercial hip hop beats. They revamped Erykah Badu's 2008 hip hop hit, "The Healer," in which she demands that hip hop, as an expression of many gods and religions, is the ultimate healer. In an act of *flippin' the script(ure)*, Hip Hopposite changed Badu's lyric of "It's bigger than religion—Hip Hop" to "It's bigger than your hip hop—Jesus Christ." While they added in a B-Love gospel rap verse "for believers," they kept Madlib's catchy and haunting hip hop beat intact. Descending bell hits and an ominous chorus of high-pitched voices pulsating in the background create a sense of spiritual immediacy. This gospel reversion makes the case for both hip hop and Jesus as transformative healers.

Despite having different methods, most gospel rappers were careful not to cross moral thresholds. For both Cue and Majesty, the logics of evangelism, marketing, and hip hop coincided and cohered under the shared imperative of circulation and affective contact with listeners; this imperative satisfied and integrated their desires to sell music, deliver a relevant message in the hopes of saving souls, and earn credibility on multiple levels. These artists sanctified the hustle of pushing and promoting their music in unique, nontraditional ways. At the same time, the act of selling underground hip hop mixtapes, drawing on relevant secular issues and locations, and deploying street slang authenticated what might otherwise be looked at as trite and disingenuous proselytizing.

REAPING WHAT YOU SOW

The payments, paybacks, and rewards of practicing gospel hip hop were not necessarily financial, nor were they necessarily spiritual. How did holy hip hoppers put gospel rap to work as a resource in various urban spaces? What kinds of social currency and extra-institutional spiritual capital did gospel rappers reap through their daily sowing?[34]

Soup the Chemist, one of the first gospel rappers in Los Angeles back in the 1980s, along with several other gospel hip hop artists, delivered an impromptu performance at one of the most notorious housing projects in Newark, New Jersey—"The Prince Street Projects"—known for both its drug trafficking and the high percentage of residents with AIDS due to shared syringe use. Soup and his crew set up a portable stage and sound system right in the middle of the four high-rise buildings. Suddenly, in the middle of one of his songs, Soup felt something hit his arm. There were people on the roofs of the buildings, flinging objects and firing BB pellets down at them. Soup saw blood running down his soundman's face after something struck him in the head.

Drug lords, committed to protecting the ongoing need for their products among the project's residents, heard Soup's performance of Christ-centered hip hop as a direct threat to their business. After weathering the storm for a while, they quickly began to pack up their equipment, but Soup kept preaching and rapping. Monetary payment for this treacherous performance came in the form of another type of shower. This time it was the older women—mothers and grandmothers—throwing money through the windows of Soup's van as it sped away, encouraging him to come back and preach his hip hop gospel to their struggling community. Soup recalled how this spontaneous concert also helped him garner street credibility and authenticity among people in that neighborhood who had previously seen gospel rappers as soft, cheesy, "wannabe" rap artists.

Holy D, a gospel rapper residing in Palmdale, California, and godbrother of Battle Cat (a hip hop producer who also made beats for Snoop Dogg), was pulled over on his way to an evening church service in Compton. He had been invited to perform a gospel rap song for his uncle's congregation. Holy D's baby blue truck was "flossed out" with rims, tinted windows, a personalized license plate, a subwoofer stereo, and a slick, two-toned paint job. It was one of the most memorable and conspicuous gospel rap vehicles I encountered, and as such, it begged to be pulled over. The cops said they stopped him because the tinting on his front windows was too dark, but Holy D was convinced they were hoping to catch him for another offense. In his words, the cops were rude, antagonistic, and distrustful of his explanation of where he was going until he showed them his holy hip hop CD, *God's Creation,* as proof of his innocence and good character. The album cover features an image of Holy D in an oversized jersey and backwards baseball cap with angel wings fanning out from behind him. Upon seeing this angelic image of the gospel rapper, the cops let him go. In a moment of visual misrecognition, Holy D's gospel hip hop CD became a critical resource that literally got him "off the hook."

FIGURE 17. Soup the Chemist, c. 2013. Photo courtesy of Daley Hake.

Gospel rappers often used their CDs as a material catalyst for face-to-face encounters that would ideally blossom into deeper conversations about God—a point of entry, a portal, a conversation piece or gift that would promote further exchanges. Their music was the milk that would warm the palette to receive the meat of the Gospel. Their automobiles were the chariots that carried them in and out of dangerous scenarios and unpredictable territories as they hustled to win souls for Christ.

DO THE HUSTLE

All of these examples demonstrate the multifaceted and unscripted nature of gospel rappers' evangelical hustle, as well as the complex ways holy hip hoppers were seen, heard, interpreted, and recognized (or misrecognized). The manner in which churches, hip hop communities, and other groups in positions of cultural and legal authority perceived and portrayed holy hip hoppers *mattered*, affecting and informing the conditions of possibility for gospel rappers' ongoing livelihoods and the strategic performance of their own subjectivities. Thus, one of the main branches of activity in evangelical hustling was the practice of authenticating oneself to Christians and non-Christians, hip hop heads and critics, both old and young, which required knowing how and when to adhere to, and disrupt, dominant structures. These earned authenticities—street authenticity, hip hop authenticity, and spiritual authenticity, among others—fused together, forming an aggregation of resources that would hopefully be *converted* into economic payback and result in the *conversion* of souls. The activities of Los Angeles gospel rappers may have translated into more souls won for Christ, but not necessarily into better paying jobs or increased credit. Conversion, as a transformative religious, musical, and economic process, held immeasurable currency in the everyday spiritual marketplace of holy hip hop.

While the music industry clearly comprises the most significant portion of the business of sounds, gospel rap practice opens up discussions of alternative economies of faith, sentiments, and livelihood defined beyond material success. The informality of gospel rap's evangelical hustle, and the acquisition of nonfinancial currencies, did not necessarily occur outside the formal economy. Rather, their activities, while privileging social collaborations and relationships over purely economic concerns, were still located within macroeconomic situations. Gospel rappers rerouted and redeemed some of the ideas, associations, and attendant forms of currency rooted in the street hustle into a hardcore urban evangelism. In so doing, they were developing what they saw as morally sound and musically sounded business ministries, born from their own individual and collective histories, and contingent on their religious beliefs, monetary realities, situated knowledges, artistic imaginations, and the expectations of specific urban populations.

In a final sequence of spin moves on the word hustle, the original meaning of "shaking to and fro" is given new significance in the dancing body of the holy hip hopper as well as in the seismic shifts of urban terrains. Participants and audience members at gospel hip hop shows often did the electric slide—a social line dance that is considered the generational offspring of the 1970s dance form the hustle. Dancers slid from side to side, flowed from back to front, forming human lines across the dance floor with their simultaneous movements. Such powerful moves suggested traversals and lateral networks of coordination and collectivity across urban spaces. Such moves demonstrated how holy hip hoppers created flow among different economic, spiritual, and social currencies circulating through territories and practices of gospel rap. Below the radar of commercial visibility, these street disciples conducted their everyday *Kingdom Business*, hustled in the here and now with their eyes on the prize of the hereafter.

5

Roads to Zion

Hip Hop's Search for the City Yet to Come

No place to live in, no Zion
See that's forbidden, we fryin'
—KENDRICK LAMAR, "HEAVEN AND HELL" (2010)

The sense of the end-times and last days must be entered in order to find the
creative imagination that can reveal paths of survival and threads of renewal
as chaos winds its wicked way back to cosmos again.
—MICHAEL MEADE

Robin D. G. Kelley, in his book *Freedom Dreams: The Black Radical Imagination*, argues that Exodus served as the key political and moral compass for African Americans during the antebellum era and after the Civil War.[1] Exodus gave people a critical language for understanding the racist state they lived in and how to build a new nation. Exodus signified new beginnings, black self-determination, and black autonomy. Marcus Garvey's "Back to Africa" movement represented a powerful manifestation of this vision of Exodus to Zion. He even purchased the Black Star shipping line in order to transport goods and people back to their African motherlands. Though Garvey's Black Star Line made only a few voyages, it has remained a powerful symbol of the longing for home. As the dream of Exodus faded, Zion has become the more central metaphor of freedom and homecoming in contemporary black cultural expressions.

Along these lines, Emily Raboteau—reggae head and daughter of the renowned historian of African American religion Albert J. Raboteau—explores Zion as a place that black people have yearned to be in her book, *Searching for Zion: The Quest for Home in the African Diaspora*.[2] In her wanderings through Jamaica, Ethiopia, Ghana, and the American South and her conversations with Rastafarians and African Hebrew Israelites, Evangelicals, Ethiopian Jews, and Katrina transplants, one truth emerges: there are many roads to Zion. One may take

128

multiple spiritual, musical, and physical routes in search of a homeland, but "To end any story," Raboteau writes, "even one far simpler than this, is a magic trick. The Promised Land is never arrived at."[3]

By way of conclusion, I would like return to holy hip hop's black religious traffics—traffics that are both multicultural and diasporic. I will move from one of the first rap music forays into Christianity (MC Hammer) to some of the most recent iterations of Christian sensibilities in contemporary hip hop (Lecrae and Kendrick Lamar) in order to connect the dots between multiple hip hop trajectories toward Zion. Tsitsi Ella Jaji argues, "black music has come to be a privileged *figure* of transnational black sensibilities and modernist expression."[4] I would like to more broadly explore the intersections of blackness, religious conversion, and postcolonial popular music in relation to holy hip hop. In seeking a place to belong, sometimes musical, religious, and physical borders are crossed and diasporic resources are employed. Hip hop artists, in their ongoing searches for a spiritual home, have assembled multiple geographies and remixed diverse black musical and religious repertoires.

DREAMING DR. KING

Just two years after Stephen Wiley released the first known Christian rap album, *Bible Break* (1985), and in the same year that Soup the Chemist recorded *Fully Armed* (1987), Oakland rapper MC Hammer joined a gospel hip hop group called the Holy Ghost Boys. While best known for his rapid rise to fame, ecstatic dance moves, signature parachute pants, and hit rap songs "U Can't Touch This" and "2 Legit 2 Quit," Hammer has also dedicated much of his life's work to serving the Lord. Now an ordained minister in the Church of God in Christ, he was raised in a Pentecostal church and joined a street ministry in 1984 after working for Charles O. Finley, then owner of the Oakland Athletics baseball team. Even as he "backslid" away from his faith during the peak years of his career, he promised to dedicate one song on each of his albums to God. The motivational 1990 hip hop anthem "Pray" is probably most well known.

After falling out of favor in the popular music industry and declaring bankruptcy, Hammer turned back to the church from whence he came. In October 1997, he began a television ministry called *M.C. Hammer and Friends* on the Trinity Broadcasting Network (the same network that gospel rapper Soup the Chemist was watching during his conversion to Christianity), insisting that MC then stood for "Man of Christ." Three years later, MC Hammer was invited by Pastor Dick Bernal to lead a gospel hip hop service on Sunday nights called "Hammertime" at the Jubilee Christian Center, an independent charismatic church in San Jose, California. "Hammertime," a term made famous in his megahit "U Can't Touch This," drew in "the unchurched and disenfranchised, including gang members, troubled youth and curious teens."⁵ Reaching such populations, as demonstrated by the work of Pastor Carol Scott and Sharon Collins at the Hip Hop Church in Inglewood, has been one of the most activist components of gospel hip hop practice.

MC Hammer intersected with a Los Angeles gospel MC in 2012. Cue—self-proclaimed "Pastorfarian" and leader of "The Church Without Walls" on L.A.'s Skid Row who found Jesus through Spike Lee's *Malcolm X*—crossed paths with Hammer in Watts at a funeral of a mutual friend, Eugene Williams. An activist pastor who founded the Los Angeles Metropolitan Churches (LAM)—a faith-based organization that sought to address high crime and poor education in communities throughout Los Angeles—Williams was also co-director of University of Southern California's Center for Religion and Civic Culture, where Cue took courses with him. Before lung cancer took his life at age fifty-two, Williams had also been working with Hammer on implementing faith-based civic engagement initiatives—work that inspired Hammer to speak to an audience of fifteen thousand youth at the first-ever "We Day" in Seattle to honor Dr. Martin Luther King, Jr.

When I came across this picture of the two men standing side by side at the memorial service at USC, mourning the loss of another spiritually minded soldier in the struggle, I thought back to Cue's original question: "How do I come with Malcolm and Martin at the same time?" Over twenty years after his conversion, Cue told me during a 2013 conversation, "I'm more in the space of Martin now. We've endured hoses. We've endured our youth being murdered in cold blood, like Trayvon Martin. There is no need to be violent. I wouldn't have said this ten years ago, but I'm at peace with nonviolent resistance now. I'm OK if someone takes my life. Malcolm and I have the same roots but I wouldn't use *any means necessary.* I'm willing to be the sacrifice."⁶ Cue reaffirmed this message on a social media post from October 25, 2016, in which he reacted to the news headline, "White Supremacists Threaten War against Black Americans if Donald Trump Loses the 2016 U.S. Presidential Election," with a lyric from the famous late rapper Notorious B.I.G.: "I'M READY TO DIE." But then he posed the question, with equal parts humor and seriousness: "Should I get strapped just in case? Y'all know I hate guns."

Over the Thanksgiving holiday in 2014, Cue led a crowd through downtown Los Angeles in a Black Lives Matter protest of the multiple police killings throughout the nation—killings in which most of the victims were black men. In Los Angeles, it was Ezell Ford, a mentally disabled African American man, who was shot dead by the LAPD in August of that same year. As a member of the Black Brown Clergy Alliance with CLUE Los Angeles (Clergy and Laity United for Economic Justice) and an organizer for SCLC—the Southern Christian Leadership Conference of which Dr. King was president at the time of his murder—Cue continues to honor Martin's legacy and fight for that city of Zion. Like his stated mission for the open mic, Klub Zyon, Cue's musical and activist work is for the city yet to come—or in his words, "a city we're anticipating with walls of jasper and streets of gold."⁷

FIGURE 18. Cue Jn-Marie and MC Hammer at the Center for Religion and Civic Culture at the University of Southern California for a memorial of their mutual friend, activist pastor and professor Eugene Williams, 2012.

Even though the Black Lives Matter movement and black evangelical Christian communities have sometimes been at odds in their visions of and methods toward black liberation, the holy hip hop artists that I worked with in Los Angeles looked to embrace this social movement. Efrem Smith, co-author of *The Hip Hop Church*[8] and president and CEO of World Impact—a missions organization committed to the empowerment of the urban poor—explains some of the "anti-church sentiments" reverberating through the Black Lives Matter movement:

As I look at the Black Lives Matter Movement and hear some of the anti-church sentiments, I realize that part of this dilemma is that the Black Church is lacking a comprehensive, contextualized, and professionalized view of youth ministry. I have witnessed this priority shift from my teen years as the Hip Hop movement came into prominence through today . . . the hard reality is that within the Black Lives Matter Movement there is anger not only at broken aspects of the law enforcement system, but also at the Black Church. This anger could stem from the perception that youth are not prioritized in annual budgets or staffing concerns. I recognize that there are a number of Black Churches that have been highly committed to youth ministry, but far too many have put other ministry initiatives above a robust commitment to youth.[9]

This lack of commitment to youth by black churches is something that holy hip hoppers and hip hop ministries have worked hard to change. Holy hip hop is in a unique position to bridge these two important cultural entities—Black Lives Matter and black churches—by offering a cultural and musical practice that can hold the complicated social and spiritual realities that young black Americans confront in their everyday lives. Smith goes on to say that Black Lives Matter, like the civil rights movement, should be understood as a complex movement made up of multiple views, agendas, and tactics that are sometimes in tension and sometimes in alignment with one another.

> The Civil Rights Movement was much larger and more complex than just the leadership of Dr. Martin Luther King, Jr. Yes, there was King and the Southern Christian Leadership Conference, but there was also the NAACP, the Urban League, the Student Non-violent Coordinating Committee, the Black Panthers, as well as leaders such as Fannie Lou Hamer and Malcolm X. These groups and leaders didn't always agree.[10]

Similarly, there is no unitary position or viewpoint that represents the Black Lives Matter movement or the holy hip hop movement. Although he rarely performs gospel rap these days, Cue embodies the complexity of holy hip hop in the way he merges the spiritual and political philosophies of the prophetic Christian leader and the militant Muslim minister in his search for Zion.

In another gospel hip hop invocation of Dr. King and Zion land, I witnessed the group Hip Hopposite perform "Road to Zion" at the weekly Christian hip hop praise party, Club Judah. The Hip Hopposite MCs took turns at the microphone, spitting lyrics about Martin Luther King, Jr. and Coretta Scott King, freedoms bells and dreams, over a laidback hip hop groove and slow crawling, ascending guitar lick. MC Crossfire rapped the final verse:

> If I get shot like Dr. King, homie, I got the dream
> Telling people black, white, young or old
> That in the middle of the ghetto I found the road

Crossfire remembers moving between various places in Los Angeles as a youth, accompanied by the voices of Tupac and Snoop Dogg. "We had a rough upbringing," he recalled to me in one of our conversations, with "broken homes and drugs and all kinds of crazy stuff."[11] He remembers finding the road in 1996, the day before Tupac's double album, *All Eyez on Me*, was released. "The night before that album dropped," Crossfire continued, "it was just like, Pow! I wasn't even in church or nothing. I had been dipping off in church, and it just hit me like, dude, you gotta abide. That's what it is. It's Jesus."

After Crossfire finished his verse, lush gospel-inspired harmonies swooped in to sing the final chorus on Hip Hopposite's instrumental track:

> I'm on the road to Zion where freedom rings on every hand
> Where there's a king named Martin and he's with his wife again

The bodies of Hip Hopposite glided across the small stage against the folds of a burgundy velvet curtain, traversing the very grounds where a Western Surplus gun store once stood, where rioters protested the police beating of Rodney King, and where the fires of destruction made way for this performance of hip hop praise. A meditative hush came over the crowd at Love and Faith Christian Center as the colorful tiled mosaic lion on the exterior of the building kept watch just beyond the walls of the sanctuary. In that moment, Dr. King's vision did not feel like a lost dream.

BROTHERS IN BABYLON

It was while standing next to the members of the Hip Hopposite collective that I first heard a Christian rap re-versioning of Nas's 1994 hip hop hit, "The World Is Yours." Nas, an MC from Queensbridge, New York, released the song on his breakout album, *Illmatic*. The hook of the song features a haunting piano progression over which Nas raps, "Whose world is this? The world is yours. The world is yours. It's mine, it's mine, it's mine. Whose world is this?" In this gospel rap version, the lyrics were changed to "The world is the Lord's." Listening to this spiritual remix, I was reminded of another pop culture quest for Zion—Damian Marley and Nas's 2005 collaboration, "Road to Zion."

Nas himself, like Cue, has stood at multiple religious crossroads. His music evokes the names of Jesus, Jah, and Allah as he positions himself simultaneously as both saint and sinner, *God's Son* (2002) and *Street's Disciple* (2004). The latter features twenty-seven tracks, just as the New Testament has twenty-seven chapters, and the cover artwork depicts Nas playing every role in the Last Supper. When asked about his main religious influences as a child, he answered, "I was surrounded by Christians . . . my grandmothers, all my family was from the South, Baptist. As I got older I got into the 5 Percent Nation, and then that pushed me toward Islam. But I'm not any religion . . . I know there's a higher power."[12]

If Nas were to rap about his own road to Zion, it would reveal a complicated navigation through multiple routes of black religiosity. His collaboration with Damian "Jr. Gong" Marley on "Road to Zion" is an exploration of Rastafarian ideas, practices, and symbols as it exposes the oppressive systems of police brutality, political dictatorship, hypermaterialism, and the prison industrial complex. Jr. Gong wails the lyrics of the hook, "I got to keep on walking on the road to Zion, man. We gots to keeps it burning on the road to Zion, man," Twenty five years earlier, Damian's father, Bob Marley a.k.a "Tuff Gong," recorded the song "Zion Train" a year before his death, in which he belts out, "Soul train is coming our way. Zion train is coming our way. Oh people, get on board!" The song also links to the American jazz standard tradition as it contains a looped sample from Ella Fitzgerald's 1958 recording of "Russian Lullaby." Ella's fluttering, melancholic hum undulates over a nostalgic harp arpeggio and a quintessentially four-beat hip hop rhythm. The original lyrics of this Irving Berlin classic also gesture toward a Zion of sorts:

> Somewhere there may be
> A land that's free for you and me

Irving Berlin, born Israel Baline to a Jewish cantor in a synagogue in imperial Russia, wrote the song in reflection of his family's quick escape to the United States in 1893 after their house was burned to the ground as part of the anti-Jewish pogroms initiated by Nicholas II, the new tsar of Russia. Ian Whitcomb describes their escape: "the Balines smuggled themselves creepingly from town to town, from satellite to satellite, from sea to shining sea, until finally they reached their star: the Statue of Liberty."[13] Always inflecting a veneer of patriotism in his songs, Berlin's Zion—"A land that's free for you and me"—was America. But Jr. Gong and Nas are more explicit in their critique of imperialism and do not offer a clear definition of Zion land, instead painting a picture of multiple Babylons.

In Rastafarian culture, Zion usually refers to the "Promised Land" of Ethiopia or the African continent more generally. But Nas's verse does not figure Africa as a utopian destination. He talks about feeling so "haunted" and "helpless" about what he sees in the world that he's "havin' daymares in the daytime." Nas elaborates on this "daymare":

> Human beings like ghost and zombies
> President Mugabe holding guns to innocent bodies in Zimbabwe[14]

Robert Mugabe, in power since 1980 when Rhodesia officially became Zimbabwe, has often been accused of conducting a "reign of terror" throughout the country.[15] Linking forms and instances of domestic and international violence, the specter of police brutality also haunts the track with Damian Marley's repeated warnings, "And police weh abuse dem authority." Nas enforces the point, "And badges screamin' at young black children stop or I will shoot." Their performance connects the terrors inflicted on black bodies and sounds multiple searches for black liberation in Babylon from Marley's Jamaica to Mugabe's Zimbabwe to Nas's New York.

The music video, filmed with Marley and Nas in Kew Gardens—an ethnically diverse neighborhood in Queens, New York, with significant immigrant populations from Latin America, Guyana, the Middle East (especially Israel), South Asia, and East Asia—features cameos from hip hop artists as well as an appearance by funk icon George Clinton. Connecting the dots, it is not hard to imagine Clinton climbing aboard his Zion Train, the Mothership, toward outer space—the only place he could truly envision freedom in a 1970s United States still wrought with deep racial and economic injustice. The map grows larger when we consider the namesake of this New York neighborhood—the Royal Botanic Gardens at Kew, an important epicenter of colonial curiosity and power, housing exotic plant specimens taken from Britain's colonies around the world. Nas and Marley, whose lives and ancestries have both been shaped by histories of British colonialism, would rearticulate this bond musically in their 2010 dub-rock/hip hop collaboration under the album title *Distant Relatives*—a name that resonates equally with Black Nationalist sensibilities and Black Atlantic circulations. As Jaji argues, "music has quite literally *rehearsed* transnational black solidarity emerging simultaneously in literature, film, and other cultural domains."[16]

In the "Road to Zion" video, Damian Marley wheels a cart of books down a cell block corridor and then passes a card to Nas through the steel bars of a prison cell. On the card is the Lion of Judah—the same lion pictured on the flag of Ethiopia, an image often used in Rastafarian culture. One interpretation of this scene would be that Jah or Rastafari is his escape route, his ticket to freedom, his "Road to Zion." In the Rastafari movement, the Lion of Judah is Emperor Haile Selassie I of Ethiopia, crowned eighty-three years ago with the titles King of Kings, Lord of Lords, Conquering Lion of Judah, Defender of the Judean faith, and the Light of the World. Rastas believe that Haile Selassie is a direct descendent of the Israelite Tribe of Judah through the lineage of King David and Solomon, and that he is also the Lion of Judah mentioned in the Book of Genesis.

Given the religious pluralism (if not confusion) expressed in Nas's music, the Lion of Judah he holds in his hand could resonate equally with the Rastafarian Movement and Christianity. In the Christian tradition, the Lion of Judah represents the triumphant Jesus who was from the tribe of Judah as is mentioned in Revelation. It is not uncommon for Christian organizations and ministries to use the Lion of Judah as their emblem or even their name, as is the case with the Love and Faith Christian Center.

LIONS IN ZION

Another Lion has been stalking hip hop's diverse religious crossroads. Born Cordozar Calvin Broadus Jr. in 1971 in Long Beach, Snoop Dogg grew up singing gospel music and playing the piano at the Golgotha Trinity Baptist Church. In sixth grade, he began rapping, developing that syncopated, laidback, molasses drawl that has become his signature sound. At the time that he was discovered by Dr. Dre in 1992, Snoop was thought to be a member of the Rollin' 20 Crips gang in the eastside of Long Beach, lending an authentic air to Dre's solo debut album, *The Chronic*, with lyrics laced with tales of street violence, gangsterism, and misogynist conquests. The following year, Snoop dropped his debut, *Doggystyle*, under Death Row Records. Scaling the *Billboard* 200 and *Billboard* Top R&B/Hip-Hop Albums charts to number one, the album sold almost a million copies in the first week of its release, became certified 4x platinum in 1994 and spawned several megahits, including "What's My Name?" and "Gin & Juice." While Snoop is best known for his myriad commercial successes, jail sentences (mainly for the possession and selling of drugs), references to cannabis consumption, and creative slang inventions, I am more interested in his diverse religious forays and incarnations as well as the ways in which his pursuit of spiritual salvation is deeply entangled with his professional and social aspirations.

It was in 2012 that Snoop Dogg announced his turn toward the Rastafarian way following a visit to Jamaica. After decades of making some of the most violent and misogynist gangsta rap, he sought a new path of peace and love. "I want to go to the White House," Snoop lamented in the documentary *Reincarnated* that chronicled his journey to Jamaica, "but what the fuck can I perform? All my songs are too hard."[17] In addition to recording a reggae-inspired album of the same name that featured Diplo, Drake, Miley Cyrus, Akon, and Rita Ora, among others, Snoop's pilgrimage to the heart of Rasta involved a visit to Tuff Gong studios, a walk through Trenchtown's western ghettos, and conversations with Rastafarian elders, including Bunny Wailer—the only remaining member of the Wailers. It was during a Rastafarian purification ceremony at a Nyabinghi temple that Snoop was rechristened Snoop Lion by a Rasta priest, his signature gangsta ruff (bow wow wow) ostensibly transforming into a regal Rasta roar.

Bob Marley, whom Snoop considers himself a reincarnation of, sang often of the "lion of Zion," referring to Haile Selassie in Ethiopia. Snoop Lion's Jamaican journey sounded these global connections as it simultaneously portrayed Kingston as a kind of Zion and Los Angeles as a Babylon, especially in light of the harsh realities of L.A.'s postindustrial landscapes, racial segregations, policing practices, and pop culture excesses. While Snoop Lion's recent reggae offerings have been widely critiqued on both their religious and aesthetic merits, his *Reincarnated* was nominated for the 2013 Grammy for Reggae Album of the Year.

During Snoop's visit with Bunny Wailer, the reggae legend donned a sweatband bearing the symbol of the Lion of Judah. Snoop blessed Bunny with some "Cali herbs" as they smoked a "chalice" together. Bunny prayed for Snoop's soul through the power of Selassie in the hopes that LBC rapper's adoption of the Rastafari faith wouldn't become too "commercialized." As it happens, the *Reincarnated* film features abundant product placement for Adidas, which sponsors Snoop and which kicked in money for the budget, according to a member of Snoop's management team. Upon seeing the film, Bunny, like many other Snoop fans and detractors, was critical of Snoop's conversion from hardcore gangsta rapper to enlightened reggae singer[18] and eventually "excommunicated" Snoop from Rastafari (on Facebook) for "outright fraudulent use of Rastafari Community's personalities and symbolism."[19] Snoop struck back in an interview with *Rolling Stone*: "It's like, people take my kindness for weakness. In the Nineties, Bunny could have never tried that because I'd have slapped the dog shit out of his old ass." But he ended his rant on a softer note: "Bunny, keep your head up. Jah bless; wisdom; guidance and protection."[20]

Bunny isn't the first spiritual advisor from whom Snoop has sought guidance. Years earlier, Snoop received counsel from his then spiritual advisor, former pimp-turned-preacher Don Magic Juan, who made a cameo on Snoop's hit single, "From tha Chuuuch to da Palace" in 2002. Snoop also visited the Honorable Louis Farrakhan at his home, commenting that Farrakhan was one of the few black leaders that supported him and fellow gangsta artists. In 1999, after Notorious B.I.G. was murdered in Los Angeles, Snoop put a call out to Minister James who then called Minister Farrakhan to hold a gathering of rappers to address the deadly nature of the East/West feud. Snoop recalled that day at the Nation of Islam Savior's Day event in Chicago on March 1, 2009: "we ended all of our beef and there was love and we've been living that way every since. Nobody ever really gave Minister Farrakhan credit for that." In that same year, it was reported that Snoop Dogg was a member of the Nation of Islam, donating a thousand dollars to the organization.[21]

Snoop's intertwined voicings of God, gangsta, Nation of Islam, Rasta, and reggae articulate a diasporic black religious pluralism. His varied musical and spiritual transformations return us to the original themes of black conversion and liberation set out at the beginning of the this book. His story reveals how he is both a highly localized product and expression of Long Beach City and a diasporic symbol of multiple black Americas. His dream to visit the White House, an ironic Zion of sorts for the gangsta rapper–turned-Rasta, finally came true in 2013, when he was invited to perform at the 36th Annual Kennedy Center Honors for Herbie Hancock.

Despite his previous lament that his hip hop songs were "too hard" for the White House, Snoop returned to his early gangsta rap sound. He donned a velvety tux while gripping a blinged-out microphone bearing his most common moniker: Snoop Dogg. In front of President Obama and the First Lady, he performed a version of the 1992 classic "Gin & Juice" over Us3's "Cantaloop (Flip Fantasia)"—an acid-jazz-rap remake of Herbie Hancock's "Cantaloupe Island." It was vintage Snoop with a few choice lyrical omissions and politically correct revisions, reincarnating himself on another island. He even got political elites, including Michelle Obama, to "Hey Ho!" along with him with waving arms and all. Afterward, Snoop humbly turned to Hancock and shouted, "Thank you for creating hip hop."

. . .

In another instance of the Jamaica–Los Angeles connection, I encountered the "Snoop Dogg of Gospel Rap" one night on the stage of Klub Zyon and across the way from a storefront Jamaican restaurant in Leimert Park. Majesty Moore, an African American female gospel rapper in her late thirties, flowed with the regal poise of a lioness over hip hop instrumentals in a smooth, understated yet potent style, reminiscent of the singsong-like quality of Snoop. I met up with Majesty about a week later on another hot and smoggy summer day in the historic black arts district of Leimert Park. We sat down at a small table on the patio of Fifth Street Dick's Coffee and Jazz Emporium across the street from the parking lot that houses the weekly Leimert Park Village flea market. A well-known hub for jazz music, Fifth Street Dick's was founded by Richard Fulton in 1991 after he was homeless for four years on the streets of L.A. and just before the 1992 riots broke out. The logo for the coffeehouse was a homeless man pushing an overflowing shopping cart—a reminder of and homage to his former life.

It was in that small storefront I learned that Majesty was originally born in Berkeley in the 1970s, where her parents were involved with the Black Panther Party. She later moved with her mom to South Los Angeles, but her dad stayed behind in Oakland and remained active in the Party. She met fellow gospel rapper Khanchuz while attending Westwood Avenue Elementary. "We were the sandbox kids," she recalled. "I knew him before he started doing holy hip hop. You should have heard some of his raps back then! You would have been scared!"[22]

In Los Angeles, Majesty's family explored and studied different religions together. "We studied with Jehovah's Witnesses. We studied with Mormons. We studied with Catholics, Lutherans, and then we studied with Christ. That was just people trying to find their way in life—which way to go—as everybody does. It was a journey and I was on a quest." She then paused in silence for minute, looking dissatisfied with this particular recounting of her journey to Christ and gospel hip hop. "Let me start my life story over for you," she continued:

> When I was leaving heaven, God said, I have a task for someone to do on earth. And of all the angels, nobody responded, 'cause usually they just raise their hand, saying, "I'll go, I'll go, I'll go do that task." But no one raised their hand on this task. None of the angels wanted to go and do this task. So, finally after a little while, I said, "I'll go." And I got these instructions, but these instructions were . . . I knew but I didn't know. It was like hidden. So when I was leaving, all the angels in heaven started crying because they didn't know if I was going to make it back to heaven again because when you leave heaven you don't know if you're gonna make it back. You have to make a choice, you gotta make a decision. And the devil is here to keep you from doing that. When I got to the earth, the devil was trying to kill me. I got a rap like that. It goes . . .

> The devil's trying to kill me. What did I do wrong?
> Is it because I praise the most high when I sing my song
> I trust no man, fear no man or woman
> on my journey through the land
> slow motion coasting on the waves of the ocean
> Elohim the grand king is hosting, we floating
> I boasting the most honorable only one
> put me down top gun now I blast y'all town

ever since I left heaven they be missing me
waiting on my safe return I must fulfill my mission see
I've been through a lot on my days on earth G
I came too far to turn back I'm in the place to be
serving lyrical pharmaceuticals on these streets
everybody know my name but ain't nobody know me
and you ain't never shot the breeze with me but you claiming you
    my homies
see I've been walking to and fro the valley of death, man
get lost in the worldliness well that's what's next, man[23]

Majesty's rap faded off as her eyes wandered across Leimert Park Village, seemingly getting lost in the world(liness) again. She then leapt back into her story abruptly: "So when I got here, when I finally reached the earth, the devil's been trying to kill me. From day one. But I'm not even going to go into all that." Our conversation went on for over an hour. Majesty shared more of her rap lyrics, but she never returned to this supernatural level of autobiographical testifying.[24] Nor did she end up telling me all the practical details of her life. Those details, she told me, were for the book that she intends to someday write about her own life story. In a parting declaration, she uttered, "I'm here to win souls for Christ *by all means necessary.*" In this one turn of phrase, Majesty conjured Malcolm X's well-known Black Power slogan, "Liberate our minds *by any means necessary,*" and rapper KRS-One's nod to Malcolm's legacy in his 1998 album title, *By All Means Necessary.* The album cover displays KRS-One, in baseball cap and dark shades, recreating the notorious photograph of Malcolm X holding a M1 Carbine assault rifle and peering out of a window—an image originally published in the September 1964 issue of *Ebony* magazine.[25] In that instant, her conversion narrative came full circle, from her early years raised under Black Panthers to her militant, Malcolm-inspired brand of gospel rap street evangelism.

HOLY HIP HOP'S AMERICAS

Houston-born Christian rap star Lecrae Devaughn Moore not only shares the same last name as Majesty, but was also raised by a single mother in a politically militant household informed by Civil Rights and Black Power politics. His mother politicized him at an early age, encouraging him to take pride in his racial identity. Lecrae remembers wearing Malcolm X hats and African medallions while sneaking off to his grandmother's house to watch rap videos. Known as "Crazy 'Crae" during his teenage years, he turned to a life of crime, stealing, and dealing drugs with his grandmother's Bible at his side as a good luck charm. At age seventeen, Lecrae hit a dead end and began attending church at his grandmother's request. But it was a performance by the Philadelphia-based Christian rap group Cross

Movement that made him realize he could be Christian and also maintain who he was culturally as *hip hop*. On his ride home, he made a quick turn on the highway, causing his car to roll, the roof to cave in, and windshield to shatter into pieces. In what should have been a fatal accident, Lecrae survived uninjured. He then committed his life to Christ, converting his smashed automobile into his Zion Train toward a new life.[26]

Now president, co-founder, and co-owner of the independent gospel record label Reach Records, Lecrae has released seven studio albums and two mixtapes as a solo Christian hip hop artist. Winner of two Grammy's and seven Dove Awards, Lecrae's music has been endorsed by many professional athletes, including former Los Angeles Laker and current Brooklyn Net Jeremy Lin, who claimed Lecrae was a staple in his pregame music mix. On his 2014 track, "Welcome to America," Lecrae unveils three Americas in three verses: one from his own perspective, one from a war veteran, and one from an immigrant. In the first verse, he raps:

> Uh, I was made in America, land of the free, home of the brave
> And right up under your nose you might see a sex slave being traded

He bemoans that in America, people "will do anything for money." As he attacks these lyrics with his usual gravitas, images of iconic American scenes bleed together: buildings ablaze in a riot, people gambling at casinos, brass bands blowing in the streets, soldiers lining in formation, subway trains bolting through underground tunnels, police arresting youth of color, and a homeless man holding out his paper cup. This is a far cry from Irving Berlin's invocation of America as the "land of the free" in "Russian Lullaby," and instead more aligned with the "daymares" experienced in Nas's depictions of American city life. And like Nas, Lecrae also lyrically leaps across the Atlantic to link local American realities with global African histories.

> I was born in the mainland; great-grandpa from a strange land
> He was stripped away and given bricks to lay

While Lecrae may feel estranged from Africa as he "was made in America," his enslaved great-grandfather connects him ancestrally to the continent—a truth he has tried to understand since a youth sporting African medallions. Sonically, Africa subtly pulses through the track as a chanted refrain—"Ta na na na muchawa, ta na na na muchawa"—projecting the continent as a diasporic source rather than an active participant in diasporic processes. A descending piano bass line enters to anchor a driving, syncopated, Southern hip hop bounce beat accented by timbale and cymbal hits. The music video fades to black on an image of the Statue of Liberty. Can Lecrae's Zion be found in this "home of the brave"?

Lecrae again questioned the state of America during his spoken word performance at the 2016 BET Hip Hop Awards. Weaving references to Donald Trump's presidential campaign, the Black Lives Matter movement, private-for-profit prisons, and cultural appropriation, Lecrae professed that he refuses to be silent. With a clear and forceful delivery, he began his spoken word poem with the line, "They tellin' us 'Make America Great Again,'" but then fervently questioned, "When was America great again?"

NO ZION

Seven years earlier, Lecrae reached out to platinum-selling, Grammy Award–winning, Compton-born rapper Kendrick Lamar after hearing the song "Faith" from Lamar's self-titled 2009 EP. The lyrics had deeply touched Lecrae and he wanted to find out more about what prompted Lamar to compose this track. The two rappers, who appear to occupy separate territories of hip hop—"secular" and "sacred"—communed over their shared tribulations as believers in the world of hip hop. Lecrae and Lamar also shared the same stage at the 2016 BET Hip Hop Awards during which Lamar was awarded "Lyricist of the Year." He also presented the "I Am Hip Hop Icon Award" to none other than Snoop Dogg—geographies of gospel and gangsta coming full circle.

Similar in structure to Lecrae's "Welcome to America," Lamar's track "Faith" features three verses from the perspective of different people struggling to maintain their faith in God despite the challenges life doles out on a daily basis. Known for his sepulchral soliloquies of the violent and unforgiving gang territories of the South L.A. that birthed him, Lamar wrestles with the real-life murder of his friend at the end of the first verse. From his release of *Good Kid, m.A.A.d. City* in 2012—after which he underwent a baptism on tour with Kanye West—to his 2017 album *DAMN*, Christian themes of good and evil, heaven and hell, apocalypse and afterlife continue to permeate Lamar's gritty reflections on black life in the City of Angels.[27] In a 2015 *Billboard* interview, Lamar commented, "We're in the last days, man—I truly in my heart believe that. It's written."[28]

Lamar sounds out the hellish landscape of these "last days" in his 2010 track "Heaven and Hell." He raps about racism and AIDS, police brutality, oil spills, burning buildings, hostages in Afghanistan, child molestation, and "earthquakes that's government tested" over a multilayered mix of melodic riffs punctuated by hard-knocking snare hits. Offering a final gloss on Hell—"No place to live in, no Zion, see that's forbidden, we frying"—Lamar then pivots toward Heaven. His Promised Land conjures an assemblage of sounds—musical, spiritual, and joyful:

> Malcolm laughing, Martin laughing, Biggie spittin, Pac is rappin,
>   Gregory tappin
> People singing, bells is ringing, children playing, angels praying

But his heavenly chorus fades away as the volume is turned down on his vocals and the listener is left with over a minute of instrumentals to ponder the departure of this divine sonic geography.

At the 2016 Grammy Music Awards, Lamar performed "The Blacker the Berry" and "Alright"—a rallying song for the Black Lives Matter movement—from his 2015 album *To Pimp a Butterfly*. Shackled in chains and donning a distinctive jailhouse-blue uniform, he shuffled onto a stage set that resembled a prison. The set then transformed into an African village scene with West African drummers and dancers moving in front of a raging bonfire. As Lamar broke free of the chain gang and staggered across the stage, he rapped, "I'm African American; I'm African." The third act concluded with Lamar rhyming topics from Trayvon Martin to struggles with sobriety to questions about how to use his fame for good. Traveling down the corridors of violence, shame, anger, and anxiety, Lamar declared, "I'm on a path with my Bible." The performance ended with Lamar's silhouette against an outline of the continent of Africa with the word "Compton" emblazoned in its center. Lamar seemed to be saying, "This is my Los Angeles."

What does it mean for the Compton MC, who recently received a key to his city, to traverse the stages of black incarceration and liberation (with his Bible)—to unlock and release Compton within Africa? Lamar's sonic and visual conversion of Compton into an African nation gestures, once again, toward Los Angeles as a geography of mobility and transformation under the shadow of apocalypse. Despite the somewhat primitivist depiction of the African village setting, Lamar's performance called attention to the ways that current racial realities are linked to oppressions and injustices that have plagued people of African descent for hundreds of years. Perhaps we (still) *frying* in the fires of Babylon. And fires, like earthquakes, generate destruction as well as the conditions of possibility for new creation.

. . .

Following these musical tracks to and through multiple Babylons and Zions, many places are made audible: Oakland, Watts, Queens, Russia, Jamaica, Zimbabwe, Long Beach City, Berkeley, Leimert Park, Houston, and Compton. Holy hip hop in Los Angeles, while a highly localized and subcultural expression, is enmeshed in a global, multivoiced cacophony of black soundings that underscores religious and social ruptures as well as transatlantic solidarities. Ruptures, despite their inherent violence, produce transformative mixtures and amalgamations. And so an important irony emerges: that something as seemingly niche as gospel rap has become a potent crossroads of black musical diversity and Afro-diasporic religious pluralism.[29] In this way, I have attempted to move discussions of black Christianity beyond a nationalist framing and beyond the thoroughly studied "black church tradition" in an effort to explore religion as a complex social, spatial, and cultural terrain.

The sound stories relayed in this concluding chapter assemble racial, religious, and musical geographies as they reveal the complex proximities of Christianity, Islam, and the Rastafarian movement in the lives of holy hip hoppers and "secular" hip hoppers alike, challenging these religious categories as uniform and fixed. These artists chose hip hop to express something that only music could communicate. What emerges is the audible interpenetration of Zion and Babylon, of Heaven and Hell, of freedom dreams and "daymares," of Martin and Malcolm, of Jesus and Jah Rastafari, of Africa and America. I weave this hip hop mix not simply to insist on black religious, political, and musical modernity as hybridity, but to illustrate how holy hip hop articulates a diasporic black pluralism that highlights the spiritual ambivalences and powerful possibilities of conversion. Redemptive practices become revolutionary acts. Deep social rifts trigger healing hip hop riffs.

Across the pages of the entire book, conversion emerges as a collective social project among the victims of organized abandonment to "save" the city by performing music that brings wholeness, holiness, and hope. I have described how a subset of black Angelenos use hip hop to create lives of religious meaning and to sustain a quest for deliverance. Holy hip hoppers enact conversion as a religious transformation, a musical transposition from secular rap to gospel rap, and as a spatial tactic of creatively repurposing the urban environment. Exploring these different iterations and practices of salvation shows us how hip hop has become an idiom of widespread conversion in the midst of black millennial unrest in the twenty-first century.

Avoiding the depiction of race as a unified entity, I have situated holy hip hop within black heterogeneous neighborhoods and black cultural traffics, but also specific structures of racial formation in the late twentieth and early twenty-first centuries. At the same time, I have offered a very up-close rendering of the intertwined life stories, conversion narratives, and daily micropractices of holy hip hoppers in an attempt to get below some of these structures. Their everyday lives provide both a window into the cruel realities and pernicious tales of black victimization, incarceration, and death *and* an antidote to these highly circulated and one-sided visions of black America.

Lastly, my aim has been to study hip hop not just as a distinct musical genre, but as an intertextual nexus of musical, social, and religious practices that transforms city spaces. While holy hip hop soundings—and the new social relations they engender—continue to reverberate across Los Angeles, the spatial transformations produced through holy hip hop often leave little to no visual trace. These fleeting geographies of conversion remind us of the many black L.A.'s that have been pushed out, systematically dismantled, or rendered invisible—but not silent. They remind us how *place is sounded*. And so let this be a call not just to further examine the intersections of pop music, race, and religion, but to attune ourselves to the many "invisible churches" and musical undergrounds that hold a microphone to unsung urban soundscapes and life stories at the margins.

The search for that divine city of Zion, through music and ministry, continues to lead holy hip hoppers down many roads, precipitating unexpected journeys and interactions—missionary trips to Africa and the Caribbean, processions through the streets of downtown Los Angeles in the name of Black Lives Matter, visits to the Moorish Science Temple on Crenshaw Boulevard to build bridges with Muslim brothers, and excursions to Chicano churches in the Inland Empire. Khanchuz still records and performs gospel rap throughout the greater Los Angeles, sometimes with his daughter, Jaysha, while Cue has stepped back from music making to focus on his Skid Row ministry and social justice work. Sharon Collins-Heads still directs the Hip Hop Church L.A. out of Inglewood, which is now in its eleventh year. Hip Hopposite no longer performs together but Celah, the lead MC, is still making gospel hip hop music. Pastor Graham leads his own church in Gardena called City of the Lord. And a new cadre of young holy hip hop MCs, DJs, and pastors are being raised in the scene. They are blazing their own roads to Zion throughout the Southland, using gospel rap as a way to remap, reconnect, and remake terrains rife with social fractures. The "City of Angels" has not yet arrived, but they must keep going toward it.

Epilogue

Aftershocks

In August 2008, just days before I left Los Angeles to move to the San Francisco Bay Area, I invited gospel rappers Khanchuz and B-Love (of the Hip Hopposite collective) to perform and speak to the students in my "Cultural History of Rap" class at the University of California, Los Angeles. Khanchuz removed his sunglasses and delivered his testimony, explaining how he used to gangbang with the 51st Street Cat-Walk Neighborhood Crips (CWC) in Inglewood, landed himself in a jail cell, and eventually gave his life to Christ. To fully demonstrate this spiritual transformation, he performed two songs. The first was a gangsta rap song he wrote while at Crenshaw High School, fully loaded with explicit language and gritty tales of his daily life in the streets of Los Angeles. By way of contrast, he then rapped the lyrics to a gospel hip hop song he wrote in the early 2000s after his conversion—"All Honor to God." Zigzagging across the room with an artful swagger, he fired his lyrics out triumphantly over the maze of desks. Khanchuz closed with "ADK (Any Demon Killa)," a track that chronicles the various emergency "house calls" he makes in his Cadillac—now converted into a holy hip hop ambulance—to stomp out demonic spirits. During this spiritual triage across the city, he sends "demons to flight" every time he "picks up the mic."

As the last line of his rhyme rang out, the classroom began to shake. The music stands huddled together along the back wall rattled against each other and I quickly realized we were experiencing an earthquake. Khanchuz, rocked by the reverberations of his seismic sounding, immediately sat down in a desk chair and prayed for the safety of his family and all the students in the room. As the tremors subsided, I heard him speak quietly under his breath: "See what happens when you speak the truth?" Quickly ushering my students outside into the bright sunlight, we stood in a circle—silent—stunned by what had just happened.

The 2008 earthquake occurred at 11:42 a.m. that morning, registering a 5.5 magnitude. The epicenter of the quake was located in Chino Hills, approximately twenty-eight miles east-southeast of downtown Los Angeles. No lives were lost but it caused considerable damage in numerous structures throughout the area and forced Disneyland and Magic Mountain to shut down their rides. I thought back to when Soup the Chemist told me about the final concert of the 1995 Holy Hip Hop tour at Magic Mountain, which included himself as well as other gospel hip hop groups such as P.I.D. (Preachers in Disguise), I.D.O.L. King, and Gospel Gangstaz. Apparently, the stage started buckling as multitudes of fans climbed atop it, eventually causing the whole structure to collapse. Soup recalled, "The Holy Ghost was in the house."

I also thought back to my first interview with Pastor Graham and his now prophetic announcement of gospel hip hop as *earthquake music:* "I call it *earthquake music* because the music shakes our souls and moves the ground we walk on." Whether the tremors that day were a product of nature, culture, or the divine, holy hip hop was again at the center of a groundswelling that had resonant effects.

I walked Khanchuz and B-Love to their cars in the UCLA parking structure. B-Love sped off quickly to pick her daughter up from daycare, but Khanchuz took his time, selecting the perfect holy hip hop track to accompany him on his drive from Westwood back to Inglewood. His metallic beige Cadillac then pulled away slowly as he headed back out into the shifting grounds of Los Angeles, leaving the hard-hitting beats of gospel rap in his wake.

ACKNOWLEDGMENTS

It is with abundant gratitude and genuine humility that I thank the following individuals, communities, and institutions for their invaluable contributions to this project and the larger orbits of my work. In particular, I must acknowledge the people whose voices animate this book—the many holy hip hop and gospel rap artists, rappers, spoken word poets, singers, DJs, mothers, fathers, preachers, pastors, clergy members, fans, and congregation members who generously shared their time, stories, and music with me over the past ten years. These words, images, and sounds exist because of them and the artful labor that is their lives. They include Carol Scott, Sharon Collins-Heads, Kenny Z and Rozzie, Kurtis Blow, Soup the Chemist, Sean and Simone Heads, Candace Jordan, Pastor Graham, Khanchuz, Purpose, Cue, Revelation, Majesty, John (a.k.a. Johnny Cash), Ikem, the Hip Hopposite crew—Celah, Crossfire, Sound Doctrine, DJ Heat, and B-Love, Slack of I.D.O.L. King, Pigeon John, the members of L.A. Symphony, DJ Technoforce, Young Chozen, Holy D, TrippL-H of G-Boy Union, Noah from the Hip Hop Church in Harlem, MC Ghandhi, Methuzelah, PK 1000's, and Jupiter 8. I am also grateful to all the folks at Holy Trinity, Club Judah, and Club Zyon who allowed me to document the many nights of music making and spirit seeking.

A few holy hip hoppers deserve special shout-outs; their words, prayers, and music have shaped this book in profound ways. Thanks to B-Love for her sisterly insights and sharing the gospel at UCLA and Pepperdine University. Barbados big-ups to Cue for his fierce honesty and trickster nature as well as for putting the "hustle" in evangelism. It is from my heart that I give extra huge praise to Khanchuz, who shared his story, his music, and his ministry so courageously. I must also thank him for reading several chapters and giving them his A.D.K. (Any

Demon Killa) stamp of approval. I am forever indebted to Sharon Collins-Heads, director of the Hip Hop Church L.A., who read and gave critical feedback on chapter 2. I thank her for believing in this research and allowing me into her life during a difficult time.

Chapters 3 and 4 began as dissertation chapters. Special thanks to my dissertation committee members Timothy Taylor, Anthony Seeger, Christopher Waterman, and my advisor Cheryl Keyes. Portions of chapter 3 appear in an article entitled "Building 'Zyon' in Babylon: Holy Hip Hop and Geographies of Conversion," published in a special edition of *Black Music Research Journal* 31, no. 2 (2010): 145–62. Thanks to Jacqueline Cogdell DjeDje, who edited the volume. Several sections of chapter 4 appear in an article entitled "Kingdom Business: Holy Hip Hop's Evangelical Hustle," published in *Journal of Popular Music Studies* 24, no. 2 (2012): 196–216.

In Los Angeles, I benefited from the support of many different UCLA entities: the Institute of American Cultures, the Ralph J. Bunche Center for African American Studies, and the Institute for Social Research. Timothy Rice, Steve Loza, Roger Savage, Tara Browner, A. J. Racy, and Helen Rees provided critical wisdom and assistance during my time in Los Angeles. Thanks to H. Samy Alim for his mentorship during the early stages of this research and for providing the invaluable space of the UCLA Graduate Working Group in Hip Hop Cultural Studies.

At home in the Bay Area, I have also been surrounded by a dynamic community of UC Berkeley professors. Thanks to Jocelyne Guilbault for support and mentorship. In particular, I clap my hands (Shona-style) to Donald Moore for the precise clarity, intelligence, and empathy of his Seeing through some difficult times and territories of suffering. I am deeply grateful for his critical insights on portions of this book and for the unique "ethics of care" he has shown my family over the years. Similarly, I must thank Jake Kosek for his friendship, keen advice, and feedback on the initial book proposal. Our shared East Bay communities and complex yet parallel familial (under)stories provide serious solidarity. To Leigh Raiford and Michael Cohen (who gave much needed feedback on the introduction), thanks for modeling what badass scholars and parents look like. And while I'm acknowledging my Berkeley brethren, I must offer thanks to Jeff Chang, who also offered feedback on portions of this work.

To the NYU professors who precipitated this ethnomusicological ride—Gage Averill, Jason King, Mercedes Dujunco, and Michael Dinwiddie—I offer my sincere and humble thanks for your early inspiration and encouragement. Jason King and his courses on R&B and hip hop are, in many ways, responsible for igniting the early passions that led to this work. To my fellow singers in the NYU All-University Gospel Choir, I thank you for the many nights and mornings of song that led to my initial encounter with gospel hip hop. Remembering musical teachers and experiences from a younger age, I must also acknowledge Doug Goodkin, who opened up many worlds of music for me.

I am beholden to my dear colleagues and comrades—now scattered across the globe—whose solidarity, friendship, and advice have carried me across many thresholds. They include Jooyoung Lee, Loren Kajikawa, Jordan Smith, Catherine Appert, Birgitta Johnson, Abimbola Cole, Selina Traylor, Sabrina Rodriguez, Ben Harbert, Beto Gonzalez, Chris Aplin, Daniel Hodge, Naomi Bragin, Jelani Mahiri, Tony Perman, and Marié Abe.

More recent thanks to those who have stepped up this past year to read and reflect on the manuscript. Gratitude to Matt Sakakeeny for mega support, second-line tips, and shared Nola networks. Humble thanks to Eileen Hayes. "Crazy Prayze" to George Lipsitz. Southland shout-outs to Oliver Wang. Martin Daughtry, thank you for last-minute heroics. And special "non-stop" thanks to Josh Jelly-Shapiro for his brilliant editorial eye and for encouraging me to write "beyond the academy." I'm grateful for our past collaborations and future projects that continue to chart and connect intersecting black star lines.

Staff, faculty, and students at Santa Clara University have provided assistance throughout the bookwriting. Thanks to the SCU Dean's Office and Provost's Office for fellowships that made the writing and "Earthquake Music" map possible. To my Music Department colleagues—Teresa McCollough, Hans Boepple, Nancy Wait-Kromm, Bruno Ruviaro, Alex Christie, Bill Stevens, John Kennedy, and Scot Hanna-Weir—thank you for your support, creativity, collaborative spirit, and good humor. To my Ethnic Studies and "Culture Power Difference" (CPD) Working Group colleagues—Tony Hazard, Courtney Mohler, Cruz Medina, Allia Griffin, Christine Montgomery, Tobias Woodford, Aldo Billingslea, James Lai, and Anna Sampaio—you keep things at SCU moving in the right directions. Special thanks to the formidable Dr. Hazard for helpful comments and happy hours.

Thanks to those at UC Press and beyond who shepherded this book through to publication: Raina Polivka, Zuha Khan, Aimée Goggins, Kate Warne, Paul Tyler, Paige MacKay, and Kevin Millham. Big shout-outs to my series editors, Guthrie Ramsey and Shana Redmond, for their backing and insights. Guy's belief in this project blazed the trail. To Molly Roy, thank you for your cartographic brilliance and artistry. You brought *earthquake music* to visual life.

To my flamenco comadres y compadres, muchísimas gracias for *duende* nights and for keeping my feet dancing throughout the many hours of writing: Melissa, Anya, Nadia, Rebecca, Yeshi, Masako, Mikelle, Laura, Molly, Lauren, Damien, Carola, Bianca, Paloma, Mareni, Nina, Valentino, David, Gopal, Azriel, and Itamar. Serious gratitude to Anya de Marie for bibliographic prowess and soulful flamenca sisterhood.

Thanks to my wise womenfolk, Kate Levitt, Raya Dueñas, and Courtney Martin, for empathetic witnessing, deep conversation, and tender care. I've needed your "Real Love" just to "Get By." To Sam Arkin, thank you for thoughtful edits and lifelong friendship, from "Nobilis" to drumming sessions in the midnight hour. Thanks to Michael Meade for mythic musings and Louis Rodriguez for profound poetry—both of which grace these pages.

Finally, to my large and extended family—the Zanfagnas, McLains, Dooreses, Di Leonardos, Chapins, Brigidis, Townsends, and Allards—I can never offer enough thanks. To my father and mother, Michael Zanfagna and Jenny McLain-Doores, who have taught me—with heart and flare—how to make art out of life, thank you for your fierce love. Gratitude to Amy for her constant championing and to Step Freddy for his constant wordplay. To my brother, Sam Doores, thank you for your music, wit, and warmth, but most importantly, for singing with me along the way. Thank you to my little sis, Sofia, for making a wish on a lucky three-leaf clover in 2009 that I would finish the dissertation, which led to this book. Abundant gratitude to Susan and Roger Sawley for their rocksteady support and devotion. To Ella and Pepukai, who have provided a necessary and joyous distraction from all things "work," thank you for your unbridled laughter, flashes of spirit, and loving embraces. May you transform the challenges, paradoxes, and uncertainties of your many worlds into a beautiful music. Lastly, always, and forever, I offer loving thanks to Duncan Allard for his unconventional wisdom, deep listening, and unyielding love. Thank you, steady drummer, for marking the mundane and magical moments with me. Thank you, noble piper, for keeping the wind in my sails.

INTRODUCTION

EPIGRAPH Quote from a speech by Frederick Douglass about the meaning of the Fourth of July. Frederick Douglass, *My Bondage and My Freedom* (Auburn, NY: Miller, Orton, and Mulligan, 1857), 444.

1. Here, I am riffing on Tricia Rose's historic 1994 monograph on the emergence of hip hop culture, *Black Noise: Rap Music and Black Culture in Contemporary America* (Hanover, NH, and London: Wesleyan University Press, 1994).

2. I will use the terms holy hip hop, gospel rap, gospel hip hop, and Christian rap interchangeably throughout the book.

3. Bakari Kitwana narrowly defines the Hip-Hop Generation (HHG) as African Americans born between 1965 and 1984. Bakari Kitwana, *The Hip Hop Generation: Young Blacks and the Crisis in African-American Culture* (New York: BasicCivitas Books, 2002). Jeff Chang says the HHG begins with DJ Kool Herc and Afrika Bambaataa, includes "anyone who is down," and ends "when the next generation tells us it's over." Jeff Chang, *Don't Stop Won't Stop: A History of the Hip-Hop Generation* (New York: St. Martin's Press, 2005), 2.

4. Josef Sorett has argued that for most of hip hop's life span, Islam and its various sects and offshoots (e.g., Five Percent Nation, Nation of Islam, Sunni, etc.) have comprised the main religious currents within hip hop. In particular, Five Percenter rap artists on the East Coast such as Rakim, Big Daddy Kane, Gangstarr, Brand Nubian, Poor Righteous Teachers, and eventually Wu Tang Clan became very commercially successful in the 1980s and '90s. While Islam continues to be a critical component of global hip hop cultures and soundscapes, the Five Percent Nation does not have the stronghold it once had within commercially successful hip hop. This is in part due to the rise of hip hop cultures and markets located outside the New York City and East Coast milieu—namely the West Coast and Southern hip hop scenes, which include more Christian members. Josef Sorett, "'Believe

Me, This Pimp Game Is Very Religious': Toward a Religious History of Hip Hop," *Culture and Religion* 10.1 (2009): 11–22. Further, Felicia Miyakawa points toward September 11 and the articulation of "Islam as terror" as precipitating a major shift in the *visibility* of Islam within hip hop. Muslim artists have found new ways to encode and submerge their religious commitments in an environment that is often skeptical of and hostile toward Islam, whereas explicit references to Christianity have become more frequent. Felicia Miyakawa, *Five Percenter Rap: God Hop's Music, Message, and Black Muslim Mission* (Bloomington: Indiana University Press, 2005).

5. Mike Davis, *City of Quartz: Excavating the Future in Los Angeles* (New York: Vintage, 1992), 284.

6. Ibid., 268.

7. These numbers refer to magnitudes based on Richter scale measurements, which quantify the energy released by an earthquake. Developed in the 1930s, Richter scale measurements are taken with a seismometer according to the base-10 logarithmic scale.

8. According to reports, the 1992 conflict was significantly more violent than the 1965 uprisings in Watts. There were 53 documented deaths, 2,383 injuries, and 16,000 arrests. Josh Sides, *L.A. City Limits: African American Los Angeles from the Great Depression to the Present* (Berkeley: University of California Press, 2003), 203.

9. As reported in Mike Davis's *Ecologies of Fear: Los Angeles and the Imagination of Disaster* (New York: Metropolitan Books, 1998), 7.

10. I draw from Donald Moore's reading and expansion of Deleuze and Guattari's use of the terms assemblages. Moore argues that "*assemblages* displace humans as the sovereign makers of history. Humans are not the only entities making mixtures not of their own choosing … Assemblages arrange provisionally, giving emergent force to contingent alignments of social relations, material substance, and cultural meaning." Donald Moore, *Suffering for Territory: Race, Place, and Power in Zimbabwe* (Durham, NC: Duke University Press, 2005), 23–24.

11. Here, I am moving from Stuart Hall's assertion that "Cultural strategies … can shift the balance of power." Stuart Hall, "What Is This Black in Black Popular Culture?" in *Black Popular Culture*, ed. Gina Dent and Michele Wallace (Seattle: Bay Press, 1992), 24.

12. Mike Davis referred to Fontana as a "Junkyard of Dreams" in chapter 7 of *City of Quartz*.

13. According to a 2012 study by the California Pan-Ethnic Health Network, "Income below Poverty Level (Los Angeles, CA 2012)," http://cpehn.org/chart/income-below-poverty-level-los-angeles-county-2012.

14. Los Angeles boasts two black mayors, Francisco Reyes elected in 1793 and Tom Bradley elected in 1973, as well as numerous African American city council members. Paul Robinson, "Race, Space, and the Evolution of Black Los Angeles," in *Black Los Angeles: American Dreams and Racial Realities*, ed. Darnell Hunt and Ana-Christina Ramon (New York: New York University Press, 2010), 21.

15. Robinson, "Race, Space, and the Evolution of Black Los Angeles," 22.

16. Darnell Hunt writes about Los Angeles's "peculiar and flexible racial order." Darnell Hunt, "Introduction: Dreaming of Black Los Angeles," in Hunt and Ramon, *Black Los Angeles*, 13. See also Tomás Almaguer, *Racial Fault Lines: The Historical Origins of White Supremacy in California* (Berkeley: University of California, 1994).

17. Anthony Macías, "Black and Brown Get Down: Chicano Music, Cultural Politics, and Hip Hop in Racialized Los Angeles," in *Sounds and the City: Popular Music, Place and Globalization,* ed. B. Lashua, K. Spracklen, and S. Wagg (New York: Palgrave Macmillan, 2014).

18. See the work of Laura Pulido and Gaye Theresa Johnson for further discussion of black and brown conflict and solidarity in Los Angeles. Laura Pulido, *Black, Brown, Yellow, and Left: Radical Activism in Los Angeles* (Berkeley: University of California Press, 2006); Gaye Teresa Johnson, *Spaces of Conflict, Sounds of Solidarity: Music, Race, and Spatial Entitlement in Los Angeles* (Berkeley: University of California Press, 2013).

19. The relationship between hip hop and Islam continues to receive ample scholarly attention: Miyakawa, *Five Percenter Rap*; H. Samy Alim, *Roc the Mic Right: The Language of Hip Hop Culture* (New York: Routledge, 2006); Miriam Cook and Bruce B. Lawrence, *Muslim Networks from Hajj to Hip Hop* (Chapel Hill: University of North Carolina Press, 2005); Sohail Daultatzai, *Black Star, Crescent Moon: The Muslim International and Black Freedom beyond America* (Minneapolis and London: University of Minnesota Press, 2012); Juan M. Floyd-Thomas, "A Jihad of Words: The Evolution of African American Islam and Contemporary Hip-Hop," in *Noise and Spirit: The Religious and Spiritual Sensibilities of Rap Music,* ed. Anthony B. Pinn (New York: New York University Press, 2003), 49–70; Su'ad Abdul Khabeer, *Muslim Cool: Race, Religion, and Hip Hop in the United States* (New York: New York University Press, 2016); and Michael Muhammad Knight, *The Five Percenters: Islam, Hip Hop, and Gods of New York* (London: One World, 2007). On the other hand, relatively few academic articles and books exist pertaining specifically to Christian rap or holy hip hop. Cheryl R. Gooch, "Rappin' for the Lord: The Uses of Gospel Rap and Contemporary Music in Black Religious Communities," in *Religion and Mass Media: Audiences and Adaptations,* ed. D. A. Stout and Judith M. Buddenbaum (Thousand Oaks: Sage, 1996); Garth Kasimu Baker-Fletcher, "African American Christian Rap: Facing 'Truth' and Resisting It," in Pinn, *Noise and Spirit,* 29–48; Josef Sorett, "Beats, Rhyme and Bible: An Introduction to Gospel Hip Hop," *African American Pulpit* 10 (2006/2007): 12–16; Eric Gutierrez, *Disciples of the Street: The Promise of a Hip Hop Church* (New York: Seabury Books, 2008); Christina Zanfagna, "Building 'Zyon' in Babylon: Holy Hip Hop and Geographies of Conversion," *Black Music Research Journal* 31.2 (2010): 145–62; Zanfagna, "Kingdom Business: Holy Hip Hop's Evangelical Hustle," *Journal of Popular Music Studies* 42.2 (2012): 196–216; Zanfagna, "Hip Hop and Religion: From the Mosque to the Church," in *The Cambridge Companion to Hip-Hop,* ed. Justin Williams (Cambridge: Cambridge University Press, 2015), 71–84; Willie Hudson, *The Holy Ghost Got a New Dance: An Examination of Black Theology and Holy Hip-hop in Inner-City Ministry* (Eugene: Resource, 2016). For other works on hip hop and spirituality see Harold Dean Trulear and N. Lynne Westfield, "Theomusicology and Christian Education: Spirituality and the Ethics of Control in the Rap of MC Hammer," *Theomusicology,* ed. Jon Michael Spencer, special issue of *Black Sacred Music: A Journal of Theomusicology* 8.1 (1994): 218–38; Philip M. Royster, "The Rapper as Shaman for a Band of Dancers of the Spirit: 'U Can't Touch This,'" *Black Sacred Music: A Journal of Theomusicology* 5.1 (1991): 61–67; James Perkinson, *Shamanism, Racism, and Hip-Hop Culture: Essays on White Supremacy and Black Subversion* (New York: Palgrave Macmillan, 2006); Guthrie Ramsey, *Race Music: Black Cultures from Bebop to Hip-Hop* (Berkeley: University of California Press, 2003); Cheryl L. Keyes, "At the Crossroads: Rap Music and Its African Nexus,"

Ethnomusicology 40.2 (1996): 233–48; Erik J. Williams, "Only God Can Judge Us, Only God Can Save Us: The Hip-Hop Soul of Thugology," *Black Arts Quarterly: Hip Hop Culture: Language, Literature, Literacy and the Lives of Black Youth* 6.2 (2001): 42–45; Daniel White Hodge, *The Soul of Hip Hop: Rims, Tims, and a Cultural Theology* (Downers Grove, IL: InterVarsity Press, 2010).

20. I define subjectivities as both the self-fashioning of identity claims and the interpellation of individuals as subjects. Subjectivity more accurately articulates the ongoing contestation between identity claims and the ways in which bodies are marked and shaped by both discursive and material practices. Through the lens of conversion, I examine how the musical practices and historically situated experiences of holy hip hoppers might further expand or reshape theories of everyday practice as well as complicate assumptions that human agency primarily consists of acts that challenge social norms as opposed to those that uphold them. In an effort to avoid the conflation of agency and resistance as Saba Mahmood has urged, I foreground the examination of holy hip hop subjectivities over discussions of identity politics. Saba Mahmood, "Feminist Theory, Embodiment, and the Docile Agent: Some Reflections on the Egyptian Islamic Revival," *Cultural Anthropology* 6.2 (2001): 202–36. See also Saba Mahmood, *The Politics of Piety: The Islamic Revival and the Feminist Subject* (Princeton, NJ: Princeton University Press, 2004). While new concepts of identity formation are celebrated for the multiple identifications they engender, discussions of identity have tended to emphasize an individual's total control over identificatory claims, thus leaving out issues of power and the ways in which cultural relativism can sometimes lead to increased intolerance and discrimination. Working from the assumption that practices of freedom do not take place outside of power or discipline, about which Foucault has written, I understand holy hip hoppers as entangled in multiple structures and thus must take into account both power and agency. Michel Foucault, *The Use of Pleasure: The History of Sexuality, Volume 2* (New York: Vintage Books, 1987).

21. Since conducting the bulk of my ethnographic research in 2007–8, we have witnessed the killing of multiple black youth and men by law enforcement, from Trayvon Martin to Mike Brown to Eric Garner and Tamir Rice, among many others. Black Lives Matter, a political ideology and platform precipitated by—but addressing issues beyond—the extrajudicial killings of black people by police and vigilantes, is offering a way for people to reignite and rebuild the black liberation movement according to more inclusive principles and with a focus on those who have been historically marginalized in the struggle for black freedom.

22. See Deborah Smith Pollard's discussion of gospel hip hop in her final chapter of *When the Church Becomes Your Party: Contemporary Gospel Music* (Detroit: Wayne State University Press, 2008).

23. Danny Rodriguez was murdered a year later in Dallas, Texas, for unknown reasons. Rodriguez saw rap music as a vehicle to reach inner-city youth in Dallas through the Street Church Academy, a ministry founded in the Buckner Terrace area of Dallas in 1983 by his parents, former drug addicts Demi and Irma "Cookie" Rodriguez. The ministry focused on antigang activities as well as fighting drug addiction. Danny had been the academy's first graduate and was one of the first Christian rappers to make extensive use of sampling.

24. Prominent scholars of black music and religion such as James Cone, Jon Michael Spencer, Michael Eric Dyson, Guthrie Ramsey, Mark Anthony Neal, Portia Maultsby, Melonee

Burnim, Samuel A. Floyd, Jr., Teresa Reed, and Deborah Smith Pollard, among others, have made these coherences a central theme in their work, and their discourses in turn feed back into cultural understandings of black music as well as the performative aesthetics of African American musicians. For specific works by these authors, please see the bibliography.

25. Formerly known as "Georgia Tom" during his days as a honky tonk pianist, he was first known for his composition of the raunchy 1928 hit record with Chicago bluesman Tampa Red, "It's Tight Like That." For more biographical information on Thomas Dorsey see Michael Harris, *The Rise of Gospel Blues: The Music of Thomas Dorsey in the Urban Church* (Oxford: Oxford University Press, 1994). For another story of blurring the borders between black sacred and popular music—this time in Los Angeles—see Jean Kidula, "The Gospel of Andrae Crouch: A Black Angelino," in *California Soul: Music of African Americans in the West,* ed. Jacqueline Cogdell DjeDje and Eddie S. Meadows (Berkeley: University of California Press, 1998), 294–320.

26. Jessie Hyde, "Hip Hop's Public Enemy," *Dallas Observer,* December 8, 2005, www. dallasobserver.com/music/hip-hops-public-enemy-6420085. The article goes on to talk about Duce—a Christian rapper with one of the more successful holy hip hop acts, The Cross Movement—who claims that an owner of a Christian bookstore in Detroit told him that Lewis's DVDs outsell all other gospel rap titles at a rate of three to one, while churches boasting congregations of ten thousand have canceled Christian rap shows after listening to Lewis speak.

27. Many postmodern theorists see the rise of *lifestyling* as an aestheticization of everyday life and central to the act of turning commodities into cultural resources to fashion particular identities. See Fred Pfeil, *Another Tale to Tell: Politics and Narrative in Postmodern Culture* (London and New York: Verso, 1990).

28. See Pradip Thomas, "Selling God, Saving Souls: Religious Commodities, Spiritual Markets, and the Media," *Global Media and Communication* 5.1 (2009): 57–76.

29. Cornel West probes this paradox in the foreword of *One Nation under God: Religion and American Culture,* ed. Margorie Garber and Rebecca L. Walkowitz (New York and London: Routledge, 1999), vii.

30. See Kai Fikentscher, *"You Better Work!" Underground Dance Music in New York City* (Hanover, NH: Wesleyan University Press, 2000); Andrew Greeley, *God in Popular Culture* (Chicago: Thomas More Press, 1998); Teresa L. Reed, *The Holy Profane: Religion in Black Popular Music* (Lexington: University Press of Kentucky, 2003); Robin Sylan, *Traces of the Spirit: The Religious Dimensions of Popular Music* (New York: New York University Press, 2002); and Timothy D. Taylor, *Strange Sounds: Music, Technology, and Culture* (New York: Routledge, 2001).

31. While this book is in conversation with the work of religious studies scholars on hip hop, most notably Monica Miller and Anthony Pinn, my theoretical framework is intentionally not based around this body of literature. I have found religious studies approaches to hip hop to be less helpful in interpreting ethnographic research than the scholarship of anthropologists and cultural theorists. Miller and Pinn's work is important in their expansion of the category of religion in hip hop to mean a conceptual "placeholder" of sorts as opposed to something that simply signifies Christianity or Islam, but their work rarely ventures beyond theoretical and theological analyses of hip hop music and lyrics. Nor does it engage significantly with broader socio-historical processes and

practices. Monica Miller and Anthony Pinn, eds., *The Hip-Hop and Religion Reader* (New York: Routledge, 2015); Miller and Pinn, *Religion in Hip Hop: Mapping the New Terrain* (New York: Bloomsbury, 2015).

32. Although similarities exist in the ways CCM artists and holy hip hoppers negotiate commercialism, creativity, and Christianity as well as how they respond to conservative movements against popular culture by evangelicals, I assert that holy hip hop is more accurately understood vis-à-vis the intra- and intercommunal relations of black communities within the context of the American metropolis—in this case, Los Angeles.

33. I have found the context and lens of urbanization, or "suburbanization" as proposed by the Los Angeles School of Urbanism, and its socioeconomic repercussions to be informative. In this regard, the work of urban sociologists such as Elijah Anderson, Sudhir Venkatesh, João Vargas, Mitch Duneier, David Grazien, Elliot Liebow, Loïc Wacquant, and Omar M. McRoberts has also been incredibly informative. Edward Soja, Mike Davis, and Allen Scott, among other scholars associated with the L.A. School, have tried to make sense of the unique arrangement of different urban restructuring processes at work in Los Angeles through the lens of capitalism. In contrast to the Chicago School, which presents a modernist theory of cities as based around central cores, the L.A. School puts forth a postmodern vision where peripheral urban communities predominate over an evacuated city center. This difference in vision engenders new concepts like "urban sprawl" and "suburbanization."

34. See Henri Lefebvre, *Writings on Cities*, ed. and trans. Eleonore Kofman and Elizabeth Lebas (Oxford: Blackwell, [1996] 1999); Michel De Certeau, *The Practice of Everyday Life* (Berkeley and Los Angeles: University of California Press, 1984); Doreen Massey, *Space, Place, and Gender* (Cambridge, MA: Polity Press, 1994); Michael Keith and Steve Pile, eds., *Place and the Politics of Identity* (New York and London: Routledge, 1993). This is a very incomplete sample of their many writings on place, space, and spatial practice.

35. See Michael Keith and Steve Pile, "Introduction Part 1: The Politics of Place," in Keith and Pile, *Place and the Politics of Identity*, 2–4.

36. See Johnson, *Spaces of Conflict, Sounds of Solidarity*; George Lipsitz, *Dangerous Crossroads: Popular Music, Postmodernism, and the Poetics of Place* (New York: Verso, 1994); Martin Stokes, "Introduction," in *Ethnicity, Identity, and Music: The Musical Construction of Place*, ed. M. Stokes (Oxford and New York: Berg, 1997[1994]); Steven Feld and Keith Basso, eds., *Senses of Place* (Santa Fe: School of American Research Press, 1997); Murray Forman, *The 'Hood Comes First: Race, Space, and Place in Rap and Hip-Hop* (Middleton, CT: Wesleyan University Press, 2002); John Connel, *Soundtracks: Popular Music, Identity, and Place* (New York: Routledge, 2002); Sheila Whiteley, Andy Bennett, and Stan Hawkins, *Music, Space, and Place: Popular Music and Cultural Identity* (Aldershot: Ashgate, 2005); David Knight, *Landscapes in Music: Space, Place, and Time in the World's Great Music* (Lanham, MD: Rowman and Littlefield, 2006); Adam Krims, *Music and Urban Geography* (New York: Routledge, 2007); Brett Lashua, Karl Spracklen, and Stephen Wagg, *Sounds and the City: Popular Music, Place, and Globalization* (New York: Palgrave, 2014).

37. By spatial practices I mean the way that people move through, use, alter, and make meaning out of space. See De Certeau, *Practice of Everyday Life*, 91–130; Henri Lefebvre, *The Production of Space* (New York: Wiley, 1992).

38. See Gupta and Ferguson for further discussion of conducting ethnography on spatially dispersed phenomena. Akhil Gupta and James Ferguson, "Discipline and Practice: 'The Field' as Site, Method, and Location in Anthropology," in *Anthropological Locations: Boundaries and Grounds of a Field Science,* ed. Gupta and Ferguson (Berkeley and Los Angeles: University of California Press, 1997), 34.

39. My understanding of the ways in which disparate locales are linked through holy hip hop resonates with Will Straw's idea of "circuits" in popular music—"the relationship of different local spaces of activity to each other takes the form of circuits, overlaid upon each other, through which particular styles of alternative music circulate in the form of recordings and live performances." Will Straw, "Systems of Articulation, Logics of Change: Communities and Scenes in Popular Music," *Cultural Studies* 5.3 (1991): 378.

40. See Williams and Kajikawa for studies on hip hop and automobiles. Justin Williams, "'You Never Been on a Ride Like This Befo': Los Angeles, Automotive Listening, and Dr. Dre's 'G-Funk,'" *Popular Music History* 4.2 (2010): 160–76; Loren Kajikawa, *Sounding Race in Rap Songs* (Berkeley: University of California Press, 2015).

41. Here I have been inspired by James Clifford's insistence that field research is predicated on travel. James Clifford, "Spatial Practices: Fieldwork, Travel, and the Disciplining of Anthropology," in Gupta and Ferguson, *Anthropological Locations,* 185–222. In addition, the prefix "loco" is also a Spanish word meaning "crazy" or "insane." Given the presence of large Spanish-speaking communities in L.A., this term *loco*-motion has added import to the ways different minority populations experience the moving grounds of the Southland. Loco-motion or crazy-motion leads to the creation of *earthquake music,* which, in turn, activates its own crazy motions and movements.

42. See Williams, "'You Never Been on a Ride Like This Befo,'" 163.

43. See De Certeau's chapter, "Walking in the City," in *Practice of Everyday Life.*

44. Mimi Sheller and John Urry, "The City and the Car," *International Journal of Urban and Regional Research* 24.4 (2000): 737–57.

45. Paul Gilroy, *Darker Than Blue: On the Moral Economies of Black Atlantic Culture* (Cambridge, MA, and London: Belknap Press of Harvard University Press, 2010), 16.

46. Ibid., 20.

47. *Black Cultural Traffic: Crossroads in Global Performance and Popular Culture* (Ann Arbor: University of Michigan, 2005), edited by Harry J. Elam, Jr. and Kennell Jackson, features essays that explore the diasporic and global connectivities of black cultural forms.

48. Here I am riffing on a turn of phrase from Jacqueline Brown, who writes, "Arguably, no scholar traffics in the local like the anthropologist." Jacqueline Brown, *Dropping Anchor, Setting Sail: Geographies of Race in Black Liverpool* (Princeton, NJ: Princeton University Press, 2005), 6.

49. See Hall, "What Is This 'Black' in Black Popular Culture?", 21–33; Paul Gilroy, *The Black Atlantic: Modernity and Double Consciousness* (Cambridge, MA: Harvard University Press, 1992); Tsitsi Ella Jaji, *Africa in Stereo: Modernism, Music, and Pan-African Solidarity* (Oxford: Oxford University Press, 2014); Maureen Mahon, *Right to Rock: The Black Rock Coalition and the Cultural Politics of Race* (Durham, NC: Duke University Press, 2004); Sorett, "Believe Me, This Pimp Game Is Very Religious."

50. Hall, "What Is This 'Black' in Black Popular Culture?"

51. In a similar argument, Jayna Brown also critiques James Clifford's assertion that African American cultures are somehow exceptional in relation to the other cultures of the black diaspora. "African American cultures, in historically specific ways, draw multiple lines of affiliation and are perhaps less circumscribed by national boundaries than Clifford implies." Jayna Brown, *Babylon Girls: Black Women Performers and the Shaping of the Modern* (Durham, NC: Duke University Press, 2008), 10.

52. In *Prophets of the Hood: Politics and Poetics in Hip-Hop* (Durham, NC: Duke University Press, 2004), Imani Perry argues that Paul Gilroy's Afro-Atlantic theory has fallen short in its application to U.S. hip hop. She defines hip hop as a product of black American consciousness "in its relationship of alterity to American power and race politics" (18), stating, "Even with its hybridity: the consistent contributions from nonblack artists, and the borrowings from cultural forms of other communities, it is nevertheless black American music" (10).

53. As Maureen Mahon argues in her insightful study of the Black Rock Coalition, "In the post–civil rights era, African Americans contend with the on-the-ground reality of black heterogeneity, white assumptions of black homogeneity, and black claims of unity that often demand uniformity" (Mahon, *Right to Rock*, 11).

54. Anthony Pinn, *Terror and Triumph: The Nature of Black Religion* (Minneapolis: Fortress Press, 2003), 170–71.

55. In discussions about black religion and black liberation, proponents of Black Nationalism have often viewed African American Christianity as complicit in black enslavement and psychological bondage. Melville Jean Herskovits, in *The Myth of the Negro Past* (Boston: Beacon, [1941] 1958), made provocative assertions about "African retentions" and innate black religiosity. He used the term "compensation" to argue that religion for African Americans was a substitute for economic deprivation, refusing to understand religion as simply an epiphenomenon of broader social and economic forces. On the other hand, Arthur Huff Fauset, in *Black Gods of the Metropolis: Negro Religious Cults of the Urban North* (Philadelphia: University of Pennsylvania Press, [1944] 2002), argued that historical exigency, and cultural, economic, and political trends, more adequately explained the prominent place of religion and the church in the lives of African Americans than Herskovits's essentialist positing of a black religious temperament or bent. Reflecting on this debate, Curtis J. Evans states, "The fear was that once one grants the claim that blacks were 'naturally religious' or differed fundamentally from whites in their religious practices, they were either complicit in their enslavement or were adherents to a religion that did not spur resistance and self-assertion in the face of racial oppression." Curtis J. Evans, "Urbanization and the End of Black Churches in the Modern World," *Church History* 76.4 (2007): 799–823.

56. Founded in the 1960s, Black Liberation Theology is about making Christianity real for black folks and understands Christianity as a matter of liberation in the here and now instead of in an afterlife. According to James Cone, Black Liberation Theology maintains that African Americans must be liberated from multiple forms of bondage. This formulation views Christian theology as a theology of liberation pertaining to existential conditions of oppression and containment. James Cone, *A Black Theology of Liberation* (New York: Orbis Books, 1986). Borrowing the Marxist critique of capitalism, Black Liberation theologians such as Cone and Cornel West have traditionally attempted to link black class politics

with race politics through the prophetic tradition of Black Christianity. Cornel West, in "Black Theology and Marxist Thought," *Black Theology: A Documentary History, Volume I, 1966–1979,* ed. James H. Cone and Gayraud S. Wiltmore (Maryknoll, NY: Orbis Books, 1980), 409–24, has complicated the concept of liberation through his analysis of the relationship between the exploiting doctrines of capitalism and imperialism. While holy hip hop is linked to a continuum of Black Liberation Theology in its attempt to counteract various modes of oppression and make Christianity relevant to the current social context and political moment, it is not explicitly about affecting political change or seeking liberation from white oppression as discussed in early arguments about Black Liberation Theology. The issues at stake in holy hip hop culture depart significantly from these core concerns of Black Liberation Theology; rather, holy hip hop intervenes in intracommunal disparities and intergenerational tensions within black communities around social difference and economic disparity.

57. Oscar Lewis coined the term "culture of poverty" in his chapter "The Culture of Poverty," in *Urban Life: Readings in the Anthropology of the City,* ed. G. Gmelch and W. Zenner (Longrove, IL: Waveland Press, [1966] 1996).

58. For a discussion of the "underclass" see William Julius Wilson, *The Truly Disadvantaged: The Inner City, the Underclass, and Public Policy* (Chicago: University of Chicago Press, 1987).

59. The "political" character of such cultural practices is not reduced here to policies and institutions of the state but instead derives, as Jocelyne Guilbault states, "from being inextricably linked with processes of exclusion, marginalization, and representation." Jocelyne Guilbault, "Audible Entanglements: Nation and Diasporas in Trinidad's Calypso Music Scene," *Small Axe* 9.1 (2005): 41.

60. I use *flippin' the script(ure)* as a metaphor that signifies multiple modes of inscription and re-inscription—the unexpected, everyday performances of religiosity that reverse, overturn, and deviate from expected norms both in and out of the church. Hip-hop MCs also use the phrase "flippin' the script" in the context of rap battles and freestyle "ciphas" to refer to MCs who create verbal "disses" out of what someone says against them, flipping the insult back on their opponent. In a broader sense, the phrase relates to a discourse of power and dominant script reversal. For more on dominant script reversals and "hidden transcripts," see James Scott, *Domination and the Arts of Resistance: Hidden Transcripts* (New Haven, CT: Yale University Press, 1992).

61. "Born again" usually refers to someone who has made a new or renewed commitment of faith, especially after an intense religious experience. In other words, this may be a return to Christianity or the adoption of a new evangelical relationship to Christianity.

62. See Talal Asad, "Comments on Conversion," in *Conversion to Modernities: The Globalization of Christianity,* ed. Peter van der Veer (New York: Routledge, 1995), 263–73; John L. Comaroff and Jean Comaroff, *Of Revelation and Revolution, Volume 2: The Dialectics of Modernity on a South African Frontier* (Chicago: University of Chicago Press, 1991); K. F. Morrison, *Understanding Conversion* (Charlottesville: University of Virginia Press, 1992); Vicente Rafael, *Contracting Colonialism: Translation and Christian Conversion in Tagalog Society under Early Spanish Rule* (Durham, NC: Duke University Press, 1993); Circe Sturm, *Becoming Indian: The Struggle over Cherokee Identity in the Twenty-First Century* (Santa Fe: School for Advanced Research Press, 2011); and Van de Veer, *Conversion to Modernities.*

63. Comaroff and Comaroff, *Of Revelation and Revolution,* 250. K. F. Morrison, on the other hand, has stated that the word "has displayed different connotations at different moments" (Morrison, *Understanding Conversion,* xiv).

64. Comaroff and Comaroff, *Of Revelation and Revolution,* 250.

65. Diane Austin-Broos, "The Anthropology of Religious Conversion: An Introduction," in *The Anthropology of Religious Conversion,* ed. Andrew Buckser and Stephen D. Glazier (Lanham, MD: Rowman and Littlefield, 2003), 1.

66. Ibid., 2.

67. Ibid.

68. We must, of course, question certain tendencies of Zionist thinking, especially as it is mapped to Judaism. The consequences of this particular geopolitical framing of Zionism (as a national movement whose goal is the return of the Jewish people to Zion or Jerusalem) continue to cause immeasurable suffering as witnessed in the Israeli/Palestinian struggle.

69. Brown, *Dropping Anchor, Setting Sail,* 9. Steven Gregory's important work on race and place is also influenced by thinking on the politics of black social spaces in relation to holy hip hop. Steven Gregory, *Black Corona: Race and the Politics of Place in an Urban Community* (Princeton, NJ: Princeton University Press, 1999).

70. In trying to foreground music's role in the formation and representation of holy hip hop subjectivities and urban spaces, I have found Jocelyne Guilbault's concept of "audible entanglements" to be quite useful. "Audible entanglements" offers possibilities for understanding the ways in which power relations are deeply enmeshed in and reconstituted through musical practices. Guilbault argues that such entanglements "*foresound* sites, moments, and modes of enunciation articulated through musical practices. So, far from being 'merely' musical, audible entanglements . . . also assemble social relations, cultural expressions, and political formations" (Guilbault, "Audible Entanglements," 40–41).

CHAPTER 1. "NOW I BANG FOR CHRIST"

1. Khanchuz, interview with the author, Los Angeles, CA, 2007.

2. Gangbanging is of course a term loaded with certain racialized and gendered assumptions about the criminality of black people, especially young black men. Black street gangs originally formed in Los Angeles to combat the racism and violence directed toward young African Americans by white residents and white gangs. For a history of the emergence of gang culture in Los Angeles, see the HBO documentary *Bastards of the Party* (2005). This film argues that the Bloods and the Crips grew out of the social and political vacuum created by the murders of several black leaders, including the head of the L.A. chapter of the Black Panther Party, Bunchy Carter. These gangs were the "bastard children" of the political parties of the 1960s and '70s.

3. For more discussion on ethnographic interviewing and modes of questioning, see Charles L. Briggs, "Anthropology, Interviewing, and Communicability in Contemporary Society," *Current Anthropology* 48.4 (2007): 551–80.

4. Furthermore, conversion narratives, as enmeshed in the history of transatlantic enslavement, can be understood as political soundings of enslaved persons refuting bondage and asserting their humanity. Every time holy hip hoppers *tell their stories,* they rearticulate cross-generational histories and discourses. Winfried Herget speaks about the importance

of conversion narratives in relation to marginalized groups and specifically itinerant African American female preachers. He states, "Originally an oral relation, the written account of the conversion came to form the core of spiritual autobiographies, which could serve as proofs for others and as documents of self-authorization in the struggle for public acceptance for those—like African-American women—who insisted that their voices be heard. To gain control over the text of their lives could, then, be a means of empowerment which, however, only very few were able to obtain." Winfried Herget, "Black Itinerant Women Preachers: Conversion to Empowerment—The Example of Jarena Lee," in *Religion in African American Culture*, ed. Winfried Herget and Alfred Hornung (Heidelberg: Universitätsverlag, 2006), 45. For further reading on testifying and religious testimony in African American cultures, see Moses N. Moore, Jr., "'Testifying' and 'Testimony': Autobiographical Narratives and African American Religions," in *Teaching African American Religions*, ed. Carolyn M. Jones and Theodore Louis Trost (Oxford: Oxford University Press, 2005), 95–108.

5. The intersecting stories also illustrate how the production of biography and history is deeply enmeshed. Religious studies scholar Josef Sorett writes, "The famous American philosopher Ralph Waldo Emerson once argued that all history is in fact biography. By this he meant that the stories humans tell say just as much about a particular author as they do about any actual historical record that an author documents" (Sorett, "'This Pimp Game Is Very Religious,'" 12). Thus, I draw on the ways that the stories told here about popular music, religion, crime, and community articulate both specific authors (gospel rappers) *and* historical knowledge.

6. Davis, *Ecologies of Fear*, 7.

7. Ibid., 8.

8. Peter King, "The Latest 100-Year Disaster," *Los Angeles Times*, March 15, 1995.

9. See Guilbault, "Audible Entanglements."

10. Soup the Chemist, *Through My Windows: The History behind Holy Hip Hop* (Dimlights, 2013), 7.

11. Soup the Chemist, interview with the author, Los Angeles, CA, 2008.

12. Stephen Wiley released an EP in 1985 with two tracks, "Bible Break" and "Rappin for Jesus." Soup the Chemist first bought the EP at a Christian bookstore.

13. Davis, *City of Quartz*, 399.

14. Ibid., 376.

15. Soup the Chemist, interview with the author, Los Angeles, CA, 2008.

16. Ibid.

17. Ibid.

18. "Interview with Sup the Chemist," *Gospelflava.com*, 2000, www.gospelflava.com/articles/sup1.html.

19. Davis, *City of Quartz*, 297.

20. Soup the Chemist, interview with the author, Los Angeles, CA, 2008.

21. John Mitchell, "The Raid That Still Haunts L.A.," *Los Angeles Times*, March 14, 2001.

22. Davis, *City of Quartz*, 268.

23. Mandalit del Barco, "Critics Decry Naming of LAPD Building for Ex-Chief," *NPR.org*, April 24, 2009, www.npr.org/templates/story/story.php?storyId = 103452604.

24. Davis, *City of Quartz*, 295.

25. Johnson, *Spaces of Conflict, Sounds of Solidarity*, 169.

26. The practice of burning music was seen previously with rock music. For instance, Eileen Luhr writes, "On November 24, 1979, brothers Steve and Jim Peters hosted their first-ever record burning at the campgrounds of Zion Christian Life Center, their church in St. Paul, Minnesota . . . The brothers continued to hold the events regularly for the next several years, and by 1984 they claimed to have destroyed over $10 million worth of secular records and tapes. Critics compared the event to Nazi book burnings, but the brothers claimed that the burnings were patterned after an episode in the New Testament in which converts burned their idols to show the sincerity of their Christian belief." Eileen Luhr, *Witnessing Suburbia: Conservative and Christian Youth Culture* (Berkeley: University of California Press, 2009), 30.

27. Davis, *City of Quartz*, 292.

28. Janet L. Abu-Lughod, *Race, Space, and Riots in Chicago, New York, and Los Angeles* (New York and Oxford: Oxford University Press, 2007), 241.

29. Ibid.

30. As quoted in Ashley Myers-Turner's article, "Forget the L.A. Riots—Historic 1992 Watts Gang Truce Was the Big News," 2012, www.scpr.org/news/2012/04/28/32221/forget-la-riots-1992-gang-truce-was-big-news/.

31. Ibid.

32. Other social programs, like Amer-I-Can, are about accepting total agency over one's life and actions and moving from a place of "I can't" to I can." For a critique of self-help ideology see Joáo Helion Costa Vargas, *Catching Hell in the City of Angels: Life and Meanings of Blackness in South Central Los Angeles* (Minneapolis: University of Minnesota Press, 2006), and Robin D. G. Kelley, *Yo' Mama's Dysfunktional: Fighting the Culture Wars in Urban America* (Boston: Beacon Press, 1998).

33. Quote taken from an interview with the *Los Angeles Times* Homicide Report. "Homicide Perspectives: Kenny Mitchell, Founder, Gangsters Anonymous," *Los Angeles Times*, October 19, 2007, http://latimesblogs.latimes.com/homicidereport/2007/10/homicide-perspe.html

34. Vargas, *Catching Hell in the City of Angels*, 212.

35. Further, Vargas points out that in certain gang prevention programs as well as Amer-I-Can "there is not the slightest suggestion that self-hatred, low self-esteem, lack of initiative, difficulties finding work, gender tensions, and propensity for drug use have some of their roots in historical and social conditions. No references are made to the role of government in perpetuating poverty" (Vargas, *Catching Hell in the City of Angels*, 207).

36. Black residents of the inner city have been systematically blocked in their attempts to relocate throughout Los Angeles. Although the Fair Housing Act of 1968 outlawed residential racial segregation, in reality, change has been minimal. The law is often not enforced and many people don't understand the specifics of the law itself.

37. Vargas, *Catching Hell in the City of Angels*, 14.

38. Khanchuz, interview with the author, Los Angeles, CA, 2008.

39. My understanding of agency has been shaped by Sherry Ortner's framing of "subaltern practice theory," which she describes in *Making Gender: The Politics and Erotics of Culture* (Boston: Beacon Press, 1996).

40. Winfried Herget notes that for many African American believers, "Salvation depends solely on God's agency." In analyzing Jarena Lee's conversion narrative, he states,

"The narrative insists on God as a causal agency. But Lee makes it equally clear how much she depends on the help of others" (Herget, "Black Itinerant Women Preachers," 54). What is absent from the dualism set up between God's agency and "the help of others" are more contemporary discourses of self-help and pulling oneself up by one's bootstraps—ideologies that gained steam under assaults on welfare programs, civil rights laws, and affirmative action programs during the Reagan–Bush years. These ideologies, which derive their moral framework from the liberal conception of the individual responsibility, were radically revived under neoliberalism.

41. Talal Asad, "Comments on Conversion," 272.

42. Ibid., 263.

43. Robin D. G. Kelley elaborates on the "gang book" genre in the preface to Vargas's book (*Catching Hell in the City of Angels,* ix).

44. Instead, journalists, pastors, church leaders, and secular rappers are often the voices heard in public discourses about gospel rap.

45. The performance of conversion narratives has historically raised questions around truth, authenticity, and sincerity, especially in contexts of slavery, colonialism, and missionization. I am less interested in whether or not holy hip hop testifyings were authentic or inauthentic than I am in gospel rappers' use of the conversion narrative as an authenticating and artful discursive technology that was often deployed in combination with other forms of testifying and modalities of performance, such as rapping, singing, recitation of scripture, and the use of hypermetaphoric speech. For holy hip hoppers, one of these forms was not enough to communicate the complex and seemingly contradictory nature of their lives, their particular anatomies of belief, and their unique brand of music-making. See Geoffrey Hartmann's chapter "Testimony and Authenticity," in *Scars of the Spirit: The Struggle against Inauthenticity* (New York: Palgrave MacMillan, 2004). Winfried Herget discusses the legitimating effects of conversion narratives, stating, "Their acceptance as 'true testimony' is not a question of actual occurrences—and suspension of belief—but one of the representation of the psychic state of suffering of 'terror and dismay'" (Herget, "Black Itinerant Women Preachers," 58). Or, as Peter Van der Veer warns, "The anxieties about the sincerity of conversion and the authenticity of speech in general seem to be embedded in a certain history of power" (Van der Veer, *Conversion to Modernities,* 16).

46. Khanchuz, interview with the author, Los Angeles, CA, 2007.

47. Ibid.

48. Ibid.

49. Ibid.

50. Khanchuz rapped these lyrics during an interview, Los Angeles, CA, 2007.

51. B-Love, interview with the author, Santa Monica, CA, 2007.

52. Ibid.

53. Ibid.

54. At the crossroads of hip hop and Christianity, it is also interesting to note that Romany Malco played MC Hammer in the 2001 VH1 movie, *Too Legit: The M.C. Hammer Story.*

55. Cue Jn-Marie, communication with the author on Facebook, February 12, 2016.

56. Cue Jn-Marie, interview with the author, Los Angeles, CA, 2008.

57. Cue Jn-Marie, interview with the author, Los Angeles, CA, 2007.

58. Of course Islam and Christianity have existed in a kind of lock-step throughout hip hop histories. As Josef Sorett states, "Alongside Islam, Christianity was a fixture in hip hop as far back as 1987 when MC Hammer's first record included 'Son of the King'" ("This Pimp Game Is Very Religious," 12).

59. Cue Jn-Marie, interview with the author, Los Angeles, CA, 2013.

60. Cue Jn-Marie, interview with the author, Los Angeles, CA, 2007.

61. Ibid.

62. Cue Jn-Marie, interview with the author, Los Angeles, CA, 2008.

63. Within the last decade, we are now witnessing young gospel rap artists being raised by parents who are gospel rappers. For instance, Khanchuz and his twelve-year-old daughter Jaysha often perform holy hip hop together throughout Los Angeles, while DJ Heat's son, Mikey, produces holy hip hop beats for members of the Hip Hopposite crew. According to DJ Heat, his son was playing too many video games on his X-Box, so he told Mikey he had to start producing more of his own music again if he wanted to be able to keep his X-Box. Mikey has since made a very dynamic track for Celah that includes samples from Led Zeppelin and secular hip hop artists.

CHAPTER 2. HIP HOP CHURCH L.A.

1. The Five Percent Nation is an offshoot of Islam to which many early hip hop artists ascribed.

2. The order of events resembled the traditional script of worship found in many mainline Protestant churches. The order of worship for Hip Hop Church services generally proceeds in the following format: PROCESSIONAL, Prayer, Announcements, RAP OF PRAISE, Choir Selection, RAP OF PRAISE, Responsive Reading, RAP OF PRAISE, Word (from scripture), Song of Praise, Offering, RAP OF PRAISE, Sermon, Altar Call & Prayer, and Fellowship.

3. Several other hip hop ministries existed in Los Angeles. Rap artist KRS-One's Temple of Hip-Hop aimed to protect, preserve and establish hip hop's common spirit while the Crenshaw Christian Center held regular "Hip-Hop Sundays."

4. Loïc Wacquant, *Urban Outcasts: A Comparative Sociology of Advanced Marginality* (Cambridge, UK and Malden, MA: Polity Press, 2007), 1.

5. Vargas, *Catching Hell in the City of Angels,* 16.

6. That said, Inglewood residents often lament the way that the city has been framed as a seedy "ghetto" by popular media.

7. Sharon Collins-Heads, interview with the author, Inglewood, CA, 2007.

8. Vargas, *Catching Hell in the City of Angels,* 17.

9. Carol Scott, interview with the author, Inglewood, CA, 2007.

10. Pastor Wallace, interview with the author, Inglewood, CA, 2008.

11. Carol Scott, interview with the author, Inglewood, CA, 2007.

12. Pastor Wallace, interview with the author, Inglewood, CA, 2008.

13. Marc Lacey, "Inside the Gates, 'a Nice Little Utopia': Inglewood: When the Residents of the City's Toniest Areas Drive past the Guardhouses, They Leave Behind the Problems of More Typical Inner-city Neighborhoods," *Los Angeles Times,* June 16, 1991.

14. Pastor Wallace, interview with the author, Inglewood, CA, 2007.

15. In a 2008 interview in Inglewood, Pastor Wallace stated, "In terms of age, it's very intergenerational. We do have many in there that are in their seventies and eighties, but like I said earlier, we have many young families. We have a preschool of sixty-five children, so we've got the little ones—preschoolers in church. We have a wide age range and an attempt to appeal to all generations."

16. Eric Pape, "Inglewood's Magisterial Mayor: Roosevelt Dorn Was Bombastic on the Bench—and He Still Is," *LA Weekly*, April 8, 1999.

17. Erin Aubry Kaplan, "10 Inner-City Stories You Didn't Read . . . Again," *LA Weekly*, January 3, 2002.

18. Vargas, *Catching Hell in the City of Angels*, 42.

19. Dennis Romero, "Gangster's Paradise Lost," *Los Angeles CityBeat*, November 6, 2003, www.lacitybeat.com/cms/story/detail/?id = 362&IssueNum = 22.

20. The racial demographics in South Los Angeles have been changing for several decades. During the 1980s, Mexican and Latin American immigrants began moving into the previously all-black neighborhoods east of South Los Angeles. Today the Latino population of South Los Angeles is larger than the black population. According to the 2000 census, the Latin American population of South L.A. had reached 58 percent and the African American population had dropped to 40 percent. Now that African Americans are no longer the largest minority group, their political and economic influence in the city is also changing.

21. For further discussion see Erin J. Aubry, "Lost Soul: A Lament for Black Los Angeles," *LA Weekly*, December 10, 1998.

22. The hospital reopened in 2015 under the name Martin Luther King Jr. Community Hospital.

23. As quoted in Pastor Carol Scott's obituary. Jocelyn Y. Stewart, "Carol L. Scott, 50; Activist Pastor Led Hip-Hop Church," *Los Angeles Times*, October 11, 2007.

24. For further discussion, see Elijah Anderson, *Streetwise: Race, Class, and Change in an Urban Community* (Chicago: University of Chicago Press, 1992).

25. Wacquant, *Urban Outcasts*, 3.

26. Aubry, "Lost Soul."

27. Vargas, *Catching Hell in the City of Angels*, 40.

28. Ibid., 16.

29. Controversy brewed as local Angeleno and columnist Larry Aubry published an article in the *Los Angeles Sentinel* (one of the oldest black newspapers in Los Angeles) just before voters rejected a proposal to speed approval of the Wal-Mart store, which accused Inglewood Mayor Dorn of accepting "at least $40,000 from Wal-Mart." Larry Aubry, "Inglewood Mayor's Tactics Should Be Denounced," *Los Angeles Sentinel*, May 19, 2004. The column ran in the April 1 issue of the *Sentinel*. The Wal-Mart initiative, known as Measure 4-A, was defeated on April 6. Dorn then sued the *Sentinel* and Larry Aubry for libel over the column, stating that he took no campaign money from the Arkansas-based retailer. The suit was eventually dismissed.

30. Aubry, "Inglewood Mayor's Tactics Should Be Denounced."

31. Ibid.

32. Carol Scott, interview with the author, Inglewood, CA, 2007.

33. Ibid.

34. Throughout the evolution of the spiritual, the words and melodies have remained fairly intact, while the rhythms and harmonies have been changed to suit current needs. Amiri Baraka keenly points out that to make a Christian song out of African music, "All that would have to be done was change the words." Amiri Baraka, *Blues People: The Negro Experience in White America and the Music That Developed from It* (New York: William Morrow Quill, 1963), 45. So is holy hip hop just old wine poured into new bottles or new wine poured in old wine skins? Is it a process of emptying out the profanity, filling it with the gospel?

35. Sharon Collins-Heads, telephone interview with the author, Berkeley, CA, 2017.

36. Stewart, "Carol L. Scott, 50."

37. Omar McRoberts elaborates on the highly "mobile" character of black churches in relationship to the proliferation of storefront churches in certain inner-city neighborhoods. He states: "They [churches] coexist by focusing on their target populations, which may or may not live in the neighborhood. This lack of identification with the neighborhood is exacerbated by the fact that churches, like poor residents, are themselves highly mobile. When rents go up for whatever reason, churches, like people, may choose to leave for another neighborhood. Church members, who are used to traveling to worship, simply follow the church. And on top of that, the ongoing threat of being priced out of a neighborhood by economic development leads some churches to actively avoid involvement in neighborhood affairs." McRoberts, "Interview with Omar McRoberts."

38. As one of the few people privy to the situation with the Hip Hop Church, Sharon's deep friendship with Carol, and witness to Sharon's immediate grief over her passing, I certainly took on a role more akin to a supporter, confidant, and friend than an academic researcher.

39. Pastor Wallace, interview with the author, Inglewood, CA, 2008.

40. At the time, Pastor Fritz had recently been appointed pastor at another Lutheran church in North Inglewood. He was also the executive director of New City Parish, which operates as a coalition of Lutheran churches in Los Angeles. Wallace chose him for his ability to attract young people from the other Parish congregations to be a nucleus for this new Hip Hop Worship night.

41. For more information on the role of women in community organizing, especially prior to Black Power ideologies, see Vargas, *Catching Hell in the City of Angels.* He highlights the work of women in the Watt's Women's Association, the Avalon-Carver Community Center, the Mothers of Watts Community Action Council, Mothers Anonymous, the Welfare Rights Organization, the Central City Community Mental Health Center, and the Neighborhood Organizations of Watts.

42. Birgitta Johnson, "Oh for a Thousand Tongues to Sing," PhD dissertation (University of California, Los Angeles, 2009), 150.

43. For instance, J. H. L. Smith, pastor at Ebenezer Baptist Church in Chicago, was instrumental in changing the tides of African American musical worship in the mid-twentieth century to include the older (and what was considered "blacker") forms of music making and worship in the church.

44. Jacqueline Cogdell DjeDje writes about the development of gospel music in Los Angeles, commenting that gospel musicians such as Eugene Douglass Smallwood and Earl Amos Pleasant formed their own churches in order to support the burgeoning gospel scene. Their churches became important centers in developing the gospel tradition in Los Angeles.

Jacqueline Cogdell DjeDje, "The California Black Gospel Music Tradition: A Confluence of Musical Styles and Cultures," in DjeDje and Meadows, *California Soul*, 133.

CHAPTER 3. BEYOND BABYLON

EPIGRAPHS bell hooks, *Yearning: Race, Gender, and Cultural Politics* (Boston: South End Press, 1990), 145. Bob Marley's "Chant Down Babylon" was released in 1983, two years after his death, on the album *Confrontation*.

1. Here, my thinking about spatial practices is informed by the work of Henri Lefebvre and Michel De Certeau. De Certeau identifies "spatial practice" as a manipulation of the fundamental elements of the constructed order and divergent from literal meanings of urban space. See Michel De Certeau, "Part III: Spatial Practices," in *Practice of Everyday Life*, 91–130. James Clifford further elaborates: "For De Certeau, 'space' is never ontologically given. It is discursively mapped and corporeally practiced. An urban neighborhood, for example, may be laid out physically according to a street plan. But it is not a space until it is practiced by people's active occupation, their movements through and around it. In this perspective, there is nothing given about a 'field.' It must be worked, turned into a discrete social space, by embodied practices of interactive travel." James Clifford, *Travel and Translation in the Late Twentieth Century* (Cambridge, MA: Harvard University Press, 1997), 54.

2. As Mike Davis argues, "Violent instability in local landscape and culture is constitutive of Southern California's peculiar social ontology." Davis, *City of Quartz*, 376.

3. Elana Zilberg, *Space of Detention: The Making of a Transnational Gang Crisis from Los Angeles to San Salvador* (Durham, NC: Duke University Press, 2011), 11.

4. Body of Christ is a term of Christian theology, implicitly traceable to Jesus's statement at the Last Supper that "This is my body" in Luke 22:19–20, and explicitly used by the Apostle Paul in 1 Corinthians 12:12–14. Body of Christ is used by some Protestants to collectively describe the believers in Christ or the Church. This is based on several passages in the Bible, including Romans 12:5, 1 Corinthians 12:12–27, Ephesians 3:6 and 5:23, Colossians 1:18 and 1:24. Jesus Christ is seen as the "head" of the body, which is the Church, while the "members" of the body are seen as members of the Church.

5. Cue Jn-Marie, interview with the author, Los Angeles, CA, 2007.

6. B-Love, interview with the author, Compton, CA, 2008.

7. Ian Condry's examination of "key sites" of hip hop performance and networking in *Hip-Hop Japan* (2006) provides some useful pathways into rethinking the mutual construction of popular music scenes by hip hop artists, audiences, and culture industries. Speaking from an ethnographic perspective, he asks: "One of the tenets of anthropological fieldwork is that you cannot understand a people without being there, but in the case of hip-hop, where is 'there'?" (4). His answer for hip hop in Japan is *genba*—key sites of cultural production where something is produced and actualized through improvisation and performance. *Genba,* he explains, draws our attention to "the ways hip-hop is constantly made and re-made in specific locations through local dialects and for particular audiences." Ian Condry, *Hip-Hop Japan: Rap and Paths of Cultural Globalization* (Durham, NC: Duke University Press, 2006), 1–2.

8. I follow Ian Condry's emphasis on "key performative locations" that bring together diverse practitioners and professionals in a multilevel embodiment of a musical scene. For

him, this emphasis is "a way of moving beyond conceptions of culture industry power in dichotomous terms" such as producers vs. consumers, global vs. local, etc. Furthermore, his call to examine "key performative locations" is not just about locating the music in a specific locale or place; rather, Condry is privileging hip hop performativity as the actualizing force that converts a space (a general field of resources) into some place (a specific located product of meaning-making practices—space made meaningful) and constructs the "there" of a musical culture as both a physical destination and an aesthetic world. I find the invocation of *genba* particularly useful because it highlights the temporary, provisional, and mobile qualities of sites of cultural production. Condry, *Hip-Hop Japan,* 88.

9. Jacqueline Cogdell DjeDje and Eddie S. Meadows, "Introduction," in *California Soul: Music of African Americans in the West,* ed. Jacqueline Cogdell DjeDje and Eddie S. Meadows (Berkeley: University of California Press, 1998), 6.

10. Mark Anthony Neal, *What the Music Said: Black Popular Music and Black Public Culture* (New York and London: Routledge, 1999). Murray Forman identifies the "'hood" as the main spatial category in hip hop culture (Forman, *The 'Hood Comes First,* 5).

11. Omar McRoberts, *Streets of Glory: Church and Community in a Black Urban Neighborhood* (Chicago: University of Chicago Press, 2003), 141. Omar McRoberts, in an interview with University of Chicago Press, states that "the experience of worshiping against the backdrop of the immediate streetscape becomes an important part of their religious experience and identity, even without religious identification with the neighborhood as such ... The world of the street supplies the raw data about the nature of evil that gets incorporated into moral teaching. So the church and street ultimately cannot be separated here. But the form that the street takes in the religious imagination discourages direct engagement with the immediate neighborhood." Omar McRoberts, "An Interview with Omar McRoberts," 2003, www.press.uchicago.edu/Misc/Chicago/562166in.html.

12. Ralph Eastman, "'Pitchin' Up a Boogie': African-American Musicians, Nightlife, and Music Venues in Los Angeles, 1930–1945," in DjeDje and Meadows, *California Soul,* 90.

13. Ibid., 96.

14. Ibid., 79.

15. Eithne Quinn, *Nuthin' but a "G" Thang: The Culture and Commerce of Gangsta Rap* (New York: Columbia University Press, 2005), 67.

16. Forman, *The 'Hood Comes First.*

17. Murray Forman, "'Represent': Race, Space and Place in Rap Music," in *That's the Joint! The Hip-Hop Studies Reader,* ed. Murray Forman and Mark Anthony Neal (New York: Routledge, 2004), 201.

18. Forman, "'Represent,'" 202.

19. Quinn, *Nuthin' But a "G" Thang,* 66.

20. Khanchuz, interview with the author, Los Angeles, CA, 2007.

21. Davis, *City of Quartz,* 304.

22. Numerous motels have remained despite deteriorating conditions. In a 2003 *LA Weekly* article on the controversy surrounding Charles Williams's proposed plan for a motel in the middle of a South Los Angeles vacant lot, Robert Greene reflects on the aftermath of the 1992 riots: "While the rubble still smoldered, neighborhood activists organized to make sure the crime magnets that made life dangerous for people just trying to get to school or work would never reopen. First on their list were liquor stores. Second: Motels. Residents

of the neat stucco houses and leaders of the storefront churches are now working hard to make sure Williams' new motel never gets built. 'A motel in this neighborhood becomes a center for prostitution,' says Pastor Roger Smith of the Southwestern Church of God. 'It's a breeding ground for it. Along with this prostitution come the drug dealers. Then alcoholism.' South Los Angeles is known for its motels, and it's not because the area is a tourist attraction. Many of the tiny lodgings were built in the 1930s and have never been upgraded. Rooms often rent by the hour. Women wearing revealing dress and the desperate looks associated with drug addiction can be spotted in front, usually at night, but often in broad daylight." Robert Greene, "No Room for the Inn: The Fight over a Vacant Lot in South L.A., Where Many Rooms Rent by the Hour," *LA Weekly*, August 28, 2003.

23. Michael Keith, *After the Cosmopolitan?: Multicultural Cities and the Future of Racism* (New York: Routledge, 2005), 73.

24. Ibid., 78.

25. See Loren Kajikawa's chapter, "Let Me Ride: Gangsta Rap's Drive into the Popular Mainstream," for an analysis of urban space and gangsta rap. In it, he argues that Dr. Dre's *The Chronic* "rearticulated blackness not as conflict and rebellion but as transcendence and mobility" (Kajikawa, *Sounding Race in Rap Songs*, 86).

26. Daulatzai, *Black Star, Crescent Moon*, 89.

27. Robert O. Self, *American Babylon: Race and the Struggle for Post-War Oakland* (Princeton, NJ: Princeton University Press, 2003), 14.

28. Paul Gilroy, "Steppin' Out of Babylon: Race, Class, and Autonomy," in *The Empire Strikes Back: Race and Racism in 70s Britain*, ed. Paul Gilroy et al. (London: Hutchinson, 1984), 292.

29. Michael Keith further argues, "Analytically we need to get under the skin of the city, to consider how the valorisation of racial subjects links to the institutional architecture of politics, economy and culture. Getting under the skin of the city is partly a task that demands an unpacking of the forms of collective memory and unruly mapping that structure our ways of thinking. But it is also about a constant iteration between the concepts and vocabularies that are being used in academic analysis and the hidden racialised genealogies of precisely these same concepts" (Keith, *After the Cosmopolitan?*, 35).

30. Kurtis Blow, along with Pastor Carol Scott and Sean and Sharon Collins-Heads, founded the Hip Hop Church Los Angeles—a monthly hip hop ministry on Friday nights housed within Inglewood's Holy Trinity Evangelical Lutheran Church. The relationship between what I am calling the "traditional" church and the hip hop ministry was fraught with distrust, miscommunications, and ultimately, some very painful betrayals. As a result, the Hip Hop Church L.A. decided to transform itself into a mobile ministry that took their service to various churches and events around the greater Los Angeles. At rapper-turned-preacher Kurtis Blow's Harlem Hip Hop Church service at Greater Hood Memorial AME, an older clergy member dressed in a formal tan pantsuit sat near the pulpit with a very disinterested gaze. She did not respond to the gospel rap performances but remained in her seat looking coolly on the crowd. The money collected from the Offering is split between the traditional church and the hip hop ministry at the Harlem Hip Hop Church.

31. Celah, interview with the author, Compton, CA, 2008.

32. Cue Jn-Marie, interview with the author, Inglewood, CA, 2007.

33. Regarding the lawsuits against L.A. hospitals that dump patients on Skid Row, see Joseph Serna, "Hospital Agrees to Pay $450,000 to L.A. to Settle Homeless Patient Dumping Lawsuit," *Los Angeles Times*, October 25, 2016.

34. Cue Jn-Marie, interview with the author, Los Angeles, CA 2008.

35. Cue Jn-Marie as quoted in the documentary *Make* by Artie Delgado in 2013, https:// vimeo.com/67363973.

36. Among the trees, they shuffled counterclockwise in a circle, swaying, clapping, stomping, and tapping their heels but never crossing their feet so as not to confuse the sacred ritual with social dancing. Accompanied by chant, this rhythmic walk moved increasingly faster until "shouters" (dancers) worked themselves into a quivering, trembling trance.

37. While Cue strongly critiques the urban church, he remains a regular attending member. He explained to me in a 2007 interview: "After being a part of this for a year, it's hard to go to church and sit down and look at the back of somebody's head. It's hard on Sunday morning. I can do it because I know the vision of the church and what the church is about and I've been blessed to do what I do without interruption and New Song has allowed me to do that."

38. We might consider holy hip hop spaces as an example of Michel Foucault's notion of "heterotopias"—spaces of paradox, the counter-sites of cultural representation and inversion that function to expose the illusions underwriting social relations. In contradistinction to inclusive utopia, heterotopia is inverted, a site where positions, places, and actions excluded from normative society are contested. Michel Foucault, "Of Other Spaces, Heterotopias," *Architecture, Mouvement, Continuité* 5 (1984): 46–49.

39. *Ciénegas* are natural springs or marshlands, many of which existed below the hills at Rancho Ciénega. "Paso de la Tijera" is often translated as "Pass of the Scissors" and was used by the imaginative Spanish settlers to describe a pass through the Baldwin Hills that resembled a pair of open scissors.

40. Josh Sides, "The Center Can Hold: Leimert Park and Black Los Angeles," *KCET*, November 12, 2013, www.kcet.org/socal/departures/leimert-park/the-center-can-hold-leimert-park-and-black-los-angeles.html.

41. The Asylumz biography on the website Sonic Bids states, "Worsh-Hop is Worship in new skins, the sound was developed by Xealot Music through the production of Mercy Diamonds, and named so by DJ Redeemed of the 12th tribe out of Bakersfield, CA." www.sonicbids.com/band/asylumz/.

42. Praise and worship is highly participatory music that often involves call and response and unison singing. It often features repetition and simple melodies in order to facilitate retention and involvement. Ethnomusicologist Birgitta Johnson writes: "Originally a product of the predominantly white contemporary Christian music (CCM) industry of the 1960s and 1970s, praise and worship music has become popular in black churches across America, and particularly in Los Angeles. Praise and worship's prominence in Los Angeles African-American churches began in the 1980s, and its incorporation into the gospel music tradition reflects a reaffirmation of traditional African-American Christian worship practices such as congregational singing and emotive worship." Birgitta Johnson, "Back to the Heart of Worship: Praise and Worship Music in Los Angeles African-American Megachurch," *Black Music Research Journal* 31.1 (Spring 2011): 108.

43. In another example, a young man who performed during the open mic was very nervous and kept using profane language and swear words in his rhymes. He got very frustrated with himself, as this was not his intention. In this instance, the crowd and event promoters did not critique him and instead applauded in support of his attempts to freestyle publicly on the microphone.

44. As quoted in Neal, *What the Music Said*, 5.

45. "Club Judah." Accessed December 15, 2008, www.loveandfaithcc.org/ministries/judah.htm.

46. Genesis 29:35.

47. "Judah" can also refer to an ancient kingdom of southern Palestine between the Mediterranean and Dead seas. It lasted from the division of Palestine in 931 B.C. until the destruction of Jerusalem in 586 B.C.

48. See AbdouMaliq Simone's article, "People as Infrastructure: Intersecting Fragments in Johannesburg," *Public Culture* 16.3 (2004): 409.

49. Khanchuz held his release party for the album *The Prophecy Project* at Club Judah in September 2015 and it remains an important venue for gospel hip hop in Los Angeles.

CHAPTER 4. THE EVANGELICAL HUSTLE

1. Canton Jones, *Kingdom Business* (2008, 2009, 2010).

2. Kellus Hill, "CantonJonesDominionaire," *Jam the Hype*, November 22, 2011, www.dasouth.com/reviews/5497-canton-jones-qdominionaireq.

3. Cross Movement, one of the most commercially successful holy hip hop groups, sells between 70,000 and 100,000 copies of their albums on average, while Eminem sold a staggering ten million copies of his last album. Jesse Hyde, "Hip-Hop's Public Enemy: G. Craige Lewis Has One Goal: Get Hip-Hop Out of the Church. Forever," *Dallas Observer*, December 8, 2005.

4. Pierre Bourdieu's framework of various "forms of capital" is related to the idea of holy hip hop resources and currencies. Pierre Bourdieu, *The Field of Cultural Production* (New York: Columbia University Press, 1993). It is also helpful here in deviating from a rigidly vertical understanding of social structures based on economic wealth, and allowing for a more complex, multidimensional, and nonlinear notion of social space. I would like to expand his theory of cultural capital to include the interplay of multiple cultural, symbolic, and spiritual *capitals*, allowing for more variation in the musical cultures of different social spaces and societies. Cultural capital is symbolic knowledge that confers status, generally acquired by education and upbringing, which is expressed through cultural preferences—from food to music, painting to sport, literature to hairstyle. As Timothy Taylor has noted, Bourdieu must be adjusted to account for generational and class issues in contemporary culture. Taylor argues that cultural capital today has less to do with high culture and more to do with being hip and trendy. Timothy Taylor, "Advertising and the Conquest of Culture," *Social Semiotics* 19.4 (2009): 405–25. The currency of hipness indicates a move from function to style, as asserted by Dick Hebdige in *Subculture: The Meaning of Style* (New York: Routledge, 1979). Similarly, Sarah Thornton refers to this as subcultural capital. Sarah Thornton in *Club Cultures: Music, Media and Subcultural Capital* (Middletown, CT: Wesleyan University Press, 1996). Gospel rappers draw from a range of acquired capitals

(some but not all conferred through class status) depending on the primary field they are operating within. These changes in cultural capital are not just reflected in popular culture, but also in the religious field, which is deeply enmeshed in a broader field of *cultural* production. See Bradford Verter, "Spiritual Capital: Theorizing Religion with Bourdieu against Bourdieu," *Sociological Theory* 21.2 (2003): 156.

5. Evangelism has always been big business. Think colonial land grabs and slave labor under the guise of civilizing and missionizing, the economic success of the growing megachurch movement, or televangelism—a little Weberian "Protestant work ethic" and a whole lot of Billy Graham. Hip hop is now a multibillion-dollar industry with cross-marketing among numerous media and corporate sectors.

6. See recent work on hip hop and authenticity: Jeffrey O. G. Ogbar, *Hip-Hop Revolution: The Culture and Politics of Rap* (Lawrence: University of Kansas Press, 2007), and Michael P. Jeffries, *Thug Life: Race, Gender, and the Meaning of Hip-Hop* (Chicago: University of Chicago Press, 2011).

7. We also see the simultaneous entanglements of missionizing/marketing, fellowshipping/networking, selling/giving, profiting/prophesizing, preaching/rapping, hip hop hooks and evangelical bait.

8. Both Peter Berger and James Hunter have argued that business ministries often respond to the "quandary of modernity" and secularization in two distinct ways: resistance to the modern secular world or accommodation to fit the modern secular world. Anne L. Borden offers a third response called "sacralization"—a fusion between Christianity and capitalism. Anne L. Borden, "Making Money, Saving Souls: Christian Bookstores and the Commodification of Christianity," in *Religion, Media, and the Marketplace*, ed. Lynn Schofield Clark (New Brunswick, NJ: Rutgers University Press, 2007), 75.

9. See Elijah Anderson's definition of streetwise: "a 'streetwise' person is one who understands 'how to behave' in uncertain public places ... becoming something more than just a reactant to public situations, the individual becomes proactive and to some degree the author of public actions." Elijah Anderson, *Streetwise: Race, Class, and Change in an Urban Community* (Chicago: University of Chicago Press, 1992), 6.

10. Pastor Graham, interview with the author, Los Angeles, CA, 2008.

11. Richard A. Peterson, "In Search of Authenticity," *Journal of Management Studies* 42.5 (2005): 1086.

12. I am referring to Richard Middleton's work on popular music and authenticity as well as Foucault's sense of disciplinary power as it relates to the ways that people self-police and self-regulate.

13. For further ethnographic work on Project Blowed, see Marcyliena Morgan, *The Real Hiphop: Battling for Knowledge, Power, and Respect in the LA Underground* (Durham, NC: Duke University Press, 2009), and Jooyoung Lee, *Blowin' Up: Rap Dreams in South Central* (Chicago: Chicago University Press, 2016).

14. Religious idleness as a sin supported the Protestant work ethic, not based on the immoral pursuit of money but on the disciplined duty of doing one's work, which is God's work—obeying your calling.

15. See Phillipe Bourgois, *In Search of Respect: Selling Crack in El Barrio* (Cambridge: Cambridge University Press, 2002). See also Sudhir Alladi Venkatesh, *Off the Books: The Underground Economy of the Urban Poor* (Cambridge, MA: Harvard University Press, 2006).

16. Soup the Chemist, *Through My Windows: The History behind Holy Hip Hop* (Dim-lights, 2013), 50.

17. Cue Jn-Marie, interview with the author, Los Angeles, CA, 2008.

18. Prosperity Theology, also known as the "Gospel of Health and Wealth," "Prosperity Doctrine," or "Name It and Claim It," is a Christian belief whose supporters believe that financial prosperity is the will of God.

19. Kaplan, "10 Inner-City Stories You Didn't Read … Again."

20. Sorett, "'Believe Me, This Pimp Game Is Very Religious,'" 14.

21. Ibid., 14–15 (emphasis mine).

22. I've also witnessed gospel MCs complain about fellow Christian rappers who "hog the mic," unabashedly promote their CDs and "on-stage" persona, or perform more songs than they were initially allotted in a church service or open mic.

23. Cue also lamented how the church will spend $5,000 to have Bishop T. D. Jakes speak but won't give an artist even $500.

24. Celah, interview with the author, Compton, CA, 2008.

25. Crossfire, interview with the author, Compton, CA, 2008.

26. Sound Doctrine, interview with the author, Compton, CA, 2008.

27. DJ Heat, interview with the author, Compton, CA, 2008.

28. Slack, interview with the author, Compton, CA, 2008.

29. This list of terms for gospel hip hop was generated from several different interviews I conducted in 2008 with gospel rappers Pastor Graham (2007), Cue (2008), Hip-Hoppo-site (2008), and PK-1000's.

30. Similarly, Ambassador, member of the Christian rap collective Cross Movement, recently named his 2008 tour "From Milk To Meat."

31. Cue Jn-Marie, interview with the author, Los Angeles, CA, 2008.

32. Majesty, interview with the author, Leimert Park, CA, 2008.

33. Compton Virtue, interview with the author, Los Angeles, CA, 2004.

34. Emily Raboteau explains that the idea of seed faith is generally credited to Oral Roberts and comes from the parable of Jesus in Matthew 4: "Because you have so little faith. Truly I tell you, if you have faith as small as a mustard seed, you can say to this mountain, 'Move from here to there,' and it will move. Nothing will be impossible for you" (Holy Bible, New International Version, 17:20). Just as the sower plants seeds that will reap an abundant harvest, the believer puts his or her faith into action, and it transforms into a miracle. Emily Raboteau, *Searching for Zion: The Quest for Home in the African Diaspora* (New York: Atlantic Monthly Press, 2013), 256.

CHAPTER 5. ROADS TO ZION

EPIGRAPH Michael Meade, *The World behind the World: Living at the Ends of Time* (Seattle: GreenFire Press, 2008), 147.

1. Robin D. G. Kelley, *Freedom Dreams: The Black Radical Imagination* (Boston: Beacon Press, 2002).

2. Emily Raboteau, *Searching for Zion: The Quest for Home in the African Diaspora* (New York: Atlantic Monthly Press, 2013).

3. Ibid., 292.

4. Jaji, *Africa in Stereo*, 4. Jaji also describes the Black Atlantic as stereophonic and offers "stereomodernism" as a "heuristic for analyzing texts and cultural practices that are both political and expressive, activated by black music and operative within the logic of pan-African solidarity." Ibid., 14.

5. "It's Hammer Time: MC Hammer Hip-Hops in His Own Weekly Church Service," *BeliefNet*, www.beliefnet.com/Faiths/2000/01/Its-Hammer-Time.aspx.

6. Cue Jn-Marie, interview with the author, Los Angeles, CA, 2013.

7. Ibid.

8. Efrem Smith and Phil Jackson, *The Hip Hop Church: Connecting with the Movement Shaping Our Culture* (Downers Grove, IL: InterVarsity Press, 2006).

9. Efrem Smith, "The Black Church, Black Lives Matter, and Youth Ministry," December 8, 2015, www.efremsmith.com/category/blog/tag/black-lives-matter/.

10. Efrem Smith, "#BlackLivesMatter and Evangelicalism," January 13, 2016, http://www.efremsmith.com/category/blog/tag/black-lives-matter/.

11. Crossfire, interview with the author, Compton, CA, 2008.

12. "Nas the Mature Voice of Hip Hop: Rapper Talks about God, Tupac, Russell Simmons, and Politics," January 4, 2005, www.today.com/id/6786474/ns/today-today_entertainment/t/nas-mature-voice-hip-hop/#.VtM8dpMrKRs.

13. Ian Whitcomb, *Irving Berlin and Ragtime America* (New York: Limelight Editions, 1988), 19.

14. A year before Robert Mugabe was elected as the prime minister of Zimbabwe, Bob Marley wrote his famous anthem, "Zimbabwe" (1979), in support of the guerillas that were fighting against the Rhodesian government in the Bush War.

15. Mugabe has also been accused of coordinating the "Gukurahundi," which led to the murders of at least 1500 people belonging to the Ndebele minority in Zimbabwe.

16. Jaji, *Africa in Stereo*, 7.

17. *Reincarnated*, directed by Andy Capper, Snoopadelic Films, 2013.

18. Other reggae artists have been more supportive of Snoop's conversion. Acknowledging Snoop's rasta tendencies (meaning his herb advocacy), Damian Marley commented, "He's shining a light toward Reggae music in his own way." The famed son of Bob Marley, Damian (Junior Gong) collaborated with Snoop on the 2006 track "Get a Light." In the same year, Nas and Snoop—hip hop's two most notorious spiritual samplers—released "Play on Playa," in which Nas raps about Jesus pieces and "kush in the weed bags." While Nas and Snoop have navigated through multiple routes of black religiosity on their road to Zion, it's clear that the sacred rasta herb is an integral part of their spiritual explorations.

19. Alexis Petritis, "Is Snoop Dogg Taking His Rastafarianism Seriously," *The Guardian*, January 24, 2013, www.theguardian.com/lifeandstyle/lostinshowbiz/2013/jan/24/snoop-dogg-rastafarianism-seriously.

20. Jonah Weiner, "Q&A: Snoop Lion Strikes Back at 'Reincarnated' Collaborator Bunny Wailer," *Rolling Stone*, April 24, 2003, www.rollingstone.com/music/news/q-a-snoop-lion-strikes-back-at-reincarnated-collaborator-bunny-wailer-20130424.

21. Rosie Swash, "Snoop Dogg Joins the Nation of Islam," *The Guardian*, March 2, 2009, www.theguardian.com/music/2009/mar/02/snoop-dogg-nation-islam.

22. Majesty, interview with the author, Los Angeles, CA, 2008.

23. Ibid.

24. This interview with Majesty illustrates the complex array of practices involved in holy hip hop testifyings that stretch over multiple times and places. Note the moves from factual testimony to supernatural autobiography to musical testifying through rapping and scripture. Notice the play of memory, forgetfulness, and exaggeration. The juxtaposition of these various forms of multimodal testifying reveals both gaps and connections between the stories of her life and reminds us that the pragmatics of discourse do not always move between fixed points in a linear fashion.

25. KRS-One also underwent a religious conversion, which inspired him to release the album *Spiritual Minded* (2002)—a sacred re-versioning of his 1993 album, *Criminal Minded*.

26. "Seconds," *I Am Second*, www.iamsecond.com/seconds/lecrae/.

27. Joe Coscarelli, "Kendrick Lamar on His New Album and the Weight of Clarity," *New York Times,* March 16, 2015, www.nytimes.com/2015/03/22/arts/music/kendrick-lamar-on-his-new-album-and-the-weight-of-clarity.html?smid=nytimesarts&_r=1

28. Joe Lynch, "Kendrick Lamar on the Biblical 'Last Days' Being Near: 'I Truly in My Heart Believe That," *Billboard,* January 8, 2015, www.billboard.com/articles/news/6436342/kendrick-lamar-on-rapture-billboard-cover-story-sneak-peek.

29. Josef Sorett has argued a similar point—that hip hop is a locus for intersecting black diasporic religiosities not bound by orthodoxies ("'This Pimp Game Is Very Religious,'" 11–12).

Abu-Lughod, Janet L. *Race, Space, and Riots in Chicago, New York, and Los Angeles.* New York: Oxford University Press, 2007.

Alim, H. Samy. *Roc the Mic Right: The Language of Hip Hop Culture.* New York: Routledge, 2006.

Almaguer, Tomás. *Racial Fault Lines: The Historical Origins of White Supremacy in California.* Berkeley: University of California, 1994.

Anderson, Elijah. *Streetwise: Race, Class, and Change in an Urban Community.* Chicago: University of Chicago Press, 1992.

Asad, Talal. "Comments on Conversion." In *Conversion to Modernities: The Globalization of Christianity,* edited by Peter Van Der Veer, 263–73. New York: Routledge, 1995.

Aubry, Erin J. "Lost Soul: A Lament for Black Los Angeles." *LA Weekly,* December 10, 1998.

———. "Ten Years and a Cloud of Dust: Crenshaw in Slow Motion." *LA Weekly,* May 2, 2002.

Aubry, Larry. "Inglewood Mayor's Tactics Should Be Denounced." *Los Angeles Sentinel,* May 19, 2004.

Austin-Broos, Diane. "The Anthropology of Religious Conversion: An Introduction." In *The Anthropology of Religious Conversion,* edited by Andrew Buckser and Stephen D. Glazier, 1–12. Lanham, MD: Rowman and Littlefield, 2003.

Baker-Fletcher, Garth K. "African American Christian Rap: Facing 'Truth' and Resisting It." In *Noise and Spirit: The Religious and Spiritual Sensibilities of Rap Music,* edited by Anthony B. Pinn, 29–48. New York: New York University Press, 2003.

Baraka, Imamu Amiri. *Blues People: The Negro Experience in White America and the Music That Developed from It.* New York: William Morrow, 1963.

Barry, Kate, and Martha Henderson. *Geographical Identities of Ethnic America: Race, Space, and Place.* Reno: University of Nevada Press, 2001.

Basu, Dipannita, and Pnina Werbner. "Bootstrap Capitalism and the Culture Industries: A Critique of the Invidious Comparisons in the Study of Ethnic Entrepreneurship." *Ethnic and Racial Studies* 24, no. 2 (2001): 236–62.

Berger, Peter L. *The Sacred Canopy: Elements of a Sociological Theory of Religion.* New York: Doubleday, 1967.

Borden, Anne L. "Making Money, Saving Souls: Christian Bookstores and the Commodification of Christianity." In *Religion, Media, and the Marketplace,* edited by Lynn Schofield Clark, 67–89. New Brunswick, NJ: Rutgers University Press, 2007.

Bourdieu, Pierre. "The Forms of Capital." In *Handbook of Theory and Research for the Sociology of Education,* edited by John G. Richardson, 241–58. New York: Greenwood Press, 1986.

———. *The Field of Cultural Production.* New York: Columbia University Press, 1993.

Bourgois, Phillipe. *In Search of Respect: Selling Crack in El Barrio.* Cambridge, MA: Cambridge University Press, 2002.

Boyd, Todd. *The New H.N.I.C.: The Death of Civil Rights and the Reign of Hip Hop.* New York: New York University Press, 2002.

Brown, Jacqueline. *Dropping Anchor, Setting Sail: Geographies of Race in Black Liverpool.* Princeton, NJ: Princeton University Press, 2005.

Brown, Jayna. *Babylon Girls: Black Women Performers and the Shaping of the Modern.* Durham, NC: Duke University Press, 2008.

Briggs, Charles. "Anthropology, Interviewing, and Communicability in Contemporary Society." *Current Anthropology* 48, no. 4 (2007): 551–80.

Brown, Saideh Page. *Can Hip Hop Be Holy?* GS Publishing Group, 2007.

Burnim, Mellonee. "Gospel Music Research." *Black Music Research Journal* 1 (1980): 63–70.

———. "Culture Bearer and Tradition Bearer: An Ethnomusicologist's Research on Gospel Music." *Ethnomusicology* 29, no. 3 (1985): 432–47.

———. "The Black Gospel Tradition: A Complex of Ideology, Aesthetic, and Behavior." In *More than Dancing,* edited by Irene Jackson, 147–67. Westport, CT: Greenwood Press, 1985.

——— and Portia K. Maultsby, eds. *African American Music: An Introduction.* New York: Routledge, 2006.

California Pan-Ethnic Health Network. "Income below Poverty Level (Los Angeles, CA 2012)." http://cpehn.org/chart/income-below-poverty-level-los-angeles-county-2012.

Carter, Eric, James Donald, and Judith Squires. *Space and Place: Theories of Identity and Location.* London: Lawrence and Wishart, 1994.

Chang, Jeff. *Don't Stop Won't Stop: A History of the Hip-Hop Generation.* New York: St. Martin's Press, 2005.

Clifford, James. *Writing Culture: The Poetics and Politics of Ethnography.* Berkeley: University of California Press, 1986.

———. *Travel and Translation in the Late Twentieth Century.* Cambridge, MA: Harvard University Press, 1997.

———. "Spatial Practices: Fieldwork, Travel, and the Disciplining of Anthropology." In *Anthropological Locations: Boundaries and Grounds of a Field Science,* edited by Akhil Gupta and James Ferguson, 185–222. Berkeley: University of California Press, 1997.

"*Club Judah.*" www.loveandfaithcc.org/ministries/judah.htm.

Comaroff, John L., and Jean Comaroff. *Of Revelation and Revolution, Volume 2: The Dialectics of Modernity on a South African Frontier.* Chicago: University of Chicago Press, 1991.

Condry, Ian. *Hip-Hop Japan: Rap and Paths of Cultural Globalization.* Durham, NC: Duke University Press, 2006.

Cone, James. *The Spirituals and the Blues: An Interpretation.* Maryknoll, NY: Orbis Books, 1972.

———. *A Black Theology of Liberation.* New York: Orbis Books, 1986.

Connel, John. *Soundtracks: Popular Music, Identity, and Place.* New York: Routledge Press, 2002.

Cook, Miriam, and Bruce B. Lawrence. *Muslim Networks From Hajj to Hip Hop.* Chapel Hill: University of North Carolina Press, 2005.

Coscarelli, Joe. "Kendrick Lamar on His New Album and the Weight of Clarity." *New York Times,* March 16, 2015. www.nytimes.com/2015/03/22/arts/music/kendrick-lamar-on-his-new-album-and-the-weight-of-clarity.html?smid=nytimesarts&_r=1

Daultatzai, Sohail. *Black Star, Crescent Moon: The Muslim International and Black Freedom beyond America.* Minneapolis: University of Minnesota Press, 2012.

Davis, Mike. *City of Quartz: Excavating the Future in Los Angeles.* New York: Vintage Books, 1992.

———. *Ecologies of Fear: Los Angeles and the Imagination of Disaster.* New York: Metropolitan Books, 1998.

De Certeau, Michel. *The Practice of Everyday Life.* Berkeley: University of California Press, 1984.

Delgado, Artie. "Make." *Brink Films* video, 09:10. Posted May 31, 2013. https://vimeo.com/67363973.

DjeDje, Jacqueline Cogdell. "Change and Differentiation: The Adoption of Black American Gospel Music in the Church." *Ethnomusicology* 30, no. 2 (1986): 223–52.

———. "Gospel Music in the Los Angeles Black Community: A Historical Overview." *Black Music Research Journal* 9, no. 1 (1989): 35–79.

———. "Los Angeles Composers of African American Gospel Music: The First Generations." *American Music* 11, no. 4 (1993): 412–57.

———. "The California Black Gospel Music Tradition: A Confluence of Musical Styles and Cultures." In *California Soul: Music of African Americans in the West,* edited by Jacqueline Cogdell DjeDje and Eddie S. Meadows, 124–75. Berkeley: University of California Press, 1998.

——— and Eddie S. Meadows. "Introduction." In *California Soul: Music of African Americans in the West,* edited by Jacqueline Cogdell DjeDje and Eddie S. Meadows, 1–19. Berkeley: University of California Press, 1998.

Douglass, Frederick. *My Bondage and My Freedom.* Auburn: Miller, Orton, and Mulligan, 1857.

DuBois, W. E. B. *The Souls of Black Folks.* New York: Vintage Books, [1903] 1999.

Dyson, Michael Eric. "Rap Culture, the Church, and American Society." *Black Sacred Music: A Journal of Theomusicology* 6, no. 1 (1992): 268–73.

———. *Between God and Gangsta Rap.* New York: Oxford University Press, 1997.

———. *Holler If You Hear Me: Searching for Tupac Shakur.* New York: BasicCivitas Books, 2001.

———. *Open Mic: Reflections on Philosophy, Race, Sex, Culture and Religion.* New York: Basic *Civitas* Books, 2003.

Eastman, Ralph. "'Pitchin' Up a Boogie': African-American Musicians, Nightlife, and Music Venues in Los Angeles, 1930–1945." In *California Soul: Music of African Americans in the West,* edited by Jacqueline Cogdell DjeDje and Eddie Meadows, 79–103. Berkeley: University of California Press, 1998.

Elam, Jr., Harry J., and Kennell Jackson, eds. *Black Cultural Traffic: Crossroads in Global Performance and Popular Culture.* Ann Arbor: University of Michigan Press, 2005.

Elden, Stuart. *Understanding Henri Lefebvre: Theory and the Possible.* New York: Continuum, 2004.

Eure, Joseph D., and James G. Spady. *Nation Conscious Rap: The Hip-Hop Vision.* New York: PC International Press, 1991.

Evans, Curtis J. "Urbanization and the End of Black Churches in the Modern World." *Church History* 76, no. 4 (2007): 799–823.

Fauset, Arthur Huff. *Black Gods of the Metropolis: Negro Religious Cults of the Urban North.* Philadelphia: University of Pennsylvania Press, [1944] 2002.

Feld, Steven, and Keith Basso, eds. *Senses of Place.* New Mexico: School of American Research Press, 1997.

Fikentscher, Kai. *"You Better Work!" Underground Dance Music in New York City.* Hanover, NH: Wesleyan University Press, 2000.

Floyd, Jr., Samuel A. *The Power of Black Music: Interpreting Its History from Africa to the United States.* New York: Oxford University Press, 1995.

Floyd-Thomas, Juan M. "A Jihad of Words: The Evolution of African American Islam and Contemporary Hip-Hop." In *Noise and Spirit: The Religious and Spiritual Sensibilities of Rap Music,* edited by Anthony B. Pinn, 49–70. New York: New York University Press, 2003.

Forman, Murray. *The 'Hood Comes First: Race, Space, and Place in Rap and Hip-Hop.* Middletown, CT: Wesleyan University Press, 2002.

———. "'Represent': Race, Space and Place in Rap Music." In *That's the Joint! The Hip-Hop Studies Reader,* edited by Murray Forman and Mark Anthony Neal, 201–22. New York: Routledge Press, 2004.

Foucault, Michel. "Of Other Spaces, Utopias and Heterotopias." *Architecture, Mouvement, Continuité* 5 (1984): 46–49.

———. *The Use of Pleasure: The History of Sexuality, Volume 2.* New York: Vintage Books, 1987.

Frith, Simon. "Towards an Aesthetic of Popular Music." In *Music and Society: The Politics of Composition, Performance and Reception,* edited by Richard Leppert and Susan McClary, 133–49. Cambridge: Cambridge University Press, 1987.

Gilroy, Paul. *The Black Atlantic: Modernity and Double Consciousness.* Cambridge, MA: Harvard University Press, 1992.

———. "Steppin' Out of Babylon: Race, Class, and Autonomy." In *The Empire Strikes Back: Race and Racism in 70s Britain,* edited by Paul Gilroy et al., 278–314. London: Hutchinson in association with the Centre for Contemporary Cultural Studies, University of Birmingham, 1984.

———. *Darker Than Blue: On the Moral Economies of Black Atlantic Culture.* Cambridge, MA: Belknap Press of Harvard University Press, 2010.

Gooch, Cheryl R. "Rappin for the Lord: The Uses of Gospel Rap and Contemporary Music in Black Religious Communities." In *Religion and Mass Media: Audiences and Adaptations,* edited by D. A. Stout and Judith M. Buddenbaum, 228–42. Thousand Oaks: Sage, 1996.

Greeley, Andrew. *God in Popular Culture.* Chicago: Thomas More Press, 1988.

Greene, Robert. "No Room for the Inn: The Fight over a Vacant Lot in South L.A., Where Many Rooms Rent by the Hour." *LA Weekly,* August 28, 2003.

Gregory, Steven. *Black Corona: Race and the Politics of Place in an Urban Community.* Princeton, NJ: Princeton University Press, 1999.

Guilbault, Jocelyne. "Audible Entanglements: Nation and Diasporas in Trinidad's Calypso Music Scene." *Small Axe* 9, no. 1 (2005): 40–63.

Gupta, Akhil, and James Ferguson. "Discipline and Practice: 'The Field' as Site, Method, and Location in Anthropology." In *Anthropological Locations: Boundaries and Grounds of a Field Science,* edited by Akhil Gupta and James Ferguson, 1–46. Berkeley: University of California Press, 1997.

Gutierrez, Eric. *Disciples of the Street: The Promise of a Hip Hop Church.* New York: Seabury Books, 2008.

Hall, Stuart. "Signification, Representation, Ideology: Althusser and the Post-Structuralist Debates." *Critical Studies in Mass Communication* 2, no. 2 (1985): 91–114.

———. "What Is This Black in Black Popular Culture?" In *Black Popular Culture,* edited by Gina Dent and Michele Wallance, 21–33. Seattle: Bay Press, 1992.

———. "New Ethnicities." In *Stuart Hall: Critical Dialogues in Cultural Studies,* edited by David Morley and Kuan-Hsing Chen, 441–49. New York: Routledge Press, 1996.

———. "The Meaning of New Times." In *Stuart Hall: Critical Dialogues in Cultural Studies,* edited by David Morley and Kuan-Hsing Chen, 223–37. New York: Routledge Press, 1996.

Harris, Michael. *The Rise of Gospel Blues: The Music of Thomas Dorsey in the Urban Church.* Oxford: Oxford University Press, 1994.

Hartmann, Geoffrey H. *Scars of the Spirit: The Struggle against Inauthenticity.* New York: Palgrave Macmillan, 2004.

Hebdige, Dick. *Subculture: The Meaning of Style.* New York: Routledge Press, 1979.

Heilbut, Anthony. *The Gospel Sound: Good News and Bad Times.* New York: Simon and Schuster, 1971.

Henderson, E. A. "Black Nationalism and Rap Music." *Journal of Black Studies* 26, no. 3 (1996): 308–39.

Herget, Winfried. "Black Itinerant Women Preachers: Conversion to Empowerment—The Example of Jarena Lee." In *Religion in African-American Culture,* edited by Winfried Herget and Alfred Hornung, 43–73. Heidelberg: Universtitätsverlag, 2006.

Herskovits, Melville Jean. *The Myth of the Negro Past.* Boston: Beacon Press, [1941] 1958.

Hill, Kellus. "Canton Jones Dominionaire." *Jam the Hype,* November 22, 2011. www.dasouth.com/reviews/5497-canton-jones-qdominionaireq.

Hodge, Daniel White. *The Soul of Hip Hop: Rims, Tims, and a Cultural Theology.* Downers Grove, IL: InterVarsity Press, 2010.

Holy Hip Hop. Directed by Christopher Martin. Deerfield: Maverick Entertainment Group, 2006. DVD hooks, bell. *Yearning: Race, Gender, and Cultural Politics.* Boston: South End Press, 1990.

Hudson, Willie. *The Holy Ghost Got a New Dance: An Examination of Black Theology and Holy Hip-hop in Inner-City Ministry.* Eugene: Resource, 2016.

Hughes, Langston. "The Negro Artist and the Racial Mountain." In *Voices from the Harlem Renaissance*, edited by Nathan Irvin Huggins, 305–7. New York: Oxford University Press, [1926] 1976.

Hunt, Darnell M. "Introduction: Dreaming of Black Los Angeles." In *Black Los Angeles: American Dreams and Racial Realities*, edited by Darnell M. Hunt and Ana-Christina Ramon, 1–20. New York: New York University Press, 2010.

Hunter, James. *American Evangelicalism: Conservative Religion and the Quandary of Modernity.* New Brunswick, NJ: Rutgers University Press, 1983.

Hyde, Jesse. "Hip-Hop's Public Enemy: G. Craige Lewis Has One Goal: Get Hip-Hop Out of the Church. Forever." *Dallas Observer*, December 8, 2005.

Jaji, Tsitsi Ella. *Africa in Stereo: Modernism, Music, and Pan-African Solidarity.* New York: Oxford University Press, 2014.

Jeffries, Michael P. *Thug Life: Race, Gender, and the Meaning of Hip-Hop.* Chicago: University of Chicago Press, 2011.

Johnson, Birgitta. "Oh for a Thousand Tongues to Sing." PhD diss., University of California, 2009.

———. "Back to the Heart of Worship: Praise and Worship Music in Los Angeles African-American Megachurch." *Black Music Research Journal* 31, no. 1 (2011): 106–29.

Johnson, Gaye Theresa. *Spaces of Conflict, Sounds of Solidarity: Music, Race, and Spatial Entitlement in Los Angeles.* Berkeley: University of California Press, 2013.

Kajikawa, Loren. *Sounding Race in Rap Songs.* Berkeley: University of California Press, 2015.

Kaplan, Erin Aubry. "10 Inner-City Stories You Didn't Read … Again." *LA Weekly*, January 3, 2002.

———. "Duped by Wal-Mart: How Annie Lee Martin Got Fooled into Becoming a Poster Girl for the Corporate Giant in Inglewood." *LA Weekly*, April 1, 2004.

Keith, Michael. *After the Cosmopolitan?: Multicultural Cities and the Future of Racism.* New York: Routledge Press, 2005.

Keith, Michael, and Steve Pile. "Introduction Part 1: The Politics of Place." In *Place and the Politics of Identity*, edited by Michael Keith and Steve Pile, 1–21. New York: Routledge Press, 1993.

Kelley, Robin D. G. *Race Rebels: Culture, Politics, and the Black Working Class.* New York: Free Press, 1994.

———. "Kickin' Reality, Kickin' Ballistics: Gangsta Rap and Postindustrial Los Angeles." In *Droppin' Science: Critical Essays on Rap Music and Hip Hop Culture*, edited by William Eric Perkins, 117–58. Philadelphia: Temple University Press, 1996.

———. *Yo Mama's Dysfunktional: Fighting the Culture Wars in Urban America.* Boston: Beacon Press, 1998.

———. *Freedom Dreams: The Black Radical Imagination.* Boston: Beacon Press, 2002.

———. "Foreword." In *Catching Hell in the City of Angels*, by Joao Helion Costa Vargas, Minneapolis: University of Minnesota Press, 2006.

Keyes, Cheryl L. "At the Crossroads: Rap Music and Its African Nexus." *Ethnomusicology* 40, no. 2 (1996): 233–48.

Khabeer, Su'ad Abdul. *Muslim Cool: Race, Religion, and Hip Hop in the United States.* New York: New York University Press, 2016.

Kidula, Jean. "The Gospel of Andrae Crouch: A Black Angelino." In *California Soul: Music of African Americans in the West,* edited by Jacqueline Cogdell DjeDje and Eddie S. Meadows, 294–320. Berkeley: University of California Press, 1998.

King, Peter. "The Latest 100-Year Disaster." *Los Angeles Times,* March 15, 1995.

Kitwana, Bakari. *The Hip Hop Generation: Young Blacks and the Crisis in African American Culture.* New York: BasicCivitas Books, 2002.

Knight, David. *Landscapes in Music: Space, Place, and Time in the World's Great Music.* Lanham, MD: Rowman and Littlefield, 2006.

Knight, Michael Muhammad. *The Five Percenters: Islam, Hip Hop, and Gods of New York.* London: One World, 2007.

Krims, Adam. *Music and Urban Geography.* New York: Routledge Press, 2007.

Lacey, Marc. "Inside the Gates, 'a Nice Little Utopia': Inglewood: When the Residents of the City's Toniest Areas Drive Past the Guardhouses, They Leave behind the Problems of More Typical Inner-City Neighborhoods." *Los Angeles Times,* June 16, 1991.

Lashua, Brett, Karl Spracklen, and Stephen Wagg. *Sounds and the City: Popular Music, Place, and Globalization.* New York: Palgrave, 2014.

Lecrae. "I Am Second." *I Am Second* video, 9:09. February 14, 2016. www.iamsecond.com/seconds/lecrae/.

Lee, Jooyoung. "Rap Dreams." PhD diss., University of California, 2009.

———. *Blowin' Up: Rap Dreams in South Central.* Chicago: University of Chicago Press, 2016.

Lefebvre, Henri. *The Production of Space.* New York: Wiley, 1992.

———, Eleonore Kofman, and Elizabeth Lebas. *Writings on Cities.* Oxford: Basil Blackwell, [1996] 1999.

Lewis, Oscar. "The Culture of Poverty." In *Urban Life,* edited by G. Gmelch and W. Zenner. Long Grove, IL: Waveland Press, 1996.

Lipsitz, George. *Time Passages: Collective Memory and American Popular Culture.* Minneapolis: University of Minnesota Press, 1990.

———. *Dangerous Crossroads: Popular Music, Postmodernism, and the Poetics of Place.* New York: Verso, 1994.

Low, Setha M. "Introduction. Theorizing the City." In *Theorizing the City: The New Urban Anthropology Reader,* edited by Setha M. Low, 1–35. Rutgers, NJ: Rutgers University Press, 1999.

Luhr, Eileen. *Witnessing Suburbia: Conservative and Christian Youth Culture.* Berkeley: University of California Press, 2009.

Lynch, Joe. "Kendrick Lamar on the Biblical 'Last Days' Being Near: 'I Truly in My Heart Believe That." *Billboard,* January 8, 2015. www.billboard.com/articles/news/6436342/kendrick-lamar-on-rapture-billboard-cover-story-sneak-peek.

Macías, Anthony. "Black and Brown Get Down: Chicano Music, Cultural Politics, and Hip Hop in Racialized Los Angeles." In *Sounds and the City: Popular Music, Place and Globalization,* edited by B. Lashua, K. Spracklen, and S. Wagg. New York: Palgrave Macmillan, 2014.

Mahmood, Saba. "Feminist Theory, Embodiment, and the Docile Agent: Some Reflections on the Egyptian Islamic Revival." *Cultural Anthropology* 6, no. 2 (2001): 202–36.

———. *The Politics of Piety: The Islamic Revival and the Feminist Subject*. Princeton, NJ: Princeton University Press, 2004.

Mahon, Maureen. *Right to Rock: The Black Rock Coalition and the Cultural Politics of Race*. Durham, NC: Duke University Press, 2004.

Massey, Doreen. *Space, Place, and Gender*. Cambridge, MA: Polity Press, 1994.

Maultsby, Portia K. "Africanisms in African-American Music." In *Africanisms in American Culture*, edited by Joseph E. Holloway, 185–210. Bloomington: Indiana University Press, 1990.

McRoberts, Omar. *Streets of Glory: Church and Community in a Black Urban Neighborhood*. Chicago: University of Chicago Press, 2003.

Meade, Michael. *The World behind the World: Living at the Ends of Time*. Seattle: GreenFire Press, 2008.

———. "An Interview with Omar McRoberts." Chicago: University of Chicago Press. www.press.uchicago.edu/Misc/Chicago/562166in.html.

Middleton, Richard. *Voicing the Popular: On the Subjects of Popular Music*. New York: Routledge Press, 2006.

Miller, Monica, and Anthony B. Pinn. *The Hip-Hop and Religion Reader*. New York: Routledge Press, 2015.

Miller, Monica R., Anthony B. Pinn, and Bernard "Bun B" Freeman. *Religion in Hip Hop: Mapping the New Terrain in the US*. New York: Bloomsbury, 2015.

Mitchell, John. "The Raid That Still Haunts L.A." *Los Angeles Times*, March 14, 2001.

Mitchell, Kenny. "Homicide Perspectives: Kenny Mitchell, Founder, Gangsters Anonymous." *Los Angeles Times*, October 19, 2007. http://latimesblogs.latimes.com/homicidereport/2007/10/homicide-perspe.html.

Miyakawa, Felicia. *Five Percenter Rap: God Hop's Music, Message, and Black Muslim Mission*. Bloomington: Indiana University Press, 2005.

Moore, Donald. "Subaltern Struggles and the Politics of Place: Remapping Resistance in Zimbabwe's Eastern Highlands." *Cultural Anthropology* 13, no. 3 (1998): 344–81.

———. *Suffering for Territory: Race, Place, and Power in Zimbabwe*. Durham, NC: Duke University Press, 2005.

Moore Jr., Moses N. "'Testifying' and 'Testimony': Autobiographical Narratives and African American Religions." In *Teaching African American Religions*, edited by Carolyn M. Jones and Theodore Louis Trost, 95–108. Oxford: Oxford University Press. 2005.

Morgan, Marcyliena H. *The Real Hip Hop: Battling for Knowledge, Power and Respect in the LA Underground*. Durham, NC: Duke University Press, 2009.

Morrison, K. F. *Understanding Conversion*. Charlottesville: University of Virginia Press, 1992.

Myers-Turner, Ashley. "Forget the L.A. Riots—Historic 1992 Watts Gang Truce Was the Big News." *Southern California Public Radio*, April 28, 2012. www.scpr.org/news/2012/04/28/32221/forget-la-riots-1992-gang-truce-was-big- news/.

Neal, Mark Anthony. *What the Music Said: Black Popular Music and Black Public Culture*. New York: Routledge Press: 1999.

Ogbar, Jeffrey O. G. *Hip-Hop Revolution: The Culture and Politics of Rap*. Lawrence: University of Kansas Press, 2007.

Ornter, Sherry. *Making Gender: The Politics and Erotics of Culture*. Boston: Beacon Press, 1996.

Pape, Eric. "Inglewood's Magisterial Mayor: Roosevelt Dorn Was Bombastic on the Bench—and He Still Is." *LA Weekly,* April 8, 1999.

Perkinson, James. *Shamanism, Racism, and Hip-Hop Culture: Essays on White Supremacy and Black Subversion.* New York: Palgrave Macmillan, 2006.

Perry, Imani. *Prophets of the Hood: Politics and Poetics in Hip-Hop.* Durham, NC: Duke University Press, 2004.

Peterson, Richard A. "In Search of Authenticity." *Journal of Management Studies* 42, no. 5 (2005): 1086.

Petritis, Alexis. "Is Snoop Dogg Taking His Rastafarianism Seriously?" *The Guardian,* January 24, 2013. www.theguardian.com/lifeandstyle/lostinshowbiz/2013/jan/24/snoop-dogg-rastafarianism-seriously.

Pfeil, Fred. *Another Tale to Tell: Politics and Narrative in Postmodern Culture.* London: Verso, 1990.

Pinn, Anthony B. "Making a World with a Beat: Musical Expression's Relationship to Religious Identity and Experience." In *Noise and Spirit: The Religious and Spiritual Sensibilities of Rap Music,* edited by Anthony B. Pinn, 1–26. New York: New York University Press, 2003.

———. *Terror and Triumph: The Nature of Black Religion.* Minneapolis: Fortress Press, 2003.

Pollard, Deborah Smith. *When the Church Becomes Your Party: Contemporary Gospel Music.* Detroit: Wayne State University Press, 2008.

Pulido, Laura. *Black, Brown, Yellow, and Left: Radical Activism in Los Angeles.* Berkeley: University of California Press, 2006.

Quinn, Eithne. *Nuthin' but a "G" Thang: The Culture and Commerce of Gangsta Rap.* New York: Columbia University Press, 2005.

Raboteau, Emily. *Searching for Zion: The Quest for Home in the African Diaspora.* New York: Atlantic Monthly Press, 2013.

Radano, Ronald. *Lying Up a Nation: Race and Black Music.* Chicago: University of Chicago Press, 2003.

Rafael, Vicente L. *Contracting Colonialism: Translation and Christian Conversion in Tagalog Society under Early Spanish Rule.* Durham, NC: Duke University Press, 1993.

Rainwater, Lee. *Behind Ghetto Walls: Black Family Life in a Federal Slum.* Chicago: Aldine, 1970.

Ramsey, Guthrie. *Race Music: Black Cultures from Bebop to Hip-Hop.* Berkeley: University of California Press, 2003.

Reed, Teresa L. *The Holy Profane: Religion in Black Popular Music.* Lexington: University Press of Kentucky, 2003.

Robinson, Paul. "Race, Space, and the Evolution of Black Los Angeles." In *Black Los Angeles: American Dreams and Racial Realities,* edited by Darnell Hunt and Ana- Christina Ramon, 21–59. New York: New York University Press, 2010.

Romero, Dennis. "Gangster's Paradise Lost." *Los Angeles CityBeat,* November 6, 2003. www.lacitybeat.com/cms/story/detail/?id = 362&IssueNum = 22.

Rose, Tricia. *Black Noise: Rap Music and Black Culture in Contemporary America.* Hanover, NH: Wesleyan University Press, 1994.

Ross, Rosetta E. *Witnessing and Testifying: Black Women, Religion, and Civil Rights.* Minneapolis: Fortress Press, 2003.

Rouget, Gilbert, and Brunhilde Biebuyck. *Music and Trance: A Theory of Relations between Music and Possession.* Chicago: University of Chicago Press, 1985.

Royster, Philip M. "The Rapper as Shaman for a Band of Dancers of the Spirit: 'U Can't Touch This.'" *Black Sacred Music: A Journal of Theomusicology* 5, no. 1 (1991): 61–67.

Scott, James. *Domination and the Arts of Resistance: Hidden Transcripts.* New Haven, CT: Yale University Press, 1992.

Self, Robert O. *American Babylon: Race and the Struggle for Post-War Oakland.* Princeton, NJ: Princeton University Press, 2005.

Serrins, John. "Klub Zyon (Crenshaw)." www.theupperground.com/index.php/Find-Sessions/Community-Centers/Klub- Zyon-Crenshaw.html.

Sheller, Mimi, and John Urry. "The City and the Car." *International Journal of Urban and Regional Research* 24, no. 4 (2000): 737–57.

Sides, Josh. *L.A. City Limits: African American Los Angeles from the Great Depression to the Present.* Berkeley: University of California Press, 2003.

———. "The Center Can Hold: Leimert Park and Black Los Angeles." *KCET,* November 12, 2013. www.kcet.org/socal/departures/leimert-park/the-center-can-hold-leimert-park-and-black-los-angeles.html.

Simone, Abdou Maliqalim. "People as Infrastructure: Intersecting Fragments in Johannesburg." *Public Culture* 16, no. 3 (2004): 407–29.

Singh, Amritjit, and Peter Schmidt. "On the Borders between U.S. Studies and Postcolonial Theory." In *Postcolonial Theory and the United States: Race, Ethnicity and Literature,* edited by Amritjit Singh and Peter Schmidt, 3–70. Jackson: University Press of Mississippi, 2000.

Singh, Nikhil Pal. *Black Is a Country: Race and the Unfinished Struggle for Democracy.* London: Harvard University Press, 2004.

Smith, Efrem, and Phil Jackson. *The Hip Hop Church: Connecting with the Movement Shaping Our Culture.* Downers Grove, IL: InterVarsity Press, 2006.

Smith, Theophus. *Conjuring Culture: Biblical Formations of Black America.* New York: Oxford University Press, 1994.

Soja, Edward. "It All Comes Together in Los Angeles." Chap. 8 in *Postmodern Geographies: The Reassertion of Space in Critical Social Theory.* London: Verso, 1989.

Sorett, Josef. "Beats, Rhyme and Bible: An Introduction to Gospel Hip Hop." *African American Pulpit* 10 (2006–7): 12–16.

———. "'Believe Me, This Pimp Game Is Very Religious': Toward a Religious History of Hip Hop." *Culture and Religion* 10, no. 1 (2009): 11–22.

Soup the Chemist. *Through My Windows: The History behind Holy Hip Hop.* Dimlights, 2013.

Spencer, Jon Michael. *Theological Music: Introduction to Theomusicology.* New York: Greenwood Press, 1991.

———. *Blues and Evil.* Knoxville: University of Tennessee Press, 1993.

Stewart, Jocelyn Y. "Carol L. Scott, 50; Activist Pastor Led Hip-Hop Church." *Los Angeles Times,* October 11, 2007.

Stokes, Martin. "Introduction." In *Ethnicity, Identity, and Music: The Musical Construction of Place,* edited by M. Stokes, 1–27. Oxford: Berg, 1997.

Straw, Will. "Systems of Articulation, Logics of Change: Communities and Scenes in Popular Music." *Cultural Studies* 5, no. 3 (1991): 368–88.

Sturm, Circe. *Becoming Indian: The Struggle over Cherokee Identity in the Twenty-First Century*. Santa Fe: School for Advanced Research Press, 2011.

Swash, Rosie. "Snoop Dogg Joins the Nation of Islam." *The Guardian*, March 2, 2009. www.theguardian.com/music/2009/mar/02/snoop-dogg-nation-islam.

Sylvan, Robin. *Traces of the Spirit: The Religious Dimensions of Popular Music*. New York: New York University Press, 2002.

Taylor, Timothy D. *Strange Sounds: Music, Technology, and Culture*. New York: Routledge Press, 2001.

———. *Beyond Exoticism: Western Music and the World*. Durham, NC: Duke University Press, 2007.

———. "Advertising and the Conquest of Culture." *Social Semiotics* 19, no. 4 (2009): 405–25.

Thomas, Pradip. "Selling God, Saving Souls: Religious Commodities, Spiritual Markets, and the Media." *Global Media and Communication* 5, no. 1 (2009): 57–76.

Thornton, Sarah. *Club Cultures: Music, Media and Subcultural Capital*. Middletown, CT: Wesleyan University Press, 1996.

Trulear, Harold Dean, and N. Lynne Westfield. "Theomusicology and Christian Education: Spirituality and the Ethics of Control in the Rap of MC Hammer." *Theomusicology: A Special Issue of Black Sacred Music: A Journal of Theomusicology* 8, no. 1 (1994): 218–38.

Van der Veer, Peter. *Conversion to Modernities: The Globalization of Christianity*. New York: Routledge Press, 1996.

Vargas, Joáo Helion Costa. *Catching Hell in the City of Angels: Life and Meanings of Blackness in South Central Los Angeles*. Minneapolis: University of Minnesota Press, 2006.

Venkatesh, Sudhir Alladi. *Off the Books: The Underground Economy of the Urban Poor*. Cambridge, MA: Harvard University Press, 2006.

Verter, Bradford. "Spiritual Capital: Theorizing Religion with Bourdieu against Bourdieu." *Sociological Theory* 21, no. 2 (2003): 150–74.

Villa, Raul Homero. *Barrio-Logos: Space and Place in Urban Chicano Literature and Culture*. Austin: University of Texas Press, 2000.

Wacquant, Loïc. *Urban Outcasts: A Comparative Sociology of Advanced Marginality*. Cambridge: Polity Press, 2007.

Watkins, Ralph C., and Jason A. Barr. *The Gospel Remix: Reaching the Hip-Hop Generation*. Valley Forge: Judson Press, 2007.

Weber, Max. *The Protestant Ethic and the Spirit of Capitalism*. Los Angeles: Roxbury, 2001.

Weiner, Jonah. "Q&A: Snoop Lion Strikes Back at 'Reincarnated' Collaborator Bunny Wailer." *Rolling Stone*, April 24, 2003. www.rollingstone.com/music/news/q-a-snoop-lion-strikes-back-at-reincarnated-collaborator-bunny-wailer-20130424.

West, Cornell. "Black Theology and Marxist Thought." In *Black Theology: A Documentary History, 1966–1979, Volume 1*, edited by James H. Cone and Gayraud S. Wilmore, 409–24. Maryknoll, NY: Orbis Books, 1980.

———. *Race Matters*. Boston: Beacon Press, 1993.

———. "Foreword." In *One Nation under God: Religion and American Culture*, edited by Margorie Garber and Rebecca L. Walkowitz, vii–viii. New York: Routledge Press, 1999.

Whalum, Kenneth T. *Hip Hop Is Not Our Enemy: From a Preacher Who Keeps It Real*. Bloomington: AuthorHouse, 2010.

Whitcomb, Ian. *Irving Berlin and Ragtime America*. New York: Limelight Editions, 1988.

Whiteley, Sheila, Andy Bennett, and Stan Hawkins. *Music, Space, and Place: Popular Music and Cultural Identity.* Aldershot: Ashgate, 2005.

Williams, Erik J. "Only God Can Judge Us, Only God Can Save Us: The Hip-Hop Soul of Thugology." *Black Arts Quarterly: Hip Hop Culture: Language, Literature, Literacy and the Lives of Black Youth* 6, no. 2 (2001): 42–45.

Williams, Justin. "You Never Been on a Ride Like This Befo': Los Angeles, Automotive Listening, and Dr. Dre's 'G-Funk.'" *Popular Music History* 4, no. 2 (2010): 160–76.

Wilson, William Julius. *The Truly Disadvantaged: The Inner City, the Underclass, and Public Policy.* Chicago: University of Chicago Press, 1987.

Zanfagna, Christina. "Building 'Zyon' in Babylon: Holy Hip Hop and Geographies of Conversion." *Black Music Research Journal* 31, no. 2 (2010): 145–62.

———. "Kingdom Business: Holy Hip Hop's Evangelical Hustle." *Journal of Popular Music Studies* 24, no. 2 (2012): 196–216.

———. "Hip Hop and Religion: From the Mosque to the Church." In *The Cambridge Companion to Hip Hop,* edited by Justin A. Williams, 71–84. Cambridge: Cambridge University Press, 2015.

Zilberg, Elana. *Space of Detention: The Making of a Transnational Gang Crisis from Los Angeles to San Salvador.* Durham, NC: Duke University Press, 2011.

SFC (Soldiers For Christ), "Listen Up" from *Listen Up* (1989)
https://www.youtube.com/watch?v=ukjPeMaDj-A

SFC, "Fully Armed" from *Listen Up* (1987)
https://www.youtube.com/watch?v=hd08WJkeIbI

SFC, "Transformed" from *Listen Up* (1989)
https://www.youtube.com/watch?v=hnZZTFIMTIk

SFC, "Kill the Spirit" from *Phase III* (1992)
https://www.youtube.com/watch?v=nhdZ0QnDgJ4

SFC, "Hoods of Good" from *Phase III* (1992)
https://www.youtube.com/watch?v=SO0ehha6m_o

Soup the Chemist, "As the Sun Rises" from *Dust* (2000)
https://www.youtube.com/watch?v=oFJLI4VoHFc

Soup the Chemist, "Is This a Dream?" from *Dust* (2000)
https://www.youtube.com/watch?v=nhdZ0QnDgJ4

Gospel Gangstaz, "I'll Be Good" (1999)
https://www.youtube.com/watch?v=k-4KnMi0axI

LA Symphony, "King Kong" (2002)
https://www.youtube.com/watch?v=Yp5oMXFaWDs

Celah, *Color Outside the Lines* (2007)
https://www.youtube.com/playlist?list=PLXR6p7Dkw7JXRky97iKT
  Im6H_RAS90c7D
https://www.cdbaby.com/cd/celahhiphop

Celah, "City Limits" (2008)
https://www.youtube.com/watch?v=wWrZmPjBEOg

Hip Hopposite performing "Road to Zion" at Club Judah (c. 2008)
https://myspace.com/redonefilms/video/road-to-zion-hip
  -hopposite/31149058

Hip Hopposite Freestyle from *Special Times with God* (2008)
https://myspace.com/djheatla/music/song/
  hip-hopposite-freestyle-17028336–16829521

Holy D, "God's Watchin Me" from *God's Creation* (2008)
https://www.youtube.com/watch?v=GgzhqP-oJbk

Holy D, "Heavenly Father" from *God's Creation* (2008)
https://www.youtube.com/watch?v=CSbQt7gxfdw

Kurtis Blow performing "The Breaks" at Hip Hop Church L.A. (c.
  2013)
https://www.youtube.com/watch?v=W4XiVJiqQEU

Klub Zyon Promo (2007)
https://www.youtube.com/watch?v=yy8eUANpGhs

Young Chozen at Klub Zyon (c. 2008)
https://www.youtube.com/watch?v=kXim_cvQkWE

Asylumz, "Crazy Prayze" from *Xealot Music Presents . . . Asylumz*
  (2007)
https://www.youtube.com/watch?v=P9xVOrlWn-4

Asylumz, "A Million MCs" (c. 2009)
https://www.youtube.com/watch?v=sJsXunNqwSk

Asylumz, "Jesus Christ Is a Healer" (c. 2009)
https://www.youtube.com/watch?v=AhO74R9VYe0

Slum Peasants, "All the Love Is Gone" from *Truth 'N' Love* (2008)
https://www.youtube.com/watch?v=e9MacZhDvRo

Khanchuz, "What the Bible Say" from *The Prophecy Project* (2016)
https://www.youtube.com/watch?v=Ho_oTyH_gR4

Khanchuz, "All Honor to God" from *The Prophecy Project* (2016)
https://www.youtube.com/watch?v=TAu-QSOC2TI

Khanchuz, "Stop It" from *The Prophecy Project* (2016)
https://www.youtube.com/watch?v=jjkHocDAbO8

Khanchuz and Pastor Graham performing "All Honor to God" at
    Club Judah (2008)
https://www.youtube.com/watch?v=8btXKjXD_L8

Pastor Graham at Club Judah (c. 2008)
https://www.youtube.com/watch?v=T4Jh0vHcygw

INDEX

Page references followed by an italicized *fig.* indicate illustrations or material contained in their captions.